The euro

The euro

Edited by
Paul Temperton
The Independent Economic Research Company
(TIER)

2nd Edition

JOHN WILEY & SONS

Chichester • New York • Weinheim • Brisbane • Singapore • Toronto

Published by
John Wiley & Sons Ltd.
Baffins Lane, Chichester
West Sussex PO19 1UD, England

National 01243 779777
International (+44) 1243 779777
E-mail (for orders and customer service enquiries): cs-books@wiley.co.uk
Visit our home page on http://www.wiley.co.uk, or http://www.wiley.com

Other Wiley Editorial Offices
John Wiley & Sons, Inc. 605 Third Avenue,
New York, NY 10158-0012, USA

WILEY-VCH Verlag GmbH, Pappelallee 3
D-69469 Weinheim, Germany

John Wiley & Sons (Asia) Pte Ltd, 2 Clementi Loop #02-01,
Jin Xing Distripark, Singapore 0512

John Wiley & Sons (Canada) Ltd, 22 Worcester Road,
Rexdale, Ontario M9W IL1, Canada

Library of Congress Cataloging-in-Publication Data

A catalog record for this book is available from the Library of Congress

British Library Cataloguing in Publication Data

A catalogue record for this book is available from the British Library

ISBN 0-471-98722-0

Designed and typeset by Nick Battley, London
Cartoons by Peter Bugh
Printed and Bound in Great Britain by Biddles Ltd., Guildford and Kings Lynn
This book is printed on acid-free paper responsibly manufactured from sustainable forestation, for which at least two trees are planted for each one used for paper production.

Contents

III: THE INSTITUTIONS OF THE EURO

IV: LEGAL ISSUES

V: PROBLEMS AHEAD?

VIII: REGULATIONS & PROVISIONS

John C. Corrigan
Chairman,
EFFAS-European Bond Commission

When the first edition of *The euro* was published just over a year ago, there were still considerable uncertainties with respect to the launch of the new single currency, ranging from who the participating countries would be to complex technical details such as the fixing of the euro exchange rates. There were also suggestions that in the lead in to January, 1999, the scheduled launch date, there might be turbulence in the foreign exchange and bond markets driven by speculative attacks on the project. It is now clear that eleven countries will be participating and that a lot of the key technical details have been satisfactorily settled, largely by the newly established European Central Bank. Moreover, European currency and bond markets have been relatively calm and orderly, notwithstanding the financial crises in Asia and, more recently, in Russia.

This book, the second edition of *The euro*, represents a very substantial revamp of the first edition, being framed against the background of the certainty now surrounding the launch of the single currency. In that context, the second edition comprehensively addresses the economic, financial and business issues to be faced in the new world of the euro. Paul Temperton, who edited the first edition, is also editor of this book. He has successfully managed both to identify all of the salient issues and to convince the recognized experts to contribute a rich analysis of these issues.

As in the case of the first edition of *The euro* this publication is also promoted by the European Bond Commission of the European Federation of Financial Analysts' Societies (EFFAS). EFFAS is a pan-European federation of some seventeen national societies of investment analysts and securities managers with over ten thousand members. The Bond Commission has been actively involved with the European Commission in Brussels and the European Central Bank in Frankfurt in the consultative process on the prospective development of financial markets in the euro. It was one of the signatories to the joint statement by European financial industry associations of July 1997 on market conventions in the euro.

I would like to extend my personal appreciation and that of my colleagues on the EFFAS-European Bond Commission to Paul Temperton, editor, and to all of the other contributing authors for what, with a little over three months to the launch of the euro, represents a timely and comprehensive evaluation. My thanks are also due to Nick Battley for his steadfast technical support. I am confident that this publication will be as enthusiastically received as the first edition.

J.C.C.

National Treasury Management Agency
Dublin, August 1998

Preface

Paul Temperton
(Editor)
The Independent Economic Research Company (TIER)

This second edition of *The euro* was put together during July and August 1998. That was just one year after the first edition was compiled. The changes to the structure and content of the book are quite marked. Of the twenty-three chapters in the book, fifteen are entirely new. Most of the chapters that appeared in the first edition contain significant and extensive amendments.

When the first edition was produced, some of the key issues surrounding the euro were 'who will be in?', 'is it a good idea?' and 'what about the practicalities?'. We now know that eleven countries will be 'in' from 1 January 1999. Some—especially in the 'out' countries, such as the UK—are still asking whether it is a good idea. But most of the attention has shifted to the practical operation of the euro. This second edition reflects that change of focus. We discuss, for example, how the euro will be created; how it will relate to national currencies; how well the 'Euroland' economy will work; and what will be the implications for markets, companies and consumers.

We concentrate, however, largely on the financial markets. That is for two reasons. First, because the book is being supported, as was the first edition, by the European Bond Commission of EFFAS (the European Federation of Financial Analysts' Societies), Second, because it is in the financial markets that the impact of the euro will be first felt. The foreign exchange, money, bond and equity markets will, to a significant extent, become 'euro' markets from the start of 1999.

I hope that the book acts as a useful contribution to the issues surrounding the introduction of the single currency.

P.T.

Chalfont St. Giles, Buckinghamshire, August 1998

Section

I

The
euro

The background to the euro

| Chapter 1 | Paul Temperton
The Independent Economic Research Company (TIER) |

Introduction

The introduction of the euro on 1 January 1999 represents, without doubt, a revolution in the way in which the monetary matters of Europe are managed. From that date onwards, the 'national currency' of the eleven countries joining in European Economic and Monetary Union (EMU)—Austria, Belgium, Finland, France, Germany, Ireland, Italy, Luxembourg, the Netherlands, Portugal and Spain—will be the euro. Legally, that is the situation. In practice, that will also be the case in the wholesale financial markets: dealing in government bonds and (listed) equities in all of the eleven countries will be in euros once the markets open for business in 1999. Euro cash—notes and coin—will not, however, arrive for a further three years. And it will be mid-2002 before existing national currencies—lira, pesetas, Deutschemarks, etc.—lose their legal tender status.

This book is organized in nine sections dealing with:

- Section I The background to the euro
- Section II The economics of the euro
- Section III The institutions of the euro
- Section IV Legal issues
- Section V Possible problems ahead
- Section VI The foreign exchange market
- Section VII Financial markets (the money market, bonds, equities and pension funds)
- Section VIII The impact on companies & consumers

In this introductory chapter we review the purpose and content of each of these sections.

The purpose of this first section—'The background to the euro'—is to discuss some of the most basic questions relating to the euro which are still frequently raised. Thus, Chapter 2 asks 'Why is the euro being introduced?' We give an explanation, which rests on both political and economic factors, and many of the themes raised recur throughout the book. We then go on to discuss (in Chapter 3) what the euro area, or

'Euroland', will look like in relation to North America and Asia. Chapter 4 deals with the euro's creation from the Ecu and its relation to the currencies of the eleven participating currencies.

The economics of the euro are addressed more fully in Section II. A form of 'cost-benefit' analysis is conducted in Chapter 5: the main sound-bite originating from that analysis is 'short-term pain for long-term gain'. In other words, the costs associated with preparing for the euro—in particular the fiscal tightening seen in all countries in recent years—will be rewarded with a boost to economic growth once the euro is launched. The fundamental economic aspects of the euro are discussed in Chapter 6. 'Can Europe work with one interest rate?' is the question addressed in Chapter 7. Specifically, will the 'one size fits all' approach to interest rates lead to greater regional disparities and even greater problems with European unemployment? Whether the UK is right to stay 'out' and the approaches the government could take to the euro are discussed in Chapter 8. The interesting arrangements in the Nordic area—with one 'in' country taking part in EMU (Finland), two 'outs' (Sweden and Denmark), and one country (Norway) not even in the EU, are discussed in Chapter 9.

Section III looks at the institutions of the euro. With its establishment on 1 June 1998, the key institution—the European Central bank—is already in place. Its operations form the subject of Chapter 10. The institution which will manage fiscal policy has been described as 'Euro-X'. But it is less an institution than a sub-group of Ecofin (the Council of Economic and Finance Ministers) and, indeed, fiscal policy will still be conducted on a national basis. We look at how the new arrangements for managing fiscal policy might work in this setting in Chapter 11.

The legal issues are dealt with in Section IV. Here, we discuss not only the features of the legislation which introduces the euro but also consider more difficult issues such as 'break up risk'.

This provides an introduction to Section V in which we ask whether there may be problems ahead. Chapter 13 examines the potential for a break-up of EMU while, in Chapter 14, Tim Congdon considers the suggestion that EMU could be Europe's 'Maoist leap forward' and assesses whether monetary union is feasible without political union.

Section VI looks at the foreign exchange market, where the euro's presence was initially felt. We ask how the new currency will trade relative to the two other main world currencies—the US dollar and the yen—in Chapter 15. In particular, arguments for the euro being a relatively strong currency are put forward. The impact of the euro on eastern European currencies is dealt with in Chapter 16.

Section VII looks at three key areas of the financial market. In the money market, new reference interest rates will be established and the European

Central Bank will determine key official interest rates for the euro area. These are discussed in Chapter 17.

Some of the benefits associated with the euro's introduction will stem from the more efficient operation of the bond and equity markets. Before a fully-functioning pan-European market is established in either of those markets, however, some transitional problems need to be overcome. In both the bond and equity chapters (Chapters 18 and 19, respectively) we discuss the transitional issues, without losing sight of the end-benefits. The much-publicized impact on pensions in examined in Chapter 20.

On a macroeconomic scale, the euro's introduction is a story of short-term costs with longer-term benefits. A similar story is often heard at the level of the individual company. Many companies have faced substantial costs as a result of adapting to the new environment: changes to their accounting practices (See Chapter 21); their systems; treasury operations; staff training and so on. As with the macro-economy, however, they also should be on the verge of reaping rewards. How companies will live with the euro is the subject of Chapters 22 and 23. Of course, 'companies' are a very heterogeneous set of institutions. We deal with two particular types of companies in these chapters: financial companies in Chapter 22 and retailers in Chapter 23. Of course, any impact on retailers necessarily has a knock-on effect upon the poor old consumer. Despite the fact that discussion of his apparent plight comes towards the end of the book, we nevertheless do our best to convince him that the undoubted upheaval that will result from the euro's introduction will be worth it in the end. For him, too, it is 'short-term pain for long-term gain'.

Chapter
2

Paul Temperton
The Independent Economic Research Company (TIER)

Why is the euro being introduced?

The answer to the question 'Why is the euro being introduced?' has both a political and an economic dimension. The most basic political impetus has been the desire to maintain peace in Europe and it is significant that the foundations of the present arrangements were laid shortly after World War Two. The economic reasons for the euro's introduction are seated in the problems of the European economy in the 1970s and 1980s—in particular, slow growth and high unemployment. The combination of the single market and the single currency will go a long way towards improving the growth rate of the European Union.

Politics of the euro

At a fundamental level, the introduction of the euro is a political move, with the aim of ensuring peace and stability in western Europe. Only a year after the end of World War Two, Winston Churchill said that the 'first step in the recreation of the European family must be a partnership between France and Germany'. The Council of Europe, the forerunner of today's European Union, was established with some (limited) supranational powers, in Strasbourg in 1949. This was followed in 1951 by the creation of the European Coal and Steel Community. The formation of the European Economic Community (EEC) with six members (Germany, France, Italy and the Benelux countries) was agreed with the Treaty of Rome in 1957, and came into existence in 1958. It was, however, some ten years later that before Europe took a significant step towards the free movement of goods: on 1 July 1968, all customs duties were abolished between the six countries. Since then, the European Community has both widened—to include more members—and deepened, with moves to the single market and single currency. Far from being in conflict with each other, these widening and deepening moves have proceeded in tandem.

For example, Spain and Portugal joined the European Community in 1986, making a total of twelve countries (Denmark, the UK and Ireland joined in 1973 and Greece in 1981), just shortly before the Single European Act was signed. Austria, Sweden and Finland joined in 1995, making a total of fifteen countries, shortly after the Maastricht Treaty had been ratified.

Fears that reunification in 1990 would lead Germany to pursue a more eastward-leaning orientation were, indeed, one reason behind the push to the single currency project. France insisted that monetary union should take place as the 'price' for agreeing to German reunification. Significantly, negotiations with five central European countries (Poland, Hungary, the Czech Republic, Slovenia and Estonia) have been put on a 'fast track' now that the single currency project is close to implementation.

Many still claim, however, that monetary union without political union will be difficult to operate and arguments along these lines are developed by Tim Congdon in Chapter 14. It may be that monetary union is a step towards political union. Indeed, Chancellor Kohl of Germany recently claimed (in *The Sunday Times* on 26 April 1998) that monetary union would give a 'mighty push' to political union although he said this would be decentralized and not a European 'superstate'.

His remarks underline the fears of many: that monetary union is just one step on the road to greater control by 'Brussels bureaucrats' and the like, with a substantial erosion of national sovereignty. For those fears to recede, it is necessary for the economic consequences of the euro's introduction to be notably beneficial.

Economics of the euro

The economic impetus behind the euro project can be found in the relatively poor performance of the European economies over the last twenty years or more. Europe has, for a long time, suffered from relatively weak economic growth. The term 'eurosclerosis' was first coined in the 1970s, but became even more pertinent in describing the performance of the European economy in the 1980s. Economic growth trailed behind that in North America and Asia; productivity gains were weak; unemployment remained persistently high; and many European countries suffered from persistently high wage and price inflation.

'Eurosclerosis' was generally thought to be caused by relatively rigid and inflexible labour markets; a high level of government involvement in the economy; a less enterprising culture compared, in particular, to that in North America; and a poorer track record of innovation and research and development. More recently, the absence of a 'stakeholder' culture and a relatively hesitant embrace of new technology and communications have been added to the list.

The European problem: weak growth...

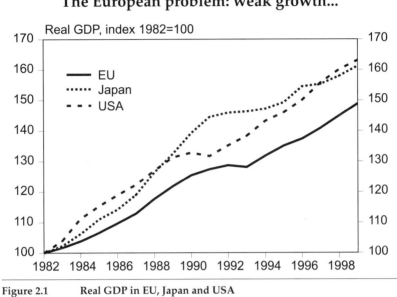

Figure 2.1   Real GDP in EU, Japan and USA

..and persistently high unemployment

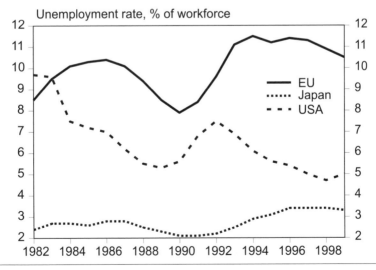

Figure 2.2   Unemployment rate in EU, Japan and USA

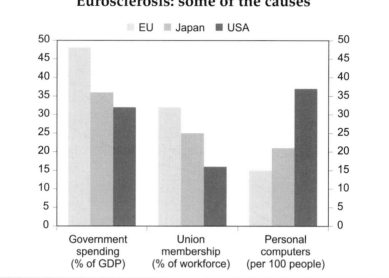

Figure 2.3   EU, Japan and USA: key statistics

In order to help correct these problems, the emphasis of European policy making in the last fifteen years has been to launch two significant projects.

First, the single European market, with the free movement of goods, labour, services and capital. This project was launched with the Single European Act of 1987 and should have resulted in such freedom of movement by the end of 1992. In reality, however, some barriers still persist.

Second, the euro project—or more correctly, the plan for European Economic and Monetary Union (EMU)—was launched the late 1980s. Jacques Delors was appointed by the 1988 Hanover Summit to look into the practical aspects of launching a single currency. He reported in 1989, and an Inter Governmental Conference that concluded at Maastricht in December 1991 broadly endorsed the Delors plan.

However, only a few months after heads of state signed the Maastricht Treaty (in February 1992), Europe entered a period of exchange rate turbulence. Between the summer of 1992 and the summer of 1993, the UK and Italy withdrew from the ERM; Sweden, Norway and Finland floated their currencies (they were previously pegged to the Ecu); and several countries devalued their currencies (Spain, for example, on three separate

The solution

Single market		EMU	
Boost to GDP growth from:		*Boost to GDP growth from:*	
Elimination of border controls	0.4	Elimination of currency conversion costs	0.5
Open public procurement	0.5	Decline in risk and uncertainty	5
Free financial markets	1.5		
Greater economies of scale	2.1		
Total	4.5	*Total*	5.5

Figure 2.4 **Impact of the single market and EMU**
Source: European Commission

occasions). The Maastricht Treaty, which envisaged a transition to a single currency via the movement to ever-narrower bands of exchange rate fluctuation, was seriously questioned. Furthermore, once exchange rate volatility receded Europe was hit by another wave of turbulence—this time in the bond markets, with bond yields rising sharply as budget deficits and stocks of outstanding debt rose sharply as a result of the recession in the early 1990s.

It was not until early 1995 that some stability returned to European financial markets and the plan for a single currency once again started to be taken seriously. In April 1995, the European Commission launched its Green Paper (a discussion document), entitled *Practical Aspects of the Introduction of the Single Currency*. This was followed by a report from the European Monetary Institute (the forerunner of the European Central Bank, which had been set up in January 1994), in November 1995. This report set the basis of the so-called Madrid scenario for the euro's introduction, which was agreed at the December 1995 Madrid Summit. Broadly, the euro is being introduced along the lines of that scenario. (The detailed timetable of that plan is set out in the next section.)

The completion of the single market and the introduction of the euro are both estimated to boost Europe's GDP significantly: by 4.5 per cent and 5.5 per cent, over ten years, respectively. Most of the single market benefits may already have been achieved. However, in combination, the measures will help to boost European growth and reduce unemployment. But two notes of caution need to be sounded. First, the single market and single currency projects do not squarely address the fundamental problems which were identified above as being the basis of 'eurosclerosis'. These two projects do not *directly* reduce the role of the state, or make Europe's labour markets more flexible, or make Europe more 'high tech'. Second, the combination of the single market and the single currency is a recipe for widespread industrial restructuring. That will necessarily entail job losses at the same time as new jobs are created by the boost to growth.

Paul Temperton
The Independent Economic Research Company (TIER)

A picture of Euroland

In this chapter, we set out some of the important features of 'Euroland', a term which is now commonly used to describe the combined economy of the eleven euro area countries. The picture given is merely an initial sketch, since greater detail is contained in subsequent chapters.

Euroland compared with the US and Japan

With an estimated population in 1999 amounting to some 287 million people, Euroland has more inhabitants than the United States (273 million) and more than double the number of Japan.

Overall, at an estimated $7 trillion in 1999, Euroland GDP is smaller than the $9 trillion of the US. Reflecting the lower GDP level and the higher population, average GDP per head in Euroland is almost one quarter lower than in the US: $24,000 per head, compared with $33,000 in the US (see Figure 3.1).[1]

The Big Three

	GDP ($bn)	Pop. (millions)	GDP/capita ($)	Trade as % of GDP
Euroland	6810	287	23,756	13.2
US	8903	273	32,622	12.9
Japan	4429	126	35,021	10.4

Figure 3.1 **Core statistics for Euroland, US and Japan**
All data are forecasts for 1999
Source: Oxford Economic Forecasting

Euroland: almost one-quarter of world GDP...

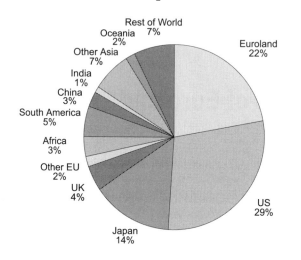

Figure 3.2   Shares in world GDP, 1999 estimates
Sources: HSBC Euroland Factbook, Eurostat Yearbook

...but only one-twentieth of world population

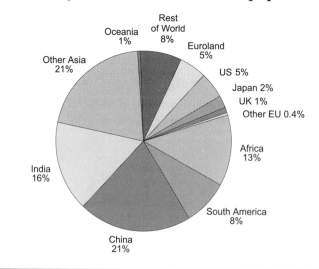

Figure 3.3   Shares in world population, 1999 estimates
Sources: HSBC Euroland Factbook, Eurostat Yearbook

Taken together, the US and Euroland account for more than half of the GDP of the entire world. Yet less than 10 per cent of the world's population lives in the two regions (see Figures 3.2 and 3.3).

As discussed in Chapter 2, European GDP growth has lagged behind that of the US and Japan for some considerable time. Over the last fifteen years, for example, growth has averaged 2.6 per cent per year in Euroland, compared with three per cent in the US. Over the first five years of Euroland's existence, however, the area is expected to grow faster than both the US and Japan.

Euroland: catching up?

	Forecast for:	Actual growth over last:		
	*Next five years**	*5 years*	*10 years*	*15 years*
Euroland	2.6	2.4	2.5	2.6
US	2.2	3.1	2.4	3.0
Japan	2.4	1.0	2.0	2.8
UK	1.9	3.0	1.7	2.5

Figure 3.4   GDP growth
Forecast for the next five years refers to 1999 to 2003
Source: Oxford Economic Forecasting

Individual Euroland economies have been used to a high proportion of their GDP being accounted for by trade with neighbouring European countries. Trade with other countries in Euroland is now, of course, 'internal' trade—similar to trade between regions of a country. As a bloc, Euroland is similar to the United States in that a relatively small proportion of its GDP is accounted for by trade outside the euro area: around 13 per cent for both Euroland and the US in 1999. This has led to some concern that Euroland may become more inward-looking. Neighbouring European countries (including those in eastern Europe) are the most important trading partners of Euroland (see Figures 3.5 and 3.6).

Euroland is an area which will has a high level of savings, being more similar to Japan than the US in this respect (see Figure 3.7). Also, to some extent reflecting that high level of savings, Euroland has a strong current account surplus. Again, there is a closer parallel with Japan in this respect. The strength of Euroland's current account position should support the value of the euro against the US dollar (see Figure 3.8).

Neighbouring European countries are...

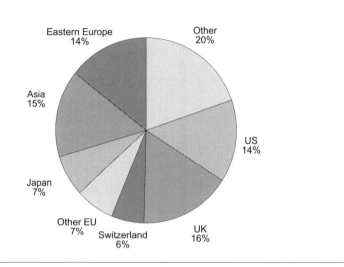

Figure 3.5   **Merchandise imports by destination, 1997**
Source: HSBC Euroland Factbook

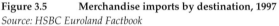

...Euroland's main trading partners

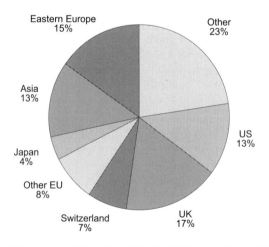

Figure 3.6   **Merchandise exports by destination, 1997**
Source: HSBC Euroland Factbook

Euroland more like Japan than the US...

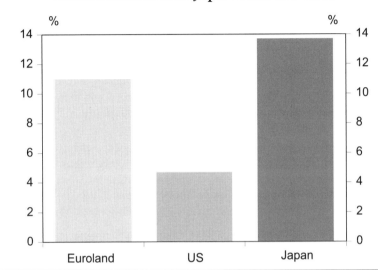

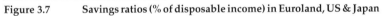

Figure 3.7   Savings ratios (% of disposable income) in Euroland, US & Japan

...with high savings and current account surplus

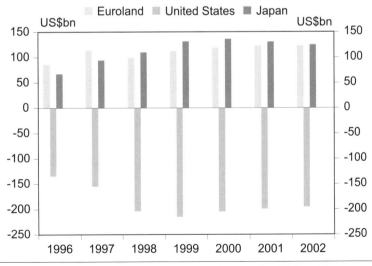

Figure 3.8   Current account balance (US$bn) in Euroland, US and Japan

Is the term 'Euroland' misleading?

In two respects, describing Euroland as one bloc is misleading. First, Euroland is just one part of the European Union, currently comprising 15 countries. 'Out' countries will be heavily influences by developments in Euroland and many companies in 'out' countries will use the euro as a currency. Indeed, with many Swiss companies intending to make active use of the euro, and Switzerland not even being a member of the EU, indicators for the entire western European economy may be more appropriate in some respects.

Second, there still exist substantial differences within Euroland. Variations in GDP per head in Euroland are much larger than within any individual European country and greater than within the US or Japan (see Figures 3.9 & 3.10). The low degree of labour mobility in Europe (see Figure 3.11), partly resulting from the high costs of moving house (Figure 3.12),

Variations in Euroland GDP per head...

Luxembourg	176
Germany	122
Spain	59
Portugal	46

Figure 3.9   **GDP per capita, 1996, index Euroland average = 100**
Source: Eurostat

..are much greater than those within the UK

South East	118
UK average	100
North East	88
Northern Ireland	80

Figure 3.10   **GDP per capita, 1996, index UK average = 100**
Source: ONS Regional Accounts

Euroland labour mobility is low...

Italy	0.5
England & Wales	1.1
Germany	1.1
France	1.3
USA	2.8

Figure 3.11   Regional moves as % total population
Source: Oxford Economic Forecasting

...partly because of the high cost of moving house

UK	5.0
USA	9.0
Germany	12.5
Spain	14.0
France	16.0
Italy	18.0
Belgium	22.0

Figure 3.12   Cost of buying or selling a house, % of total price
Source: Oxford Economic Forecasting

but also from social and linguistic differences, means that these differences maybe difficult to overcome. That is but one of the challenges facing Euroland in the years ahead.

Notes for Chapter 3

[1] *These calculations are on the basis of projected exchange rates for 1999 of DM1.75/US$ and ¥115/US$. Some calculations use PPP, or purchasing power parity, exchange rates in calculations of GDP per head. If PPP rates were, say, DM1.50/US$ and ¥100/US$, then GDP per head on a PPP basis would be higher in both the euro-11 and Japan: approximately $28,000 and $40,000 respectively. Still, the euro-11 would be some way behind the US.*

Chapter

4

The euro

Pat McArdle
Ulster Bank Markets[*]

How the euro is being created

Introduction

The euro is born on 1 January 1999. Legally, the euro becomes the national currency of the eleven countries participating in EMU on that date. The euro comes into existence in two ways. First, one Ecu becomes one euro. The official Ecu basket ceases to exist and the Ecu, renamed the euro, becomes a currency in its own right. Second, fixed conversion rates for each of the eleven national currencies to the euro come into force. From then on, these rates must be used for conversion either way between the euro and the national currency units. Conversions between national currency units must be done via the euro using the conversion rates instead of the traditional bilateral rates. Three years later, at the beginning of 2002, the national currencies will cease to exist and only the euro will remain. The birth of the euro is displayed diagramatically in Figure 4.1. This chapter explores the mechanics of the euro's creation in detail.

Background

The legal framework for the introduction of the euro is contained in two council regulations.

One of them, Council Regulation (EC) No. 1103/97 of 17 June 1997 on 'certain provisions relating to the introduction of the euro', contains provisions on matters which it was felt were most in need of legal certainty, such as the 1:1 relationship between the Ecu and the euro, continuity of contract and rounding details. The second, Council Regulation (EC) No. 974/98 of 3 May 1998 on 'the introduction of the euro', provides for, *inter alia*, the name of the new currency and its substitution for the national currencies at the conversion rates.

[*]*The views expressed are personal and do not necessarily reflect those of Ulster Bank Markets.*

Official provisions concerning euro conversion rates

'At the starting date of the third Stage, the Council shall, acting with the unanimity of the Member States without a derogation, on a proposal from the Commission and after consulting the ECB, adopt the conversion rates at which their currencies shall be irrevocably fixed and at which irrevocably fixed rate the ECU shall be substituted for these currencies, and the ECU will become a currency in its own right. This measure shall by itself not modify the external value of the ECU. The Council shall, acting according to the same procedure, also take the other measures necessary for the rapid introduction of the ECU as the single currency of those Member States.'

Article 109l(4) of Maastricht Treaty

'The European Council therefore decides that, as of the start of Stage Three, the name given to the European currency shall be euro. . . The specific name euro will be used instead of the generic term 'ECU' used by the Treaty to refer to the European Currency Unit.

A Council regulation entering into force on 1 January 1999 will provide the legal framework for the use of the euro. From that date, the euro will be 'a currency in its own right' and the official ECU basket will cease to exist. This Regulation will have the effect that the national currencies and euro will become different expressions of what is economically the same currency.'

Madrid Summit December 1995

'Every reference in a legal instrument to the ECU. . . shall be replaced by a reference to the euro at a rate of one euro to one ECU. . . from 1 January 1999 . . .'

Council Regulation (EC) No. 1103/97

'The euro shall be substituted for the currency of each participating Member State at the conversion rate'.

Council Regulation (EC) No. 974/98

'The current ERM bilateral central rates of the currencies of the Member States. . . will be used in determining the irrevocable conversion rates for the euro. . . The central banks of the Member States adopting the euro as their single currency will ensure through appropriate market techniques that on 31 December 1998 the market exchange rates . . . are equal to the ERM bilateral central rates. . . The final official ECU exchange rates calculated accordingly and released on 31 December 1998 will be proposed by the Commission for adoption by the Council on the first day of Stage Three, i.e. on 1 January 1999, as the irrevocable conversion rates for the euro for the participating currencies.'

Joint Communiqué on the Determination of the Irrevocable Conversion Rates for the euro May 1998

Figure 4.1

On 1 January 1999, one Ecu becomes one euro and...

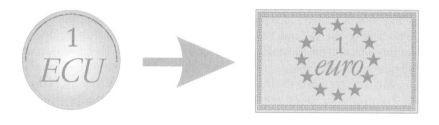

...11 national currencies have their rates irrevocably fixed to one euro

DEM	1.96267
BEF	40.4810
LUF	40.4810
NLG	2.21142
ITL	1,943.05
ESP	166.969
PTE	201.183
FRF	6.58252
IEP	0.790322
ATS	13.8104
FIM	5.96750

Figure 4.2   The euro's birth
Note: Conversion rates are indicative; actual rates will be announced on 31 December 1998

Neither the Maastricht Treaty nor the regulations, which were drawn up in the latter part of 1996, deal with the question of how the conversion rates should be set. This led to a major debate in the markets and various options were proposed. This process was brought to an end by the issue, on 2 May 1998, of a 'Joint Communiqué on the Determination of the Irrevocable Conversion Rates for the euro' (See Appendix A, at the end of this chapter). The participants to the communiqué included the ministers of the member states adopting the euro as the single currency, the governors of the Central Banks of these member states, the European Commission and the European Monetary Institute (EMI). They agreed that the current ERM bilateral central rates of the participating currencies will be used in determining the irrevocable conversion rates for the euro. While the communiqué does not have legal force, it clearly commits the authorities to a particular course of action and it has received widespread acceptance.

The announcement was credible in the markets

For much of 1998, the decision to use ERM bilateral central rates as the irrevocable conversion rates for the euro was well signalled in advance and was, therefore, anticipated in the markets. It was also widely expected that these rates would be pre-announced around the time of the decision in early May on the member states which qualified to participate in the third stage of EMU. For the half dozen or so core currencies, these rates are unchanged since the late eighties and in recent times all of the likely participants have traded close to their central rates. It was, thus, possible for the authorities to claim that 'these rates are consistent with economic fundamentals and are compatible with sustained convergence among the member states which will participate in the euro area.' In the period since the May announcement, market rates have moved even closer to the pre-announced conversion rates. At end-July 1998, forward exchange rates in seven of the eleven member states had converged completely, while in the remainder, the difference was only a fraction of one per cent.

The danger of speculation has receded

The objective of the pre-announcement of the conversion rates was to guide the markets and thereby lessen or eliminate potential speculation in the latter part of 1998. The potential for speculation, however, still exists, given that the conversion rates will not be formally fixed until 1 January 1999. To this end, the central banks of the member states adopting the euro have committed to 'ensure through appropriate market techniques that on

31 December 1998 the market exchange rates..are equal to the ERM bilateral central rates.' Though they do not say so explicitly, it is clear that the words 'appropriate market techniques' are code for unlimited intervention, should this be necessary. This means that the Bundesbank, which was once thought to have reservations about such co-operation in advance of the transfer of its powers to the new European Central Bank (ECB) on 1 January 1999, has thrown its full weight behind the agreement. Provided that the central banks are, indeed, committed to such unlimited intervention they can secure any desired exchange rate with a high degree of certainty. In practice, however, the credibility with which the announcement was greeted, and which is now widely expected to continue, should ensure that market rates remain convergent without the need for any significant further action on the part of the authorities.

Ecu/euro rates cannot be announced until 1998 year end

Article 109l(4) of the Maastricht Treaty provides that the rates at which the euro will be substituted for the currencies participating in the euro area will be adopted at the start of Stage Three of the Economic and Monetary Union, i.e. on 1 January 1999. The adoption of the irrevocable conversion rates for the euro shall by itself not modify the external value of the official Ecu. Likewise, Article 2 of the Council Regulation of 17 June 1997 on certain provisions relating to the introduction of the euro stipulates that every reference in a legal instrument to the official Ecu shall be replaced by a reference to the euro at a rate of one euro to one Ecu. Therefore, the irrevocable conversion rates for the euro have to be identical to the value of the official Ecu expressed in units of the participating currencies on 31 December 1998.

Since the Ecu is a currency basket, which includes the Danish krone, the Greek drachma and the pound sterling (currencies of member states not participating in the euro area), it is not possible to announce before the end of 1998 the irrevocable conversion rates at which the euro shall be substituted for the participating currencies. It was possible to announce that the bilateral central rates of the currencies participating in the euro area will be used on 31 December 1998 for computing the exchange rates of the official Ecu (and thus in computing the irrevocable euro conversion rates for these currencies) because the authorities will ensure that market rates on 31 December are, for all pratical purposes, identical to the pre-announced rates. The three 'out' currencies will, however, continue to fluctuate thereby influencing all Ecu rates in the process. Their levels on 31 December 1998 cannot be accurately predicted and we will have to wait until then to see what the precise final Ecu rates will be.

We have, however, a fair idea of what the euro rates will be

The Ecu/Deutschemark rate on 30 July 1998 was 1.96825. Details of how this and other Ecu rates are calculated are given in Appendix B. Figure 4.3 contains indicative calculations of the likely Ecu/Deutschemark rate on 31 December 1998. In it, we assume that the pre-announced bilateral rates against the Deutschemark will be achieved and simply substitute them for the 30 July rates shown in Appendix B. It is obviously much more difficult

Euro conversion rates can be approximated...

	Amount of national currency units in the Ecu basket		Pre-announced DM rates DM 1 =	Equivalent in DM of national currency amount
Nine 'ins'	(a)		(b)	(c) = (a) / (b)
1 Ecu equals	0.6242	DEM	1	0.6242000
Plus	3.301	BEF	20.6255	0.1600446
Plus	0.130	LUF	20.6255	0.0063029
Plus	0.2198	NLG	1.12674	0.1950761
Plus	151.8	ITL	990.002	0.1533330
Plus	6.885	ESP	85.0722	0.0809313
Plus	1.393	PTE	102.505	0.0135896
Plus	1.332	FRF	3.35386	0.3971543
Plus	0.008552	IEP	2.48338*	0.0212379
Three 'outs'			**Forward rates as at 30/07/98**	
Plus	0.1976	GBP	2.85404	0.2506989
Plus	1.440	DKK	3.81922	0.0517383
Plus	0.08784	GRD	172.202	0.0083623
			1 EUR = 1 ECU = DEM	1.9626691

Figure 4.3   Approximation of euro conversion rates
*The pre-announced rate was actually DEM = IEP 0.402676, i.e. the reciprocal of that used here, which is the usual quotation.
Note: The calculations in this table are shown via the DEM in order to facilitate exposition. In practice, the dollar will be used – see Appendix B.

to predict what the rates for the three 'out' currencies will be. We have used the forward rates (on 30 July 1998) for 31 December 1998. These are the markets' current forecasts based on the forward points which in turn, reflect interest rate differentials—the reality could, and frequently does, turn out to be quite different. If, however, the markets' predictions were to be realized then the euro conversion rate for the Deutschemark on 31 December 1998 would be that given in Figure 4.3, rounded to six significant figures, viz., 1.96267. The other euro conversion rates can be obtained by crossing the respective Deutschemark rates. Conversion rates for all eleven participants obtained in this manner are given in Figure 4.1. These data are shown to six significant figures as required by Regulation 1103/97. The uncertainty which remains regarding the evolution of sterling and the other two non-participant currencies means, however, that they are best regarded as the centre of a range of possible outcomes.

At the very least, we can provide a narrow range

There are different views as to what the British pound/Deutschemark rate will be on 1 January next. Some pundits believe that it will be closer to

...but not with precision as sterling may fluctuate*

| | Range of likely euro conversion rates | | | |
| | GBP = DM 2.85 | GBP = DM2.75 | GBP = DM 2.95 | *c minus b* |
	(a)	*(b)*	*(c)*	*% difference*
DEM	1.96	1.95	1.97	0.9
BEF	40.5	40.3	40.7	0.9
LUF	40.5	40.3	40.7	0.9
NLG	2.21	2.20	2.22	0.9
ITL	1943	1934	1951	0.9
ESP	167	166	168	0.9
PTE	201	200	202	0.9
FRF	6.58	6.55	6.61	0.9
IEP	0.79	0.79	0.79	0.9
FIM	5.97	5.94	5.99	0.9
ATS	13.8	13.7	13.9	0.9

Figure 4.4   **Range of euro conversion rates**
* *The DKR and GRD may also fluctuate but their weights are low and their impact on the euro rates correspondingly small. They are assumed to remain constant at the forward rates in Figure 4.3.*
Note: The number of significant digits used in the above table has been reduced to facilitate the exposition. In reality, each conversion rate will be given to six significant digits.

DM2.75 than the DM2.85 indicated by the forward rates on 30 July 1998. Others think it could be as high as DM2.95. Figure 4.4 shows what the euro conversion rates would be at each of those extremes which lie either side of the central proposition set out in Figure 4.1. If sterling were to evolve as predicted by the market, it would go to DM2.85 and the euro/ Deutschemark rate would be 1.96. If sterling were to fall to DM2.75, it would drag down the Ecu, and by extension the euro/Deutschemark rate, closer to DM1.95. On the other hand, if sterling were to rise to DM2.95, the euro/Deutschemark conversion rate would go up to 1.97. The difference between these upper and lower reaches is just less than 1 per cent. (The impact on the euro rates can be derived by multiplying the percentage increment in the sterling rate, in this case 7.3 per cent, by its weight in the Ecu basket, 12.77 per cent (7.7 × .1277 = 0.93) to get the resultant percentage). The impact on all Ecu rates is the same because the sterling rate is the only one which we allow to vary—see footnote to Figure 4.4.

The likely euro conversion rates based on the pre-announced bilateral rates and forward levels of sterling, the Danish krone and the Greek drachma are set out in column (a) of Figure 4.4. One euro would be equal to DM1.96, BEF40.5 etc. These rates are approximately midway between the upper and lower bounds which sterling movements might give rise to. We could, therefore, envisage a half per cent movement in either direction at most. This, in turn, means that the eventual euro/Deutschemark conversion rate is likely to lie in the range DM1.95 to 1.97. The corresponding ranges for the other currencies are set out in Figure 4.4.[1]

Notes for Chapter 4

[1]*The central banks have announced that the 'bilateral rates between the euro area participating currencies obtained by crossing the respective US dollar rates recorded by the EU central banks will be equal to the pre-announced ERM bilateral central rates, up to the sixth significant digit only' —see Appendix B. Once the euro conversion rates are fixed, they must be used henceforth per Regulation 1103/97. The use of bilateral rates between participating national currency units is prohibited unless they produce the same result as the triangulation algorithm (i.e. conversion via the euro), laid down in the regulation. So far, it has not been possible to prove rigorously that alternative methods of calculation do produce the same results as the triangulation algorithm and the onus of proof, as well as the legal risk, rest with the person using an alternative method. Many banks intend, however, to show bilateral rates, e.g. IEP/DEM for illustrative purposes. Crossing the euro conversion rates may not, however, give the exact pre-announced bilateral central rates because of the rounding phenomenon noted above. The European Bankers Federation have asked the authorities to produce a consistent matrix of bilateral rates for all eleven currencies but the central banks are reluctant to do this because they want to de-emphasize the bilateral rates as much as possible after 1 January 1999.*

Chapter

4

Joint Communiqué on the Determination Of The Irrevocable Conversion Rates for the Euro

In accordance with Article 1091 (4) of the Treaty, the irrevocable conversion rates for the euro will be adopted by the Council, upon a proposal from the Commission and after consultation of the European Central Bank (ECB), on the first day of Stage Three, i.e. on 1 January 1999.

With a view to guiding markets in the run-up to Stage Three, the Ministers of the member states adopting the euro as their single currency, the Governors of the Central Banks of these member states, the European Commission and the European Monetary Institute (EMI) have agreed on the method for determining the irrevocable conversion rates for the euro at the starting date of Stage Three.

The current ERM bilateral central rates of the currencies of the member states which, on the first day of Stage Three, will adopt the euro as their single currency, will be used in determining the irrevocable conversion rates for the euro. These rates are consistent with economic fundamentals and are compatible with sustainable convergence among the member states which will participate in the euro area. The central banks of the member states adopting the euro as their single currency will ensure through appropriate market techniques that on 31 December 1998 the market exchange rates, recorded according to the regular concertation procedure used for calculating the daily exchange rates of the official Ecu, are equal to the ERM bilateral central rates as set forth in the attached parity grid.

The procedure agreed upon by all parties to this Joint Communiqué will ensure that the adoption of the irrevocable conversion rates for the euro will by itself, as required by Article 1091 (4) of the Treaty, not modify the external value of the Ecu, which will be replaced on a 1:1 basis by the euro. The attached annex provides detailed information on this procedure* (*—not attached, see Appendix B). The final official Ecu exchange rates calculated accordingly and released on 31 December 1998 will be proposed by the Commission for adoption by the Council on the first day of Stage

	DEM	BEF /LUF	ESP	FRF	IEP	ITL	NLG	ATS	PTE	FIM
	100 =	100 =	100 =	100 =	1 =	1000 =	100 =	100 =	100 =	100 =
Germany DEM										
Belgium /Lux. BEF/LUF	2062.55									
Spain ESP	8507.22	412.462								
France FRF	335.386	16.2608	3.94237							
Ireland IEP	40.2676	1.95232	0.473335	12.0063						
Italy ITL	99000.2	4799.90	1163.72	29518.3	2458.56					
Netherlands NLG	112.674	5.46285	1.32445	33.5953	2.79812	1.13812				
Austria ATS	703.552	34.1108	8.27006	209.774	17.4719	7.10657	624.415			
Portugal PTE	10250.5	496.984	120.492	3056.34	254.560	103.541	9097.53	1456.97		
Finland FIM	304.001	14.7391	3.57345	90.6420	7.54951	3.07071	269.806	43.2094	2.96571	

Figure 4.5   **ERM bilateral central rates to be used in determining the irrevocable conversion rates for the euro**

Three, i.e. on 1 January 1999, as the irrevocable conversion rates for the euro for the participating currencies.

In compliance with the legal framework for the use of the euro, once the irrevocable conversion rate for the euro for each participating currency has been adopted, it will be the only rate which will be used for conversion either way between the euro and the national currency unit and also for conversions between national currency units.

Chapter

4

APPENDIX B

the euro

Extracts from the Annex to the 2 May 1998 Communiqué[*]

Calculation of the exchange rates of the official Ecu on 31 December 1998.

To calculate the exchange rates of the official Ecu on 31 December 1998, the regular daily concertation procedure will be used. According to this procedure, the central banks of the member states communicate the representative exchange rate of their respective currency against the US dollar.

Step 1: Determination of the EU currencies' concertation exchange rates against the US dollar

At 11:30 a.m. (CET), the EU central banks, including those with currencies which are not components of the Ecu basket, provide to each other in the context of a teleconference, the US dollar exchange rate for their respective currencies. These exchange rates are recorded as discrete values lying within the market bid-ask spreads. While, as a rule, the discrete values are equal to the mid-points of the bid-ask spreads, the EU central banks, as is allowed by the current concertation procedure, will take into account the need to ascertain exchange rates expressed with six significant digits, like for the pre-announced rates. The bilateral rates between the euro area participating currencies obtained by crossing[**] the respective US dollar rates recorded by the EU central banks will be equal to the pre-announced ERM bilateral central rates, up to the sixth significant digit. The EU central banks participating in the euro area stand ready to ensure this equality, if necessary, through the use of appropriate market techniques.

---

[*]*The material on calculations via the Deutschemark has been added by the author.*
[**]*For example, FRF/DEM = FRF/USD ÷ DEM/USD*

	Step 1	Step 2		Step 3
	Amount of national currency units in the Ecu basket	USD exchange rate on 30 July 1998	Equivalent in USD of national currency amount	Ecu exchange rates
		$1 =		Ecu 1 =
	(a)	(b)	(c) = (a) / (b)	(d) = (USD/ECU) × (b)
DEM	0.6242	1.76500	0.3536544	1.96825
BEF	3.301	36.3975	0.0906930	40.5889
LUF	0.130	36.3975	0.0035717	40.5889
NLG	0.2198	1.99020	0.1104412	2.21939
DKK	0.1976	6.72680	0.0293750	7.50144
GRD	1.440	293.700	0.0049030	327.522
ITL	151.8	1741.63	0.0871597	1942.19
ESP	6.885	149.870	0.0459398	167.129
PTE	1.393	180.640	0.0077115	201.442
FRF	1.332	5.91800	0.2250760	6.59950
GBP	0.08784	1.64450	0.1444529*	0.678113
IEP	0.008552	1.42410	0.0121789*	0.783061
		1 Ecu = USD	1.1151571	
FIM	Nil	5.36560		5.98349
ATS	Nil	12.4190		13.8491
SEK	Nil	7.89650		8.80584

Figure 4.6   **Calculation of the official Ecu exchange rates *vis-à-vis* all EU currencies on 30 July 1998**

The dollar exchange rate for the GBP and IEP is the number of dollars per currency unit rather than the number of currency units per dollar. Column (c) is therefore calculated for each of these two currencies by multiplying the value in column (b); and column (d) by dividing the dollar equivalent of the Ecu (i.e. US$/Ecu) by the rate in column (b).

	Step 1		Step 2	Step 3
	Amount of national currency units in the Ecu basket	DM exchange rate on 30 July 1998	Equivalent in DM of national currency amount	Ecu exchange rates
		DM 1 =		*Ecu 1 =*
	(a)	(b)	(c) = (a) / (b)	(d) = (DM/Ecu) × (b)
DEM	0.6242	1	0.6242000	1.96825
BEF	3.301	20.6218	0.1600733	40.5889
LUF	0.130	20.6218	0.0063040	40.5889
NLG	0.2198	1.12759	0.1949290	2.21938
ITL	151.8	986.759	0.1538370	1942.19
ESP	6.885	84.9122	0.0810838	167.129
PTE	1.393	102.346	0.0136107	201.443
FRF	1.332	3.35297	0.3972597	6.59949
IEP	0.008552	2.51354	0.0214958	0.783060
DKK	0.1976	3.81122	0.0518469	7.50145
GRD	1.440	166.402	0.0086537	327.521
GBP	0.08784	2.90254	0.2549591	0.678114
		1 Ecu = DEM	*1.9682530*	

Figure 4.7   Calculation of Ecu rates via the Deutschemark

Step 2: Calculation of the exchange rate of the official Ecu against the US dollar.

The rates as recorded by the EU central banks are thereafter communicated by the National Bank of Belgium to the Commission, which uses them to calculate the exchange rates of the official Ecu.[*] The USD/Ecu exchange rate (expressed as 1 Ecu = x USD) is obtained by summing up the US dollar equivalents of national currency amounts that compose the Ecu.

Step 3: Calculation of the exchange rates of the official Ecu against the EU currencies participating in the euro area.

The official Ecu exchange rates against the EU currencies are calculated by multiplying the USD/Ecu exchange rate by their respective US dollar exchange rates. This calculation is performed for all EU currencies, not only the ones which are components of the Ecu basket.

These Ecu exchange rates are rounded to the sixth significant digit. Exactly the same method of calculation, including the rounding convention, will be used in determining the irrevocable conversion rates for the euro for the euro area currencies.

For illustrative purposes, the calculation of the official Ecu exchange rates *vis-à-vis* all EU currencies on 30 July 1998[**] is shown in Figure 4.6.

Calculation of Ecu rates via the Deutschemark

The calculation of the Ecu via the dollar reflects precedent and the historic position of that currency in global forex markets. The calculation could, however, be done via any other currency. For example, had we used the Deutschemark, the result would be as shown in Figure 4.7.

The results are essentially the same though in seven out of the twelve cases the final digit of the Ecu rate is different because of rounding factors.

Anyone attempting, on 1 January 1999, to recreate the pre-announced bilateral conversion rates by crossing the new euro irrevocable conversion rates will encounter similar rounding inaccuracies i.e. there will be differences at the level of the sixth significant digit.

---

*These are published daily on Reuters page FXEZ.
**To make the calculations more realistic, the numerical example is based on 30 July 1998 instead of 31 December 1997 data.

Section

II

The
euro

The economics of the euro

Nikolaus Keis

HypoVereinsbank, Munich

The costs and benefits of the euro: a case study for Germany

Short-term pain for long-term gain

In this chapter, we look at the effects on the German economy of the introduction of the euro. The framework used is to identify the economic costs and benefits, both in the run-up to the euro's introduction and after it has been implemented.

The main costs in the run-up to the introduction of the euro were that:

- fiscal policy had to be tightened, not only in Germany, but also in other European countries; and that

- short- and long-term interest rates in Germany and core Europe were higher as a result of an EMU risk premium.

There were two benefits to economic growth:

- the 'risk premium' also led to a weaker value of the Deutschemark against the US dollar and the yen, helping to improve competitiveness and bring a boost to German exports; and

- the euro's introduction also required additional investment spending on the part of business to gear up for the euro.

The conclusion of the analysis in this chapter is, however, that the benefits only provided a minor offset to the substantial costs and that German economic growth was substantially reduced as a result of the preparations for the euro's introduction. In aggregate, German growth may have been reduced by up to one per cent in 1997, the year in which the costs were most evident.

Once the euro is introduced, however, economic growth will be boosted by three factors:

- the elimination of foreign currency transactions costs between euro area countries;

- the elimination of exchange rate risk in the euro area;

- additional supply-side effects brought about by continued fiscal discipline, lower wage growth and structural improvements in capital markets.

On balance, compared with the path the economy would have taken without the euro's introduction, growth was depressed in 1997, 1998 and 1999. But, by 2002, the losses seen in the run-up to EMU will have been offset by the post-EMU gains; and, by 2005, the accumulated gains to the German economy are expected to be substantial. In a nutshell, the story is one of short-term pain for long-term gain.

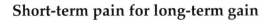

Short-term pain for long-term gain

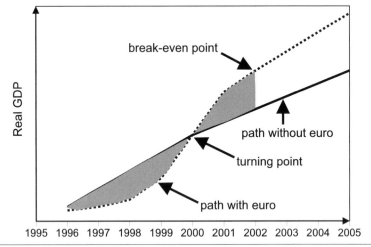

Figure 5.1   German growth — with and without the euro

Before the euro[1]

Fiscal tightening in Germany

Germany's public sector deficit was 3.8 per cent of GDP in 1996. In early 1997, it was generally thought that, without any tightening of fiscal policy, the budget deficit would probably have amounted to about 3.5 per cent of GDP. In an attempt to meet the three per cent target, a package of measures was introduced early in 1997, cutting government spending by DM40bn. Even so, it looked likely by mid-1997 that the three per cent target would still be exceeded. This led to a proposal by the Finance Ministry to use the profit from revaluing the gold reserves to reduce the budget deficit; the plan was, however, dropped following Bundesbank opposition. Further tax increases and spending cuts were therefore implemented in the second half of 1997 and the end result was that the budget deficit amounted to 2.7 per cent in the year.

The direct effect of the fiscal tightening, according to our estimates, was to cut GDP growth in 1997 by around 0.7 per cent. It would not be correct, however, to ascribe all of this reduction in output to the introduction of the

Short-term pain

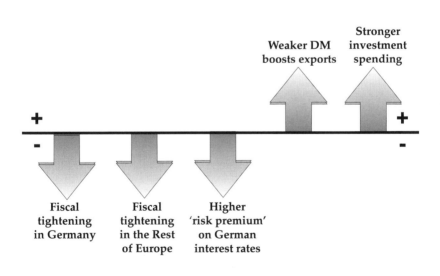

Figure 5.2   Effect on German growth: before the euro

euro. Even without the euro preparations, the deficit would also have been tackled in 1997. On balance, we assume an EMU-induced real GDP loss in 1997 of DM15bn, representing 0.4 per cent of GDP.

Fiscal tightening in other countries

With the exception of Luxembourg, all prospective EMU members were in the position in early 1997 of having to reduce their public deficits, sometimes considerably, in order to meet the deficit and debt criteria contained in the Maastricht Treaty.

In our simulations, we have applied the Maastricht criteria rather strictly. All EMU core members must have reduced their public sector deficit to three per cent of GDP in 1997. In addition, the debt ratio—in as far as it exceeds 60 per cent—must be moving downwards. These requirements also apply in subsequent years. The other EU countries are projected to fulfil the criteria, to a large extent, by the year 2000. Fiscal retrenchment is generally assumed to take place via a reduction of government expenditure. The effects on the various countries are strongly contradictory. In several countries, real government spending has to be reduced by more than three per cent. The losses in GDP for the core countries amounted to some 1.5 per cent of GDP in 1997. For some non-core countries the effects are even larger.

Lower growth in other EU countries reduced the demand for German exports. According to our simulations, the reduction in GDP from this effect also amounted to around 0.4 per cent of GDP in 1997.

The EMU risk premium: higher bond yields

It is clear that, in the run-up to EMU, the bond market has at times set a 'risk premium' on German long-term interest rates. It is difficult to measure this precisely, but one indication is given by the yield differential between Germany and the USA, adjusted for inflation. This shows that 'real' interest rates in Germany were as much as 175 basis points higher than in the USA at times during 1995. We estimate the EMU-induced risk premium was 50 basis points on average during 1996, 75 basis points in 1997, and 25 basis points in 1998.

The EMU risk premium: a weaker Deutschemark

We assume that the anticipation of EMU led to a 10-15 pfennig weakening of the Deutschemark against the dollar in the run-up to the euro's introduction. As other euro area currencies were broadly stable against the Deutschemark in that period, there was an overall improvement in the

'Risk premium' on German rates

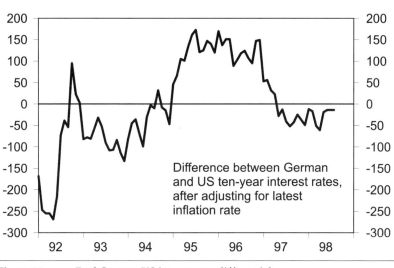

Figure 5.3   Real German-US interest rate differential

euro area's competitiveness *vis-à-vis* the USA. The resulting improvement of price competitiveness led to stronger exports (and weaker imports) after a time lag (the well-known 'J-curve effect').

Investment spending: a boost for growth in the run-up to EMU

In the run-up to the introduction of the euro many sectors of the economy had to carry out additional investment spending. Additional spending is necessary to put into place a dual or multi-currency accounting system; staff training for the euro will be required and additional information will have to be provided to consumers.

Reliable cost estimates are not available. According to a survey of the European Bank Union in spring 1994, the outlays of banks in all 15 EU countries during the three years up to 1999 would amount to Ecu20bn (around DM38bn). Corresponding to its share in the EU economy (23 per cent), German banks would have to spend almost DM9bn. However, the same survey mentions a figure of two per cent of current costs of banks, which would imply a cost of DM2bn for German banks. On the other hand, if one uses some of the bank-specific estimates (Bayerische Vereinsbank: DM120m, Deutsche Bank: DM250m) and project a total figure—assuming a greater than proportional cost for smaller organizations, who will not be able to take advantage of economies of scale—the cost would work out to be almost DM4bn. We also need to take into account that the costs of large projects are often underestimated initially.

Bearing in mind these considerations, we assume the costs to be DM5bn for the banking sector and DM10bn for the total financial sector (including insurance and social insurance).

We see the adjustment expenditures for most of the goods producing firms as relatively modest. The *Middelstand* (small businesses) will adjust its accounting system later, when the costs of doing so will probably be lower; while large, internationally-orientated companies already have to transform transactions in several currencies, making then more easily adaptable to the introduction of the euro.

On balance, we assume that the additional DM10bn of investment spending was undertaken over the three years—1996 to 1998 inclusive—up to the euro's introduction. The maximum effect on GDP is reached in 1999, when GDP is marginally higher than would otherwise have been the case.

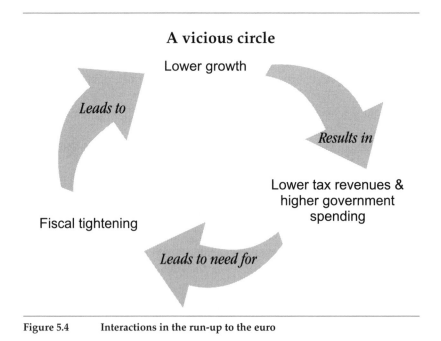

A vicious circle

Lower growth

Leads to

Results in

Lower tax revenues & higher government spending

Fiscal tightening

Leads to need for

Figure 5.4   Interactions in the run-up to the euro

Aggregate effect

We can add together the effects of fiscal tightening in Germany and other European countries, a higher risk premium on interest rates and on the currency, as well as the effect of higher investment spending, to obtain an estimate of the overall effect on German GDP.

On this basis, the greatest 'cost' to German GDP growth was in 1997, when GDP was 0.8 per cent lower than would have been the case if the country had not been preparing for the euro.

These calculations, of necessity, do not take into account any effect that the preparations for EMU have on general business and consumer confidence. It has certainly been the case that many European countries have, at times, been caught in a 'vicious circle', whereby fiscal tightening and the dampening effect on economic growth has led to even slower growth, resulting in a larger budget deficit, and so on. Such effects, which would increase the costs of preparing for the euro, are not specifically taken into account. More recently, both business and consumer confidence has improved. Partly in anticipation of the euro's introduction.

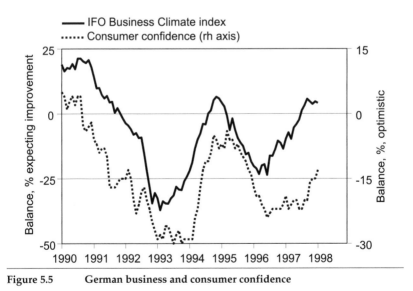

Figure 5.5   German business and consumer confidence

After the introduction of the euro

In assessing the benefits to the German economy after the introduction of the euro, we have—as a first step—based our work on the estimates produced by the European Commission in 1990.[2] That is, the real output gains from the euro are assumed to be five per cent over a time span of 10-15 years, or about 0.4 per cent per annum.

The main gains stem from:

- the disappearance of exchange rate related transaction and information costs; and

- the disappearance of exchange rate risks and the related reduction of investment risks.

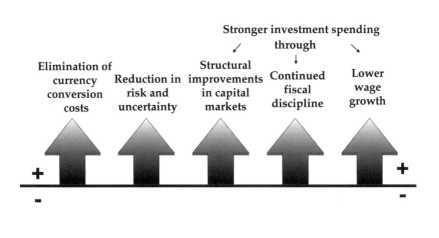

Figure 5.6   Effects on German growth: after the euro

These changes lead to a better allocation of resources and a more efficient market. They are also likely to stimulate stronger investment spending, giving a further boost to growth.

However, there are four reasons for thinking that the actual gains from the euro may be somewhat higher than these estimates:

- **First,** there may be greater structural consequences. For example, the European capital market will become more liquid, deeper in many segments and more diverse in terms of the range of instruments available. For companies issuing debt and equity, this implies lower capital costs. For the financial sector in general, there will be increased competition and greater 'pressure to perform'. Even with a small number of countries in the euro area, the European bond market would become the second largest in the world—behind the USA, but ahead of Japan. It could therefore become more independent from US interest rate movements. The financial infrastructure will be modernized and thus more productive. All these factors will help to bring lower European interest rates.

- **Second**, the 'shareholder value' concept—familiar in the US—may become a more prominent feature of German business.

- **Third,** the introduction of the euro will make differences in wages throughout the euro area much clearer. Just as the euro illustrates quickly to the Portuguese worker how much one can earn in Germany, it helps clarify to German employers and employees how much hourly wage costs are in Portugal. Real wage growth could be more modest, which should lead to more employment and growth.

A virtuous circle?

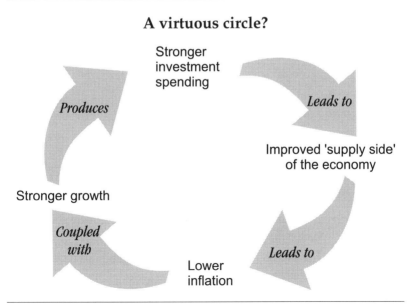

Figure 5.7   Interactions after the euro's introduction

Finally, we also expect a medium-term gain from improvements in supply conditions triggered by the euro. The Maastricht criteria and the stability pact require a change in fiscal policy. Countries will find it much more difficult to run up government debts, which should lead to lower real interest rates. According to an IMF estimate, the rise in the debt ratio in industrial countries from 40 per cent to 70 per cent between 1980 and 1995 led to an increase in real interest rates of 100 to 250 basis points. The corollary is that real interest rates will fall as the stock of debt in relation to GDP tends to fall. This may allow lower taxes and greater freedom for the private sector of the economy.

The growth effects arising from the improvement in the supply-side of the economy and structural improvements are very difficult to quantify, not least because they may generate a 'virtuous circle' of stronger growth. We see, however, no reason why they should be any lower than those identified in the European Commission's earlier study. Nevertheless, we err on the side of caution and thus assume that they will add one half of the effects identified by the European Commission (i.e. to boost GDP growth by 0.2 per cent p.a.).

Overall effects & conclusion for the German economy

Taking into account the costs incurred in preparing for the euro and the subsequent benefits the following picture emerges for the German economy:

- Preparation for the euro implies an initial reduction in German economic growth.

- The highest 'cost' was in 1997, when we estimate that real GDP was around 0.8 per cent lower than would otherwise have been the case.

- With the introduction of the euro in 1999, the expansionary effect on the economy begins to come through.

- By the year 2000, the level of GDP will be back to the level it would have been in the absence of the costs of preparing for the euro.

- By the year 2002, the pre-euro losses will have been made good by the post-euro gains.

- In 2005, real economic activity will be higher by almost DM100bn (at 1991 prices).

- Over 10 years, the net wealth gain (aggregated real GDP discounted by an assumed five per cent p. a.) amounts to DM140bn.

Notes for Chapter 5

[1]*The first version of this study was completed at the end of 1995. What was at that time a forecast—namely the developments in the run-up to the euro—is now already history. But in retrospect, we can be content with our analysis of the adjustment phase before 1999, i. e. that Germany and Europe would have to accept slower growth. The minor adjustments which we would have to make on the basis of what we know today would, by and large, offset each other: there was a lower risk premium on interest rates than we assumed and the boost to investment spending may have been stronger, but the fiscal tightening was more aggressive than we first expected. We judge that the quantitative effects in the preparatory phase for the euro are not substantially different to those which we initially estimated. There has been nothing to change our fundamental assessment of the post-euro benefits.*

[2]*European Commission (1990), 'One market, One Money' European Economy Number 44, October.*

Professor David Miles
Merrill Lynch &
Imperial College, London

Chapter
6

Fundamental economic implications of EMU

What is really driving monetary union?

It is almost universally accepted that economic and monetary union is primarily a political, rather than an economic, enterprise. The implication of this proposition is that political goals (the avoidance of another European war, the desire to cement Franco-German relations) are what is driving the process forward. Wise commentators tell us that EMU will happen not because of economic forces, but in spite of them. This is all much too glib, and ignores the economic factors which make monetary union for many (but perhaps not all) European countries a sensible arrangement. It is economic conditions that make this so; they make a single currency for many European countries the best system. This is a strong statement. But 'best' is synonymous with 'least bad'. It is completely implausible that monetary union is a panacea for many European countries' problems. But it is plausible that having permanently-fixed exchange rates against a country's closest trading partners is, in many cases, a less bad option than having volatile ones.

Economic factors behind monetary union are much more important than political ones . . .

The key economic factor that lies behind the move towards European monetary union is the realization that three things are mutually inconsistent. These are:

- free capital movements;
- national autonomy over monetary policy;
- fixed exchange rates.

It is impossible for a country to have a fixed exchange rate, for there to be free movement of capital and for that country simultaneously to set its monetary policy by reference to domestic economic conditions. If a country wants the value of the exchange rate against some other currencies to be stable it must be prepared—in the absence of exchange controls and with free flows of capital—to use interest rates to achieve that. Interest rates cannot be set at the level that domestic economic conditions suggest is appropriate. European governments have come to see the advantages of free capital movements; the substantial rise in the amount of intra-European trade has, at the same time, increased the damage done by sharp fluctuations in exchange rates between European countries. So, what has happened over the last twenty years is that many governments have been forced to give up much of their national autonomy over monetary policy precisely because they see the advantages of free capital movements *and* a substantial degree of stability in their exchange rates. It is the perceived economic advantages of stability in exchange rates and free capital movements that has been the key factor behind the next logical step of giving up national autonomy over monetary policy.

. . .recognizing the primacy of economic forces is intellectually liberating

So it seems that economic factors have actually been the key behind monetary union; one does not need to be a Marxist to believe that ultimately it is economic factors that are the key behind what appear to be forces determined by politicians. Recognizing the primacy of economic forces in driving the EMU process is liberating. Rather than seeing the whole thing as being driven by idealistic, and possibly misguided, politicians one is instead led to focus on the underlying and fundamental economic forces at work. In this chapter, the aim is to think about the big economic factors behind monetary union. In particular, we want to consider some of the major implications of monetary union for households, non-financial companies and for financial institutions.

Some economic fundamentals

At the outset it is helpful to think in a fundamental way about what monetary union does. Forming a currency union is a process which will:

- further reduce obstacles to trade between members of the currency union;

- substantially increase substitutability of assets issued by governments and companies in different parts of the currency union;

- potentially cause inflation and also economic business cycles to be more closely aligned than they would otherwise be; and, finally

- quite probably make interest rates within countries less suited, on average, to local conditions that they otherwise might have been.

Some of these implications of the formation of a monetary union—such as reductions in obstacles to trade—are good. Others—such as interest rates becoming somewhat less suited to local conditions—are bad.

Monetary union effectively increases the size of the market for many firms . . .

The most obvious 'good' is the further reduction in obstacles to trade. One can think of this as effectively increasing the size of the market for firms producing and selling within the currency union. There are two different reasons why this might increase the average size of European firms (brought about either by rapid growth of some firms or through mergers and takeovers). In some industries, the size of national markets may have prevented economies of scale being exploited to their fullest extent. To the extent that monetary union effectively increases the size of markets, it may allow firms in some sectors to take advantage of economies of scale that are only fully exhausted at very high levels of operation. Conceivably, such economies of scale may exist within financial services and, if they do, one would expect some firms to substantially increase their size at the expense of others.

A second process has little to do with economies of scale. It may just be that some companies are substantially more efficient than others. Again, to the extent that currency fluctuations gave them a disadvantage in foreign markets, the complete removal of currency variability enhances their ability to take advantage of greater efficiency. The result, once again, is that some firms come to take a bigger share of the new larger market.

. . . and can be expected to lead to consolidation in many markets

The implication of these simple economic propositions is that, across a range of different markets in Euroland, we might expect to see some firms gaining market share substantially at the expense of others; and the overall average size of firms within Europe may become larger. In turn, this has indirect implications for the structure of financial markets. One expects that larger firms are more likely than smaller firms to use securities markets, so one factor behind the greater use of securities markets (bond and equity markets), and the lesser use of funds intermediated through the banking sector, is rationalization and increased scale across different European markets.

Portfolio shifts

Portfolios of wealth in Europe are currently strikingly biased towards domestic assets . . .

A second, and perhaps more obvious, implication of the removal of currency risk is the impact it has on portfolio allocation. One thing that is strikingly true across all European countries (indeed across all developed countries) is the spectacular degree of international *non*-diversification of portfolios. Figures 6.1 and 6.2 give a snapshot of the portfolios of financial assets held by the private sectors in the major economies at the end of 1996. (Here, we add together all financial assets held directly by households to financial assets held on their behalf by pension funds, insurance companies and in unit trust, mutual funds, etc.). Figure 6.1 shows that, in

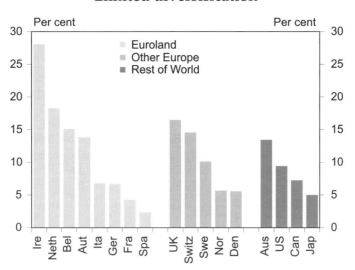

Limited diversification

Figure 6.1   Proportion of total private sector financial assets held in overseas assets (1996)*

The sum of financial assets held by households plus financial assets of pension funds, insurance companies and collective investment schemes (mutual funds, unit trusts, etc.).
Source: Intersec

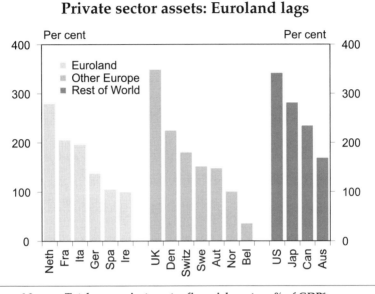

Private sector assets: Euroland lags

Figure 6.2   Total gross private sector financial assets as % of GDP*

*The sum of financial assets held by households plus financial assets of pension funds, insurance companies and collective investment schemes (mutual funds, unit trusts, etc.).
Source: Intersec

most European countries, less than 10 per cent of total financial assets are claims on companies or governments in overseas countries. Even in countries where international diversification is relatively high (the UK and Netherlands) more than 80 per cent of assets are claims on domestic firms and the national government.

. . .whether and by how much this will change depends on several factors

The extent to which one would expect all this to change in Europe as a result of monetary union depends crucially on the degree to which currency variability has been the key factor in pushing people toward domestic assets in the past. How important that factor has been varies across countries and across institutions within countries. Figure 6.3 shows the current rules which constrain portfolio allocations of pension funds and insurance companies in different countries.

National regulations . . .

In nearly all cases, insurance companies face the requirement of being currency matched up to 80 per cent; monetary union clearly has a major

National regulations

Country	Pension funds	Insurance companies
Austria	Minimum 50% in home currency bank deposits or bonds; max 35% in foreign currency assets	80% currency matching
Belgium	Max 50% in foreign assets; max in equity of 65%	80% currency matching
Denmark	80% currency matching; max 40% in equity	80% currency matching
Finland	80% currency matching	80% currency matching
France	5% ceiling on foreign assets; minimum of 34% in state guaranteed assets	5% ceiling on foreign assets; minimum of 34% in public debt instruments
Germany	80% currency matching; 30% ceiling on EU equity	80% currency matching
Italy	33.3% currency matching rule (but ECU assets are considered matched).	80% currency matching
Neth.	Limits on employer-related investment	80% currency matching
Norway	20% limit on equity; 30% limit on foreign assets	80% currency matching
Portugal	Ceiling on foreign, OECD securities of 20%	80% currency matching
Spain	No limits on equity or on currency composition	80% currency matching
Sweden	Foreign asset ceiling of 5-10%	80% currency matching
UK	Self-investment restricted to 5%; 'Prudent-Person' rules	Subject to matching and localization rules.

Figure 6.3   Restrictions on asset allocations of European institutional investors
Source: IMF 'International Capital Markets', November 1997

impact on the extent to which this particular constraint binds. However, for pension funds, other constraints are likely to prevent significant portfolio diversification after monetary union because, in many cases, there are currently limits on the amount of foreign assets that can be held. Also, in many countries, there are quite low ceilings on the proportion of assets that can be held in the form of equities. Whether these restrictions will persist is unclear; if monetary union makes European equity markets deeper and more liquid, it would be a sensible response of national regulators of pension funds to allow more assets to be held in stocks and shares.

Direct holding of wealth by individual households is not subject to such restrictions.

... and the degrees of correlation in returns are the key factors

Perhaps the key factor in determining the degree of cross-border portfolio diversification within the monetary union will be the degree of correlation of equity and bond returns across different countries. The greater the national factors in determining rates of return on national assets, the larger the benefits of diversification. So, perhaps paradoxically, those who believe that Euroland will fall well short of being an optimum currency area—precisely because business cycles do not move closely in line—should perceive the benefits of diversification to be high. One could make the same point in a slightly different way. One would need to believe that the degree of correlation between financial markets in different European countries is phenomenally high for there to be no benefits from greater international portfolio diversification.

The balance sheets of companies and households

The maturity, duration and overall magnitude of debt for companies and households varies a lot in Europe . . .

While European countries' portfolios of assets are similar in the extent of the home-country bias, there are substantial differences in the allocation of wealth to different types of asset. Also, there are big differences in the balance sheets of corporates and households on the liabilities side. Figures 6.4 and 6.5 bring out some of the big differences that currently exist. As is well known, households in some European countries (most notably the

Big differences in household indebtedness

UK	79	(1995)
Norway	70	(1993)
Spain	58	(1995)
Germany	56	(1995)
Sweden	54	(1994)
France	50	(1995)
Finland	41	(1994)
Italy	24	(1995)

Figure 6.4   **Financial liabilities of the household sector (% of GDP)**

Source: OECD Non-Financial Enterprises Financial Statements

UK) have substantially more debt than the European average. At the same time, a much higher proportion of that debt in some countries is at floating rate, or of short maturity. In the UK and Italy, households and corporates are affected more rapidly by changes in short-term interest rates than is the case in most other countries. One interesting question is whether one might expect convergence in the structure of debt.

. . . in part this reflects past patterns of inflation which are likely to change as a result of EMU

To a large extent the reliance on floating-rate debt in the UK (by households and corporates) and Italy (by the government) is a reflection of high and variable inflation in their recent past, which has made long-term, fixed rate contracts risky for both providers and users of funds. To the extent that monetary union affects the level and variability of inflation it will have an impact here.

The importance of equity markets

Equity markets are set to become more important . . .

However, perhaps the greatest differences within Europe now are in the composition of financial assets held, rather than in the levels of debt of households and companies. Figure 6.5 shows the importance of equities,

---

Big differences in corporate indebtedness

Italy	76	(1994)
Norway	74	(1993)
Sweden	66	(1993)
Finland	64	(1993)
France	61	(1994)
Germany	60	(1994)
Spain	60	(1994)
Belgium	59	(1994)
Netherlands	56	(1993)
Denmark	54	(1994)
Austria	53	(1994)
UK	**38**	**(1994)**

Figure 6.5   **Liabilities of non-financial enterprises as % of total assets**

Source: OECD Non-Financial Enterprises Financial Statements

Differences in portfolio structure

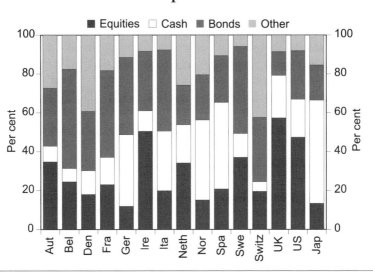

Figure 6.6   **Portfolio allocation of the private sector - 1996***

*Distribution of financial assets by category. Total assets are the sum of gross financial assets held by households, by pension funds, by insurance companies and in collective investment schemes.
Source: Intersec

bonds, cash and other assets in the portfolios of the private sectors of most European countries (portfolio allocation for the US and Japan is also shown). Equities are dramatically more important for the private sectors in the UK, Ireland and the US compared with most other countries. Might we expect convergence here?

... crucial here is the way in which pension arrangements evolve in the light of demographic shifts

The answer depends crucially on how European governments respond to the implications of demographic change. It is well know that aging populations will put increasing strains on government-run, unfunded pension systems. At the same time, they alter the advantages of funded systems relative to unfunded systems. The point can be made simply: the lower the rate of growth of the aggregate wage bill in the future, the lower the rate of return on contributions to unfunded state systems. Demographic shifts will reduce the rate of growth of the labour force and reduce the effective rate of return on contributions to unfunded schemes. Figure 6.7 shows an estimate of the rate of return to contributions made to unfunded government pension systems relative to an estimate of the rate

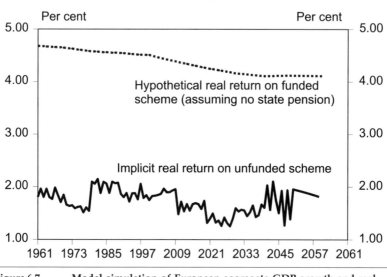

Funded vs. unfunded pension schemes

Figure 6.7   Model simulation of European aggregate GDP growth and real rates of return

Source: Miles, 1997

of return that can be earned on funds. The rate of return on funds is a hypothetical figure based on an assessment of where returns on assets would be if there were no unfunded state pensions and private savings were higher as a result.[1] What the chart suggests is that rates of return on assets has been, and will remain, substantially higher than the kind of rates of return that implicitly are earned on government-run pension systems.

So it seems likely that there are economic forces which will push European governments toward encouraging their citizens to make greater funded provision for their own retirement and rely less upon state pensions. Since equities would likely form a substantial part of the portfolios of efficiently-run pension funds, it would follow that greater private sector funding of pensions will see the overall proportion of private sector wealth invested in the equity markets rise in Europe over the longer term. Funds will be invested in marketable securities, so the proportion of assets in bonds and equities combined is likely to rise relative to the proportion in cash (i.e. in banks). There is an obvious implication of all this for financial institutions within Europe. If long-term savings markets are set to increase substantially, one expects fund managers to be in a healthy economic environment. The position for banks is less clear.

Some implications for banks

The efficiency of banks varies significantly across countries in Europe . . .

While providers of long-term savings products, and managers of the assets, are likely to do well, banks may be in a more difficult situation. Where we start from in Europe is a position where banks in different countries differ quite markedly in rates of return, in the degree of excess capacity, and in the margins between interest rates charged on assets and liabilities. Figures 6.8 to 6.10 give an indication of the degree of variability that currently exists. Net interest margins have been relatively low in the UK and Netherlands, but relatively high in Italy, Germany and France. At the same time, profitability has tended to be higher in countries where net interest margins have tended to be lower. There also is a positive correlation between a crude measure of excess capacity (number of branches per person in the population) and net interest margins. All of this suggests that cost differences between banks in different countries may be substantial and that countries where net interest margins have been fairly high in the past are those where banks have needed a substantial margin to cover high costs. If monetary union substantially changes the extent to which banks based in one country can compete in the markets of banks based in another, then there could be major changes in the structure of banking. There would be big winners and big losers.

. . .as does profitability and excess capacity

However, at least in the retail financial markets, there will remain substantial barriers to cross-border competition. Loyalty to recognized national names is likely to be much greater in retail banking than in wholesale markets. At the same time, public ownership of banks remains substantial in some countries. And there are several examples of explicit tax breaks that favour domestic banks. For example, in France, tax-exempt special savings accounts are available only from two institutions (The French Post Office and the Caisse d'Epargne) and tax-exempt share savings plans are restricted to investing exclusively in French shares. And as the IMF recently noted: '*In Italy and Portugal, the interest paid on loans from non-residents is subject to a withholding tax, which practically excludes non-residents from lending to domestic non-banks .... in some countries insurance premiums are tax deductible only if the insurance contract is with a company having its headquarters in the national territory*'.

Wide variation in banks' net margins...

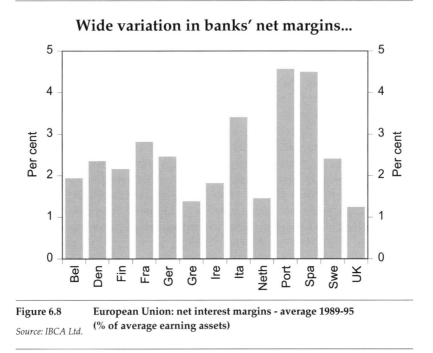

Figure 6.8   **European Union: net interest margins - average 1989-95**
Source: IBCA Ltd.   **(% of average earning assets)**

...and the number of bank branches

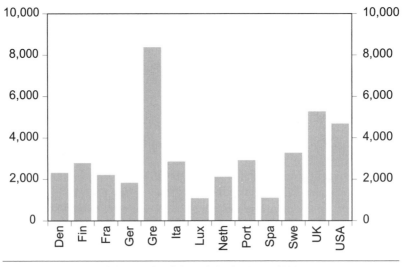

Figure 6.9   Population per bank branch in the EU and USA, 1994
Source: Schinasi (1997) based on data from Organisation for Economic Cooperation and Development (OECD), Bank Profitability: Financial Statements of Banks 1985-1994 (Paris OECD, 1996).

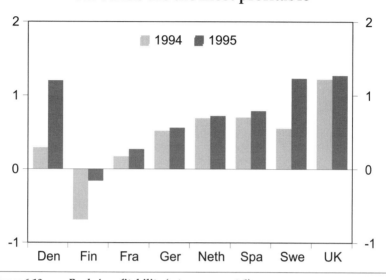

UK banks are the most profitable

Figure 6.10   Banks' profitability (return on assets*)

*Pre-tax profits of major banks (IBCA data).
Source: Schinasi (1997) based on data from IBCA Ltd. and Organisation for Economic Cooperation and Development as adapted from Bank for International Settlements, 66th Annual Report (Basle: Bank for International Settlements, 1996).

In an environment where the relative scale of flows of funds intermediated through the banking sector may fall . . .

So, changes in the structure of retail financial markets may well be slow and the death of less efficient firms may be a drawn out and painful affair. However, because economies of scale may be large in the provision of financial services—and more importantly because cost and efficiency differences are currently substantial—then ultimately there may be more changes in the structure of European financial markets than in most other sectors.

. . .there will be losers

The IMF has recently gone on record as singling out the banking sectors of some countries as being likely gainers from the completion of the single European market. They also imply where the losers are. Here is what they said in the latest (November 1997) edition of *International Capital Markets*: *'The UK banking system is the most competitive in the European Union and the one in which restructuring is most advanced. UK banks have a high return on equity even though they operate in an environment with low net interest margins, few impediments to cross-border competition, and a highly developed financial market, which exposes them to the risk of dis-intermediation. Their performance is explained by a large and increasing share of non-interest income, below-average and falling cost-to-income ratios, a constant decline in the density of branches, and intense merger and acquisition activity. Only the Nordic countries and Ireland have also experienced some of the restructuring observed in the United Kingdom: although their banking systems are not as profitable, their costs tend to be relatively low and the density of their branch networks has been falling for several years.'*

Notes for Chapter 6

[1]*The calculations are based on a simple economic model of the European economy which takes account of the impact of big changes in demographic structure on both the return on assets and on the growth in aggregate wages. The implicit real return on the unfunded scheme is the rate of growth of aggregate real wages; at a constant contribution rate, this is the effective rate at which payments made to the state during work get remunerated over the period until retirement. The line marked 'Implicit real return on unfunded scheme' in Figure 6.7 moves around largely because of demographic shifts which alter the size of the labour force and have a big influence on the total wage bill. The model is described in 'The Implications of Switching from Unfunded to Funded Pension Systems'. National Institute Economic Review, no 163, January. Miles, D (1998).*

Chapter
7

Paul Mortimer-Lee
Paribas

Can Euroland work with one interest rate?

The aim of this chapter is to assess how well the Euroland economy will work, especially in the context of the area having one common level of interest rates.

In broad terms, it is not difficult to assume that the monetary union will work imperfectly—no economy does. One simply has to look at the UK or Japan now, or the US in the early 1990s, to find examples of economies that do not work very well. The structural changes brought about by EMU will represent major challenges to the economies, markets, policies and politics of Europe. That is, of course, part of the point of EMU—to be a major step in the integration of Europe. To acknowledge the challenges is not to be critical of EMU, but rather to contribute to the debate on how to make it a success. It is in that spirit that this chapter is written.

The analysis is in four main sections. First, we start with an examination of the convergence process, both in relation to the Maastricht requirements and on both a shorter-and longer-term perspective. The main conclusion is that there is clearly evidence of a convergence of inflation rates over a long period of time. However, two notes of caution are sounded: there is little evidence of convergence in other areas of economic performance; and inflation performance might already be starting to diverge. We then raise the question of whether the recent low rates of inflation may be due simply to a large output gap and high unemployment, and whether inflation rates might diverge once more. We argue that there is a serious risk of such divergence occurring. This leads on to an assessment of the adjustment mechanism in Euroland once such inflation divergence starts to occur. The concern which is highlighted is that the 'automatic' adjustment mechanism via an appreciation of the real exchange rate, lost competitiveness, reduced demand and a dampening of inflationary pressures may take too long to be effective. The other main adjustment mechanisms one would expect to operate—fiscal policy—may also not function effectively. It is constrained by the Stability and Growth Pacts and the fact that most countries have eased up on efforts to reduce their structural budget deficits. Moreover, there are concerns both theoretically and practically about the use of fiscal policy as a fine tuning instrument. In short, the euro will work—but only if there are further structural changes in fiscal policy, the labour markets and the political institutions to make it function more effectively.

Convergence

In the subsequent sections we look at the behaviour of convergence in the euro-11 countries in four different ways:

- on the basis of the Maastricht Treaty 'snapshot';

- immediately pre-and post-1997;

- on a longer-term basis, taking into account forecasts to 1999;

- on the basis of the reactions of different euro-area countries to external shocks.

The Maastricht Treaty snapshot

Convergence of economic performance was a central requirement of the Maastricht Treaty which was signed in 1992. The treaty set out convergence requirements which countries had to meet in order to qualify for membership of EMU. These were specified for the behaviour of inflation, budget deficits, the stock of government debt, long-term interest rates and exchange rate stability. A summary of the criteria and countries' performance in relation to the criteria are set out in Figures 7.1 and 7.2, respectively.

A vast amount has been written on whether countries truly met the convergence requirements or whether they were 'fudged' in some sense. The purpose of this section is not to comment further on that question, but to set the data for 1997 convergence in perspective. This is done in three ways. First, we look at convergence immediately before and after the 1997 'reference year'. Second, over a longer period—from the early 1970s onwards. Third, we look at how, in the future, different countries in Euroland might react to external shocks.

Immediately pre-and post-1997

In its convergence report published in November 1996,[1] the EMI concluded that there was still insufficient convergence (relative to the Maastricht Treaty requirements); yet, by March 1998, eleven countries

Maastricht convergence criteria

Budget deficit	Not to exceed 3% of GDP, unless excess is small and temporary.
Government debt	Not to exceed 60% of GDP, unless the ratio is approaching 60% at a satisfactory pace.
Inflation	Not to exceed by more than 1.5 percentage points the level in the three lowest inflation countries.
Bond yield	Long-term government bonds not to exceed by more than 2 percentage points the level in the three lowest inflation countries.
Exchange rate	Must remain in the normal ERM fluctuation bands for the two previous years without severe tensions. No unilateral devaluation of currency's central rate permitted in that period.

Figure 7.1   Maastricht Treaty convergence criteria

Convergence criteria: 1997

	Govt. deficit (-) or surplus (+) *(% of GDP)*	General govt. debt *(% of GDP)*	Inflation rate *(% p.a.)*	Long-term bond yield *(%)*	Currency stability achieved?
Austria	-2.5	66.1	1.1	5.6	✔
Belgium	-2.1	122.2	1.4	5.7	✔
Denmark	0.7	65.1	1.9	6.2	✔
Finland	-0.9	55.8	1.3	5.9	✔
France	-3.0	58.0	1.2	5.5	✔
Germany	-2.7	61.3	1.4	5.6	✔
Greece	-4.0	108.7	5.2	9.8	✗
Ireland	0.9	66.3	1.2	6.2	✔
Italy	-2.7	121.6	1.8	6.7	✔
Luxembourg	1.7	6.7	1.4	5.6	✔
Netherlands	-1.4	72.1	1.8	5.5	✔
Portugal	-2.5	62.0	1.8	6.2	✔
Spain	-2.6	68.8	1.8	6.3	✔
Sweden	-0.8	76.6	1.9	6.5	✗
UK	-1.9	53.4	1.8	7	✗

Figure 7.2   Convergence performance in 1997

Reference values are those set out in the Maastricht Treaty (see Figure 7.1). For inflation, the average of the lowest three inflation countries was 1.2%, so the reference value was 2.7%. The average bond yield in the lowest three inflation countries was 5.8%, so the reference value was 7.8%.

were deemed suitable to join in monetary union.[2] So convergence came late in the run-up to EMU, only in 1997.

For certain variables, there has been a remarkable degree of convergence in the relatively recent past. For example, Figure 7.3 shows that, in the period to 1997, the dispersion of inflation decreased markedly. It has to be noted, however, that since the middle of 1997 there are some signs of inflation becoming less similar in the euro-11 countries. Fiscal deficit performance has also converged. There has been less progress in ensuring a satisfactory convergence of debt levels, where Belgium and Italy still have debt/GDP ratios over twice the supposed Maastricht limit of 60 per cent. Moreover, there are some big differences in unemployment rates—a theme to which we return later.

Inflation convergence...and divergence?

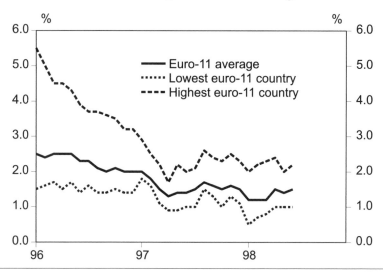

Figure 7.3   Euro-11 average inflation rate and highest/lowest individual country rates

While the criteria for convergence will almost certainly continue to be met by participating member states in 1998, it is difficult to be certain that convergence is truly durable on the basis of just two years' data.

A longer perspective: nominal convergence, real divergence

We have compiled estimates of the degree of disparity between the economic variables in the euro-11 countries over a longer time period: from the early 1970s up until 1999. (For 1998 and 1999, we are taking the

European Commission's own economic forecasts, released in their Spring 1998 report). These are shown in Figure 7.4. Generally, there is clear evidence of convergence in the 'nominal' variables—inflation, budget deficits and interest rates—which were the basis of the Maastricht requirements. Arguably the most compelling evidence of the success of the EMU convergence process has come with regard to inflation. But there is very little evidence of such convergence for the real economy—for GDP growth, current account and unemployment. Indeed, the divergence of annual rates of GDP growth has, on average, become slightly more pronounced through the past decade. More recently, this may be explained by varying degrees of fiscal consolidation across the EU, though, based on the Commission's own data, the divergence in growth rates will moderate only slightly up to the year 2000.

Have we seen real convergence?

Degree of disparity	1974-85	1986-90	1991-95	1996-99	1999
'Maastricht Treaty' variables					
CPI inflation	5.5	3.1	1.6	0.4	0.5
Government deficit	4.2	3.9	1.9	1.3	1.4
Government debt	22.8	34.1	37.0	34.1	29.3
Long-term interest rates	n/a	3.2	2.1	0.4	0.1
Short-term interest rates	n/a	3.2	2.2	1.0	0.0
'Real' variables					
Current account	8.4	8.7	6.6	5.1	5.6
GDP	0.6	1.1	1.9	2.0	1.7
Unemployment	3.0	5.1	5.4	4.8	4.5

Figure 7.4   Convergence of selected EU indicators
The degree of disparity is measures by the root mean square standard deviation of the economic variables. A declining trend indicates a lower degree of disparity.
Data for 1996-99 are based European Commission forecasts.

The current account data paints a similar picture and the Commission forecasts imply that the divergence will be slightly *more* pronounced in 1999 compared to the 1996-99 average. In mitigation, the significance of the individual current account positions will diminish in Euroland, which will be more similar to the US and Japan; a relatively closed economy which, incidentally, will run a huge net surplus. Diverging unemployment rates may be more of a problem as there is little evidence of convergence in this area, notwithstanding differences in national definitions.

Other work using a variation of this methodology reaches similar conclusions: that is, the clear evidence of convergence in inflation performance is not matched with evidence of convergence in other (particularly 'real economy') measures.[3]

It must also be remembered that the convergence of inflation performance that has been seen has been achieved against the background of:

• a generally benign environment for inflation throughout the world;

• generally subdued demand in the euro-11 countries, with none operating significantly above trend output;

• a much faster pace of fiscal consolidation in some countries (e.g. in Southern Europe) than in Germany and France; and

• significant differences in nominal and real short-term interest rates (higher in Southern Europe than in the core).

Thus the historically most inflation-prone economies have had significantly more restrictive macroeconomic policies imposed on them than have the core countries. There is thus little wonder there has been inflation convergence. These observations raise one other important issue: has inflation simply been held down by the existence of an output gap and high unemployment? Before going on to discuss that, we turn to the subject of prospects for convergence—bearing in mind the different reactions in different countries to external shocks.

Asymmetric shocks

An important issue in assessing the durability of convergence is the different responses of the various euro-11 economies to external shocks. Different shocks have different effects on different economies and, indeed, a simple form of 'shock'—such as a 10 per cent appreciation of the euro—could have an impact on Irish, Dutch and Austrian GDP of about twice the size as that on German GDP (according to a recent study by the OECD).

Such asymmetries exist in current monetary unions, for example, the US or the existing European states themselves. To assess whether or not Europeans face a qualitatively larger problem, the IMF looked at the correlations between 'anchor areas' in the US and the potential EMU. They took the anchor area in the US to be the Mideast, and in Europe to be

How shocks affect US states...

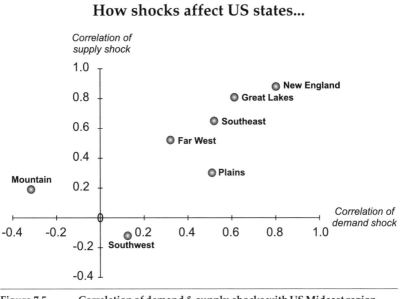

Figure 7.5   Correlation of demand & supply shocks with US Mideast region

...and European countries

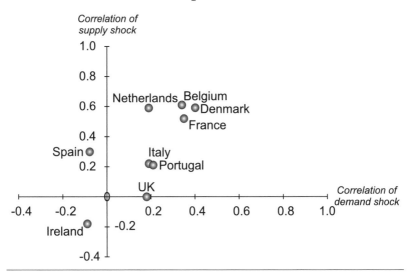

Figure 7.6   Correlation of demand & supply shocks with Germany

Germany. They found correlations with the anchor area were larger in the US than in Europe, though in both there was evidence of a 'core' which was highly correlated. This consisted of Germany, France, Belgium, Austria and the Netherlands in Europe. This gives some support to those who argue that EMU's chances of success would have been improved by starting with a relatively small group.

The IMF also examined the extent to which European and US regional demand and supply shocks were correlated with the anchor region. Supply-side shocks include shifts in technology and commodity prices and can be expected to have long-lasting effects on output. Demand-side shocks include changes in export performance, business or consumer confidence and behaviour, the mix of fiscal and monetary policies (e.g. following German unification), and have relatively short-lived effects on the level of output, but more persistent effects on the level of prices.

Figure 7.5 and 7.6 show the correlations of demand- and supply-side shocks with the anchor areas. The charts suggest that the effects of such shocks were more asymmetric in Europe than the US over the period 1962-1988.

However, the IMF concludes that the differences for the core group of European countries were not large. It should also be recognized that the correlations between European countries' growth rates have increased after the end of the data period that the IMF examined.

Moreover, the advent of EMU should itself serve to insulate the member states which participate from asymmetric shocks. An interesting example is provided by the different reactions to two recent currency crises. The currency turmoil of 1995, sparked by the Mexico crisis, produced a sympathetic reaction in European currency markets and damaged European growth severely. This contrasts with the negligible reaction within Europe to the much larger Asian external shock of 1997/1998. The difference in the markets' reaction is largely explained by anticipation that EMU would start on 1 January 1999 with a large group.

Wage setting in Euroland

Is inflation low just because unemployment is high?

We raised the question above: is inflation in Euroland low just because of a large output gap and high unemployment. We venture an answer to that question in this section.

The degree to which a persistent output gap, i.e. high unemployment, has been important in achieving a reduced level of inflation throughout Euroland may be examined by looking at the process of wage formulation.

Figure 7.7 traces the shift in the link between wage growth and unemployment in the EU in the past 20 years, distinguishing two periods that are significant from a statistical point of view (1975-79 and 1988-97). The results are, in fact, those expected from the Phillips curve (an inverse correlation). However, there has also been a recent flattening in the curve, suggesting that wage increases have not been curbed solely by unemployment—for example the abolition of the *Scale Mobile* in Italy has helped considerably there. The flatter curve than in earlier years suggests that any pick-up in wage inflation as the economies recover in 1998 and 1999 may be relatively modest. This is good news for sustaining convergence, since previous episodes suggest that inflation variability

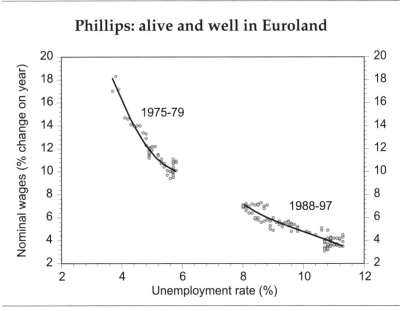

Figure 7.7   EU Phillips curve

between economies and over time tends to rise with the level of inflation.

In fact, most international macro-econometric models include wage equations embodying an augmented Phillips relationship: the level of unemployment is a relevant explanatory variable for the increase in nominal wages, but inflation remains the inescapable major determinant. What changes from one estimate to another is the speed at which wages respond to a change in the inflation rate. As shown in Figure 7.8, which measures the response of the growth in wages to a change in the inflation

Wages: responding to inflation

	Impact elasticity to inflation rate changes[1]	Impact elasticity to the unemployment rate[2]
Germany	0.88	-0.71
Austria	0.86	-0.97
Belgium	0.61	-0.67
Denmark	0.51	-0.57
Spain	0.63	-0.45
Finland	0.85	n.a.
France	0.74	-0.57
Greece	n.a.	-0.73
Ireland	n.a.	-0.27
Italy	0.75	-0.90
Netherlands	n.a.	-0.93
Portugal	0.56	-2.19
United Kingdom	n.a.	-0.20

Figure 7.8   Nominal wage equation coefficients

[1]*The degree of sensitivity of nominal wages to an acceleration in inflation. For example, a coefficient of 0.88 in Germany indicates that a 1 percentage point increase in the inflation rate results in a 0.88 percentage point increase in nominal wage growth rate in the first period.*
[2]*Taking again the case of Germany, it means that a 1 percent decrease in the unemployment rates results in a 0.71 percentage point increase in the nominal wage growth rate in the first period.*
Source: OECD and Paribas

rate, the degree of response is less than unity—that is, wage growth does not immediately compensate for more rapid inflation. 'Real' variables, such as unemployment and productivity, seem to play an increased role in wage determination in many countries of Europe.

Negotiation systems: a comparison

To use a fashionable term, the labour markets have moved in the direction of greater flexibility: real wages are no longer as 'sticky' on the downside, especially in the depressed phases of the business cycle. To see this, one only has to remember that, in Italy (a country hardly enjoying a reputation for discipline as regards wage inflation), wage purchasing power declined three years running (1993-1995) and is still below its 1992 level. Spanish

EU wage systems

	Legal minimum wage as % of average wage (1)	Degree of centralization of negotiations (2)	Coverage by branch collective bargaining (3)	Percentage of trade union membership (4)	Real wages, y/y % change (1987-97) (5)
Germany	-	Intermediate	92	29	1.1
Austria	-	High	98	42	1.6
Belgium	48	High	90	54	1.6
Denmark	-	Intermediate	69	76	1.5
Spain	42	Intermediate	78	19	1.1
France	59	Intermediate	95	9	0.9
Finland	-	High	95	81	2.3
Greece	44	n.a.	n.a	n.a.	0.7
Italy	-	Intermediate	82	39	1.7
Ireland	-	n.a.	n.d	n.a.	2.3
Luxembourg	47	n.a.	n.d	n.a.	0.8
Netherlands	49	Intermediate	81	26	0.5
Portugal	59	Intermediate	71	32	3.5
Sweden	-	Intermediate	89	91	2.1
United Kingdom	-	Low	47	34	1.5

Figure 7.9   Principal features of collective bargaining systems in the EU

wages have undergone practically the same evolution since the beginning of the decade. It is this restraint on real wages that has in Italy and Spain resulted in a convergence in nominal wage growth.

In the final analysis, this mechanism leads to a fairly similar behaviour of nominal variables within the EU-15, apart from Greece and Portugal. The dispersion around 3.2 per cent (the average wage increase in 1997) is very small (a standard deviation of 0.9). The same goes for inflation (a standard deviation of 0.6 around a mean of 1.8 per cent in 1997). This convergence has been attained at a time when the process of wage determination—despite the general slowdown—is far from uniform. Broadly outlined in Figure 7.9, the methods of collective bargaining retain national characteristics that, a priori, have an impact on the outcome of each country's wage negotiations.

The relative 'generosity' of the various systems is measured, in column 5, by the average annual rate of increase in real wages (strongly correlated with nominal wages) over the period 1987-97. As might be expected, the unionization ratio has an influence as regards the preservation of purchasing power (Figure 7.10). There does not seem to be any obvious link between the rate of wage growth and the extent of collective bargaining or the existence of a minimum wage. One possible explanation

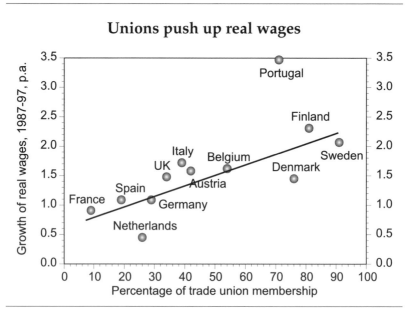

Unions push up real wages

Figure 7.10   Trade union membership and real wages
Sources: OECD Employment Perspectives, July 97; European Commission Annual Report

of this is that minimum wages and collective bargaining result in a wage level above the market clearing price which raises unemployment and therefore reduces the rate of wage increase for those earning more than the minimum wage.

The degree of centralization of the negotiations (column 2 of Figure 7.9) is probably the criterion most abundantly discussed in the theoretical literature when it comes to comparing the efficiencies of various methods of wage determination. This degree is judged to be high when the negotiated wage increase results from agreements that are mostly reached at a national level between trade unions, employers, and, in certain cases, governments (Austria, Belgium, Finland). It is intermediate when the increases are mainly determined through sector-level agreements (Germany, France, the Netherlands, Spain, Portugal and, to a lesser extent, Italy, Sweden and Denmark) and low when bargaining takes place at the level of the company or factory level (the UK).

According to the calculations by Paribas reproduced in Figure 7.11, the fall in unemployment rates in the countries mentioned is likely to lead to an acceleration in the rate of wage increases, of at least half a percentage point during 1998. The acceleration in wage growth will not be uniform. This is because the impact effects of unemployment in the various national wage equations are different. If the emerging differences in growth rates, and therefore unemployment trends, are more than just transitory, then the behaviour of wages and prices will be more different, and will stay more different in the future than we have seen in the recent past. However, the

Euroland wages: a real mixed bag

% change on year	1997	1998 (estimates)
Germany	1.4	2.0
Spain	4.5	3.5
France	2.8	2.7
Italy	4.4	3.5
Netherlands	2.5	3.0
UK	4.5	4.6
Sweden	4.3	4.3

Figure 7.11   Negotiated wage rises
Source: Paribas

move to structural reforms in labour markets (for example, the greater flexibility achieved in Germany in recent years) and the fact that firms in the traded goods sector will know that there will be no devaluation escape hatch from excessively high wage increases, means that wage performance should be much more similar in the future than in the more distant past. There is cause for concern, but not for pessimism.

The growth-inflation divide

In general, an economy's structural propensity to encounter inflation problems can be assessed by its inflation-growth divide, i.e. how a demand shock will be split between output growth and inflation. This is also a key question for monetary policy as, in the case of a monetary growth target, the central bank can only provide the liquidity for a certain amount of nominal growth. The split of nominal growth between real growth and inflation is then determined by the economic agents in the economy. The Fisher equation, which is the theoretical backbone for money supply targeting, implies that money is neutral with respect to output (the major statement which triggered the monetarist revolution) as it assumes that a change in money supply will translate into an equal change in inflation. Obviously, evidence, at least with regard to the short term, contradicts this statement (for example, the Phillips curve). This is reconciled by the monetarist proposition that the neutrality of money only applies in the long run.

A working paper produced by the IMF elaborates on the inflation/growth divide. The author estimates how the difference between the rate of nominal income growth and the potential rate of growth, which is called excess income growth (EIG), affects inflation and growth. This EIG variable is used to estimate two equations: one describing the change in inflation, and the second the change in (real) output growth. Given that the rises in inflation and real growth are equal to nominal growth, the coefficients for EIG in both equations are restricted so that they add up to one. We have replicated this work (Figure 7.12), which shows that while there is a close similarity between the inflation/growth split in Germany and France (encouraging from the perspective of maintaining convergence). Italy looks less favourable, though again we would draw attention to the change in indexation arrangements in the labour market in recent years.

Plugging the exogenous variables into our model yields an average inflation rate of 1.3 per cent in 1998. In 1999, the annual average will increase to two per cent, but with an acceleration through the year to 2.5 per

The growth/inflation divide

	Growth (1)	Inflation (2)	Sum 1/(columns 1+2)
US	0.73	0.22	0.95
Japan	0.17	0.79	0.96
Germany	0.68	0.28	0.96
France	0.64	0.31	0.95
UK	0.59	0.35	0.94
Italy	0.40	0.53	0.93
Canada	0.40	0.55	0.95

Figure 7.12   **Major industrial countries: estimated inflation and growth effects of nominal income gap (1971-95)**

(1) Growth = deviation of actual output growth from its potential rate
(2) Inflation =the change in the inflation rate
Source: Paribas

Euroland inflation

	1996	1997	1998	1999
Germany	1.5	1.8	1.3	2.1
France	2.0	1.2	1.0	1.2
Italy	3.9	1.8	1.9	2.3
Spain	3.6	2.0	2.1	2.6
Netherlands	2.1	2.2	2.4	2.8
G7	1.9	2.0	1.3	1.8
EU-11	2.5	1.7	1.5	2.0

Figure 7.13   **Euroland consumer prices (% change on year)**
Source: Paribas

cent in the second half. The model prediction is pretty much in line with the aggregated country forecasts produced by Paribas' analysts(Figure 7.13). However, half of the rise in Euroland inflation will come from Germany (which accounts for roughly one-third of total Euroland), where we expect further increases in indirect taxes—which are not included in our model forecast. The projections suggest that there will be significant differences in the inflation rates of France (and if we exclude tax changes, Germany also) and Spain, suggesting that inflation divergence is likely to become a more important issue in mid-1999/2000 than it is now.

What if inflation diverges?

If inflation were to begin to rise in a regional sub-economy in EMU then, in contrast to the situation with independent monetary policy, real interest rates would fall (not rise) and growth and inflation would be stoked up as a consequence rather than being held back. In the absence of counteraction through fiscal policy, the situation would be brought into check by an appreciation of the real exchange rate (defined either as a rise in the price of non-tradables relative to tradables, or as a rise in ratio of domestic to foreign prices and wages).

This appreciation of the real exchange rate would cause a loss of net 'exports' to other member states and to countries outside the EMU. This which would reduce demand, lead to the emergence of an output gap (unemployment) which would eventually cool inflation and result in the relative price level declining again. This long-run analysis could be taken to suggest that there would not be much of a problem, because the real exchange rate would eventually return to its equilibrium level and all would be well.

That is far too cosy an analysis. The real problem is not that there will be adjustment, but the speed at which that adjustment takes place. History tells us that inflation has had a strong inertia in a number of countries, with a high correlation of inflation in one year with its previous values. This has been more prevalent in some countries, e.g. Spain, than in others (Germany has had an unusually low correlation of inflation with its more distant previous values—see Figure 7.14).

Once an inflationary cycle sets in, it may take a very substantial output gap to kill it. Moreover, to restore output to capacity, the real exchange rate may not only have to return to its equilibrium level, but actually to undershoot it because, once production facilities move elsewhere, they will need an incentive to move back—merely returning to the prior equilibrium exchange rate will not be enough.

Germany is different

	t-1	t-2	t-3	t- 4	t-5
Germany	0.7	0.3	-0.0	-0.3	-0.4
France	0.9	0.8	0.7	0.6	0.5
Italy	0.9	0.8	0.7	0.6	0.6
Spain	0.9	0.9	0.9	0.9	0.8
Netherlands	0.8	0.5	0.4	0.4	0.4
Finland	0.8	0.7	0.7	0.7	0.7
Ireland	0.8	0.7	0.5	0.5	0.5
Portugal	0.8	0.6	0.4	0.5	0.6
Belgium	0.8	0.6	0.4	0.3	0.4

Figure 7.14 Correlation coefficient for inflation in year t with inflation in year t-x
Source: Datastream/ICV

Even returning the exchange rate to its equilibrium level may take an extraordinarily long time. This is because inflation in the EMU region as a whole is likely to be low—around 2 per cent. Once competitiveness is lost, a rate of inflation below this Euroland rate will be needed to regain competitiveness. Since many prices—in particular wages—are inflexible downwards, the crawl back to competitiveness from a brief inflationary splurge may take several years, implying continued unemployment during that period. Thus the problem is not that real exchange rate changes will not take place within the EMU, but that they will take time to be ground out, perhaps a long time.

This analysis should not in truth be particularly surprising. After all, monetary policy is pretty blunt weapon which does not differentiate much between the needs of various sectors. A good example was the UK in 1997 and 1998: the level of interest rates which was appropriate for the manufacturing sector was much lower than the appropriate rate for the consumer sector, resulting in a 'dual-speed' economy'. Similarly, US regions have obviously not grown at the same speed as each other in the past—has the rate of interest appropriate for California been exactly the same as that appropriate for, say, Texas (e.g. during the banking crisis there), or to the rust belt? Clearly not.

There is nothing new—nor should it be surprising—in saying that a one-size monetary policy will not fit all perfectly in Euroland—it corresponds to readily-observed reality in economies today. What is different is that those economies have much more developed mechanisms—flexible labour markets and/or a system of automatic or discretionary inter-regional transfer mechanisms—than does Euroland to make the inevitable rough justice of monetary policy a little less rough. Moreover, the degree of political integration in existing nation states enables trade-offs between the needs of their various sectors and regions to be made more smoothly than is likely in a more homogeneous Euroland.

There may be further problems also. The areas where there will be most danger of inflation will be in the sectors sheltered from international competition. This not only includes labour employed in services but also in the property sector—both residential and non-residential. If monetary policy cannot respond to fast asset price inflation there are likely to be excesses. This will not only be driven by residents, but also by non-residents. One could argue that there are parallels with south-east Asia before the 1997 collapse—fixed exchange rates and interest rates below the level necessary for domestic equilibrium led to asset price bubbles, notably in property. The consequence of bubbles in Euroland regional economies could be very serious for national banking systems. One example would be the Irish housing market. There, prices have already—with interest rates several hundred points above the core—doubled in the last three years. The potential is high for a bubble, over-extension of the banking system, and a subsequent bust—especially if the British pound falls relative to the euro, which seems inevitable. However, it should be noted that regional banking crises are not unknown in the US, where regulatory restriction, rather than inertia-driven regional specialization of some banks in the EU, led to trouble.

The recognition of the potential problems arising from making one nominal interest rate fit all in Euroland is not, however, a reason to conclude that the project will fail. The appreciation of the problem has led to increased awareness that fiscal policy will be important in balancing economic developments in various economies, with some prominent officials suggesting that the faster-growing economics should tighten their fiscal policy more aggressively in 1999 than the slower-growing economies (especially Germany). It is therefore to fiscal policy that we now turn.

Fiscal policy

Krugman is one of the many economists that have argued that 'in a monetary union old-fashioned Keynesianism with its emphasis on fiscal policy comes back into its own.[4] The problem in the Euroland context is that the use of fiscal policy is quite severely constrained. The current constraints on using fiscal policy for economic management are discussed in Chapter 6. Those constraints are imposed by the operation of the Stability and Growth Pact and the fact that many countries are already close to, and some may be in danger of breaching, the three per cent deficit limit. There are two other problems with fiscal policy discussed here: the issue of whether changes in fiscal policy would, in fact, have the desired effect; and, second, the practicalities of using fiscal policy as a fine-tuning instrument.

Fiscal policy fine-tuning: useful?

For fiscal policy to be a good fine-tuning device, it must have a real effect. There are theoretical arguments as to why fiscal fine-tuning may make for bad economics. The usual monetarist arguments are that fiscal policy causes only nominal, rather than real, changes in the economy. Government investment is seen as displacing private sector investment rather than complementing it (through a crowding-out effect). Neo-Ricardians would argue that, since a higher deficit today implies more taxes tomorrow (to service the debt), agents with perfect foresight who maximize economic welfare over the future, as well as today, will act in such a way that fiscal policy has no effect. However, the crowding-out effect primarily results from higher interest rates than otherwise. In a monetary union, the crowding-out effects will be spread throughout the entire union, not just in the country which pursues an expansionary fiscal policy. Therefore, fiscal efficacy may rise in EMU (which is, of course, one reason why the Stability Pact was needed to stop governments being tempted by this). Monetarists tend to argue that a government should encourage aggregate demand by creating an environment where there are as few government-made obstacles as possible, i.e. keeping the budget in balance and hoping the private economy will do the rest of the work. But, in Euroland, fiscal policy is the only weapon governments will possess, they will need to use it regardless of whether it is useful in the long term, so long as it may do some good in smoothing the bumpy ride of the economic cycle.

Moreover, whatever the theoretical arguments, it looks to us as though fiscal policy has had an effect in the last few years. This is easily explained by the fact that some agents are cash-constrained—thus, even if they would have behaved in the neo-Ricardian way (which is doubtful), cash constraints prevent them doing so. Contractionary fiscal policy exacerbates cash constraints, expansionary policy eases them.

Fine-tuning: practicalities

Changes in government expenditure can have a direct impact on aggregate demand, and therefore on output and employment. It is not, however, easy to manipulate government expenditure in a fine-tuning manner. Fiscal policy is a clumsy tool:

- Government spending programmes take some time to affect fully the economy, with long feed-through times reducing the ability of the government to act in a timely fashion. The long lags between fiscal policy being put into action and the effect on aggregate demand could exacerbate the business cycle and lead to boom and bust rather than a smoother path for aggregate demand.

- It is difficult to bring about changes in spending quickly, e.g. parliamentary agreement is needed and bureaucracy is often cumbersome. Government expenditure programmes tend to take a long time to plan and then a long time to complete. It is often difficult to contain spending plans for large government programmes, as they have a tendency to escalate out of proportion.

- Once government spending programmes are in place, it is politically difficult to remove them when aggregate demand needs cooling down. Abandoning a project once it has been started would be difficult, wasteful and unpopular.

- Much of government expenditure consists of payment of public sector salaries. Declines in this component of government expenditure can only be achieved by reducing the quantity of labour employed by the government. Decisions to reduce the level of government employment are very unpopular and take time to implement.

- Though tax rates can be varied more quickly and have, therefore, been the primary instrument of fiscal short-run stabilization policies, there are problems here, too. Indirect tax changes affect consumer spending directly and fairly quickly, but they are also very unpopular as they tend to be borne disproportionately by the poor.

- The history of fiscal fine-tuning via tax changes is chequered: tax rises are infrequently reversed—suggesting that, as an instrument of fine-tuning, it tends to work only one way.

- Due to the ratchet effect of government spending (easy to raise, difficult to cut), it can often lead to unsustainable public finance problems and escalating debt burdens, which take many years of fiscal austerity to correct. A budget deficit will lead to an increase in government debt, which will have to be serviced in the future. If the interest rate on the government debt were greater than the real growth rate of the economy, the government debt/GDP ratio could increase progressively (depending on the level of the primary government deficit (i.e. excluding debt interest), requiring often severe corrective action. Fiscal policy is, therefore, an expensive tool to use, and one which cannot be resorted to too often.

- Fiscal policy on its own can only really deal with one economic problem at a time. In the past, fiscal fine-tuning has proved inadequate to deal with, for example, stagflation in the UK in the 1970s because there were two different objectives. Fiscal policy was needed both to reverse increases in unemployment and to lower inflation. Two incompatible problems. With two different objectives, fiscal policy alone could not work effectively.

- Finally, perhaps the biggest problem of fiscal fine-tuning is that the political cycle can often get in the way of good fiscal management. Governments are insufficiently objective to be good fiscal fine-tuners. The political cycle is also influential. Cosetti and Roubini (1993), in *The design of optimal fiscal rules for Europe after 1992*, conclude that the effect of elections on budget deficits is significant both statistically and economically. Their empirical analysis estimated that after controlling other determinants, fiscal deficits tend to be higher in election years by more than 0.6 percentage points of GDP in industrialized countries.

Politically-inspired fiscal expansion can also increase the 'one-way' nature of fiscal fine-tuning mentioned above; governments are unlikely to cut spending prior to an election, so raising the likelihood of public spending becoming unsustainable.

One further drawback should be noted, which applies particularly to small, very open economies (and, therefore, a large number of potential EMU member states). The problem is that, if imports account for a large proportion of domestic demand, any impact of a more expansionary fiscal stance on domestic activity will be severely deflated by 'leakages' into imports.

Fiscal policy co-ordination

With fiscal policy so difficult a tool to use, particularly for fine-tuning, how will asymmetric shocks which occur within EMU be dealt with? Optimal currency area theory tells us that there are two safety valves in this situation: the first being labour market flexibility (and, particularly, labour mobility), and the second being supranational fiscal policy. With labour mobility in Europe fairly low, the burden falls once again to fiscal policy.

The first option for supranational fiscal policy is to centralize national government budgets, or a significant part of them. In the same way that a national government will tend to take in more revenues from a capital city, and then distribute them to high unemployment regions (in the form of extra subsidies, unemployment benefits, government building projects, etc.), a supranational budget will also distribute from more to less prosperous areas. Though some governments may be willing for this to take place and see federalism as the next step after EMU, other governments (and electorates) disagree vehemently about this way forward. Progress in this direction will not be easy, as a fresh treaty would be required, possibly followed by referendums—which, on EMU matters, have faced difficulties in the past. A less formal approach would be through 'co-ordination', e.g. through the Euro-X Committee or in Ecofin, under the 'Broad Guidelines' provisions of the Maastricht Treaty. But moving to an 'economic government' in this way could be problematical if, say, one government was facing political pressure at home and so was unwilling to act in a way consistent with the interests of Euroland as a whole.

The last (small) safety valve

Even in the US, Blanchard and Katz showed that, after a state-specific shock, unemployment grew and took six years to fade, demonstrating that there is still a need for some counter-shock policy at the regional level. In the US, state governments make no effort to use their budgets as a stabilization tool. In fact, almost without exception, they have balanced budget requirements. The automatic stabilization role is therefore played by the federal budget. As we discussed above, Europe does not (yet) have such a budget.

The main problems with the issue of fiscal transfers are:

- Fiscal transfers which would cope with asymmetric shocks of the size likely in EMU would have to be large, at least much larger than the size of the EU budget at present. Though the EU budget has risen sharply over the years (in real terms it has more than doubled since 1985), it still only represents about 1.2 per cent of EU GNP and 2.5 per cent of public expenditure in member countries. Any increase in the size of the budget would take some time.

- The legal requirement for zero balance between revenue and expenditure for the EU budget greatly limits its role for allocation and redistribution.

- Despite the small size of the EU budget, it has still caused much animosity between European nations, with the redistributive elements being particularly keenly fought over. This is not a good omen for the budget taking a key role in the future. The European Union seems to lack the social cohesiveness needed to support the size of fiscal transfers that may be needed from one region to another. As Goodhart (1989, in *Money, Information and Uncertainty*) stated 'The optimal currency area is a function not so much of geography but rather of social psychology'.

Fiscal policy conclusions

Fiscal policy is a clumsy fine-tuning tool, which, in EMU, will have a tremendous workload. It will have some of the responsibility of smoothing national economic cycles, as well as easing the adjustment to asymmetric shocks. The leeway provided by the Stability Pact is fairly narrow given the burden that fiscal policy will be under. This suggests that Stability Pact targets will be breached fairly frequently, particularly as EMU participants are unlikely to have budget balances on average over the cycle as the Pact intends. With national fiscal policies shackled, adjustment mechanisms such as the movement of labour and fiscal transfers will be crucial. EU fiscal transfers are too small at the moment to perform this function sufficiently under the added strains of EMU. Obstacles to these fiscal transfers increasing are large, but if this fails to occur the prospects for EMU are gloomy. We therefore expect to see a move towards a more centralized fiscal transfer mechanism within five to ten years. This would take the Maastricht Treaty's concept of 'an ever closer union' a stage beyond simple monetary union. But if EMU is to work well, there is no real alternative.

Having said this, there are instances where fiscal fine-tuning would be appropriate—where one country is out of synchronization in the cycle, for example, though national interest politics may get in the way of that, too. Reducing the extent of national sovereignty to set budgets (already implicit in Maastricht's three per cent limit and the rules of the Stability Pact) would make the process more flexible, as would automatic stabilizers through a federal budget that nationally transferred income from fast-growing economies to slower-growing ones. However, the intense debate that has recently centred on contributions to the EU suggests that this is a step Europe is not yet ready to take. It may well take a period of stress, with symptoms that Euroland cannot treat properly with one interest rate, to give the impetus for the tough political decisions that will be needed to make these reforms.

Overall conclusions

We see real problems in the EMU area in coming years, but they are far from insurmountable and certainly within the range of experience in Europe in the last half decade. The main conclusions are as follows. First, there is a likelihood that the inflation convergence of recent years will unwind, especially as there is likely to be an upturn in economic activity in coming years. The fact is that the economies are going into monetary union after a prolonged period of disequilibrium, so that we cannot be at all confident that the constellation of real exchange rates will prove appropriate to the new world. Second, fiscal policy will have to play a more active fine-tuning role in making one interest rate fit all. But the scope for the use of fiscal policy is seriously constrained by the lack of progress in reducing structural budget deficits and the three per cent deficit/GDP ceiling. Furthermore, the practical difficulties of employing fiscal policy as a fine-tuning mechanism are considerable. This leads to the third main conclusion: that a reduction in fiscal autonomy and a more democratic Europe are needed to realize the full benefits of the EMU. Euroland can work with one interest rate, but it will require further structural changes in fiscal policy, the labour market and political institutions.

Notes for Chapter 7

[1]*European Monetary Institute, Convergence Report, November 1996.*

[2]*European Monetary Institute, Convergence Report, March 1998.*

[3]*See, for example, work using cluster analysis, as in 'The Credibility of European Economic Convergence by Groeneveld, Koedijk and Kool; Weltwirtschaftliches Archiv, No. 134'. In this study, inflation shows the most convergence. Furthermore, as in other research, in terms of standard deviation calculations, there is no significant decline in cross-country variations across a range of economic indicators—again with two key exceptions, inflation and public finances.*

[4]*Krugman, 1992, 'Lessons of Massachusetts for EMU'.*

Chapter
8

Professor David Miles
Merrill Lynch &
*Imperial College, London**

The options for the UK

This chapter analyses the policy implications for the UK of the euro. It does not say whether it is right or wrong for the UK to join EMU, but emphasizes that, whatever decision is taken there will be big changes in the economic environment which will require policy responses. The aim of the chapter is: to analyse the changes in microeconomic and macroeconomic policies that will make the euro work better if the UK does join; and to investigate how policies might need to change so as to reduce any costs, and increase any benefits, of not joining. We conclude by considering the three main strategies for EMU available to the UK, namely: make a decision soon to enter in a few years' time (say, 2002 or 2003); 'wait and see'; and 'stay out'.

Issues if the UK does join the euro area

If the UK joins the euro area, then:

- it will lose the power to set national interest rates. Short-term interest rates for countries participating in EMU will be set by the European Central Bank;

- longer-term interest rates will differ only marginally from those in other countries in the euro area, mainly reflecting differences in risk premiums;

- it will be unable to change its exchange rate against other countries participating in the euro.

The significance of these changes depends on several factors: the size of economic shocks that are specific to the UK; the degree of flexibility in labour markets; and differences in the way that a common European monetary policy would affect countries in the euro area.

This chapter is an abridged version of The Ostrich and the EMU: Policy Choices Facing the UK published by the Centre for Economic Policy Research (telephone 0171 878 2900), London, in June 1997 with support from the Esmee Fairbairn Charitable Trust.

Clearly, the UK's economic cycle has recently been out of line with the cycle on the continent. This partly reflects differences in monetary policy, and, to that extent, joining EMU would make the UK cycle more like that of other members. But even EMU would not eliminate some distinguishing features of the UK economy. The obvious structural differences include:

- **Oil production:** The UK is a sizeable net exporter of oil, and the only EU country that is a net exporter of all primary energy. This will continue for some time. (see Figures 8.1 and 8.2).

- **Personal debt:** The UK's stock of household debt is, and is likely to remain, substantially higher than the EU average (see Figure 8.3).

- **Company borrowing**: Corporate use of the bond market is relatively low in the UK, and reliance on short-term bank loans has been above the EU average (see Figure 8.4).

- **Public expenditure**: As a proportion of GDP, government expenditure and taxes are lower in the UK than in most EU countries (see Figure 8.5).

- **Trade**: The proportion of UK trade that is currently with other EU members is below average (see Figure 8.6).

Of course, most countries are unusual in some respect and it is useful to use a wider measure of how far countries are subject to specific shocks. One simple guide is the correlation of national GDP with growth in the EU as a whole (see Figure 8.7). On this measure, the UK is indeed in the group of economies which have not been highly correlated with the EU cycle. Some studies using more sophisticated econometric techniques have come up with similar findings. For example, Figure 8.8 shows correlations between aggregate supply and demand shocks estimated by Bayoumi and Eichengreen.[1] They found that the UK had a relatively low correlation of both demand and supply shocks, though Finland and Ireland were even more out of line with the EU norm.

Any such conclusions are based on the past, while the more important question is whether the idiosyncrasies of the UK economy will persist into the future, especially if the UK joins EMU. One of the likely benefits would be increased trade and integration, which would affect the structure of economies, probably making them more synchronized—but even that is not certain. It is conceivable that the lower costs of cross-border trade would encourage more specialization, so that individual EMU member countries became more dependent on particular industries. Even if shocks were uniform across the euro area, individual countries would still have different degrees of labour mobility and would have different responses to interest rate changes.

This analysis has major implications for fiscal policy, an issue to which we now turn.

The UK is a net exporter of oil...

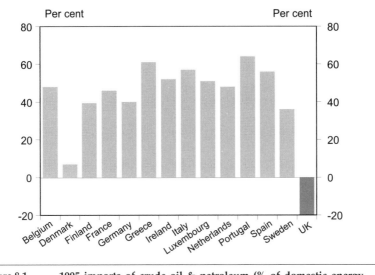

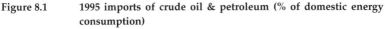

Figure 8.1   1995 imports of crude oil & petroleum (% of domestic energy consumption)

...and of primary energy in general

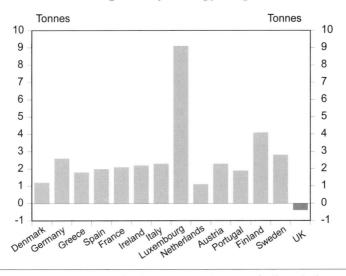

Figure 8.2   Net imports of primary energy (tonnes of oil equivalent per person)

UK households are highly indebted...

	% of GDP	Year
UK	79	1995
Norway	70	1993
Spain	58	1995
Germany	56	1995
Sweden	54	1994
France	50	1995
Finland	41	1994
Italy	24	1995

Figure 8.3   **Financial liabilities of the household sector (% of GDP)**
Source: OECD balance sheets of non-financial sector

...and UK companies make little use of the bond market

Sweden	69.5
Germany	31.2
Belgium	55.5
Austria	36.5
Switzerland	35.8
Norway	19.2
Finland	19.2
Italy	13.7
France	11.6
Iceland	9.6
Netherlands	7.6
Spain	6.1
Ireland	3.2
UK	2.9

Figure 8.4   **Corporate bonds outstanding in 1995 (% of GDP)**
Source: Merrill Lynch 'The Size & Structure of World Bond Markets', October 1996

The UK has relatively low taxes...

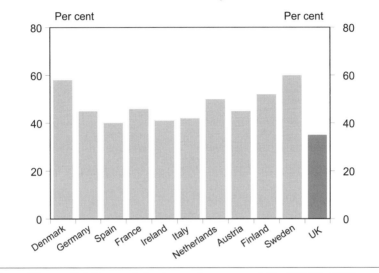

...and is relatively less dependent on EU trade

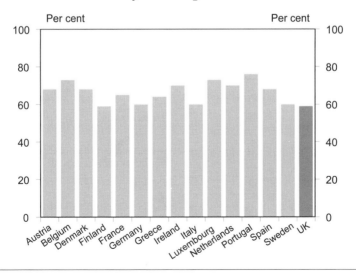

UK growth is not strongly linked with the rest of the EU...

France	0.91
Belgium	0.87
Germany	0.85
Italy	0.79
Spain	0.79
Austria	0.78
Portugal	0.76
Netherlands	0.75
Denmark	0.69
Sweden	0.67
Greece	0.66
Luxembourg	0.64
UK	0.63
Finland	0.59
Ireland	0.20

Figure 8.7   **Correlation of the annual growth of national GDP with EU GDP, 1961-1993**

...and the UK does not respond like Germany to shocks

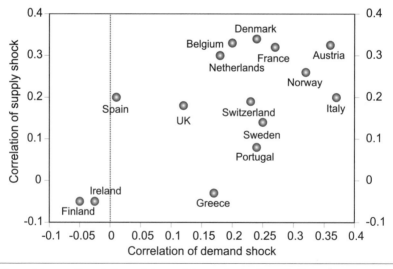

Figure 8.8   **Correlations of demand & supply shocks with Germany**
Source: Bayoumi and Eichengreen (1996)

Fiscal policy

Could fiscal policy mimic monetary policy?

If the UK lost control over short-term interest rates, then fiscal policy would have to play a larger role in counter-cyclical policy. One way of thinking about this is to ask whether fiscal policy could mimic the effects which changes in interest rates would have had on the economy. It is possible to think of several such methods, but all have inherent difficulties.

First, tax deductibility of interest could be reduced—thereby raising the post-tax interest rate—when it was desired to slow economic growth, and vice versa. Unfortunately, this approach would require frequent changes in tax rates, which is both difficult and undesirable.

Second, sales taxes (VAT and excise duties) could be varied. If macroeconomic policy needs to be tightened, a temporary increase in sales tax may persuade consumers to postpone spending. The one major weakness of this approach is that in an overheating economy, raising indirect taxes adds to inflationary pressure at just the wrong time.

Third, government expenditure could be varied, but it is not desirable (nor politically feasible) to reverse decisions on big items of government expenditure at short notice.

Other schemes could be developed. For example, taxpayers could receive income tax refunds if GDP falls or they could hold back some tax payments in a downswing. But to run through all of these options is to highlight their inherent weaknesses. There are no simple and non-distortionary ways of boosting fiscal flexibility to offset the loss of monetary policy autonomy.

What about the Stability Pact?

At the EU Dublin summit in December 1996, governments agreed on penalties for running excessive deficits. It is hard to know whether these rules will be applied in practice but, in principle, the fines for exceeding a budget deficit of three per cent of GDP could be very large. For example, over the last thirty years the average UK budget deficit has been three per cent of GDP. The deficit was less than three per cent of GDP in fewer than half of those years.

Faced with such fines, the strategy of aiming for a small surplus could be sensible. This would allow, in a downturn, greater scope for loosening fiscal policy without hitting the three per cent limit.

Would fiscal policy still be autonomous?

The autonomy of fiscal policy could be affected at two levels

First, a national government's ability to raise revenue to finance national spending could be reduced. If people can easily move to countries where taxes are low, then some of the better-off may opt out of a redistributive tax and spending system. In principle, labour mobility is likely to be enhanced by EMU; in practice, the effect is unlikely to be great, as language and cultural differences (for example) probably have much more influence on migration.

In fact, more problems are likely to arise from labour immobility. If some countries have high and rising unemployment, they may seek greater fiscal transfers from the EU.

Second, the freedom of governments to have their own tax and benefit systems may be affected. The Maastricht Treaty has no direct implications for the harmonization of tax structures and welfare programmes, but a single currency would probably affect the substitutability of goods, services and financial assets. We consider these implications under four headings: indirect taxes; income taxes and benefits; taxes on companies; and capital taxes.

Indirect taxes

There are currently EU restrictions on the VAT rates that EU governments may set: the standard rate cannot be under 15 per cent and no more than two reduced rates are allowed.[2] Despite these restrictions, VAT rates still vary widely across the EU and neither rates nor exemptions have converged much over the last ten years. Would the introduction of the euro require rapid and complete harmonization of taxes? The experience of the United States suggest not. There, individual states have rates of sales tax that differ as much as in EU countries. It seems that non-currency factors ensure that such differences persist. Cross-border tax-driven shopping is already important in many EU member countries and will probably increase when the euro is introduced, but it seems unlikely that this will attain sufficient importance to necessitate harmonization of indirect taxes. The European Commission has recently published proposals for a much greater harmonization of VAT systems, but such an introduction is not formally linked to the introduction of the euro.

Income taxes and benefits

In or out of EMU, countries are less likely to harmonize their income taxes and welfare systems, than their indirect taxes. Mobility of labour within Europe is low and people are unlikely to migrate in large numbers for tax reasons alone. The same goes for welfare payments and public services, which already vary widely across the EU and have not prompted much migration. It is not obvious that any of this inertia would change simply because the euro came into existence.

Taxes on companies

In contrast, once currency risk is eliminated, companies may well pay more attention to differences in the costs of doing business in different countries. As an 'in', the UK (with relatively low employment and corporate taxes) would become more attractive for businesses wishing to sell in Europe. Precisely for that reason, other euro area members may try to harmonize company taxes. Pressure to harmonize corporate taxes would probably be just as strong if the UK were 'out'. If its corporate tax system were thought to be attracting companies from the Continent, EMU members would probably complain that the UK was making the whole project more difficult.

Capital taxes

If companies are more footloose than people, financial capital is positively nomadic. With currency risk eliminated, all euro-denominated assets will become closer substitutes for one another, no matter where they are issued. The implication is that, for investors facing a particular set of tax rules, the expected post-tax returns on assets should be closer once the euro is introduced. It is not clear, however, that national rules on capital taxes therefore need to be closer. Currently, double tax agreements mean that holdings of many classes of foreign assets are taxed as if they were domestic assets. Although this heightens incentives to live and be taxed in a particular country, tax exiles are unlikely to become much more numerous purely because of a single currency.

The transmission mechanism

The balance sheets of UK households, companies, banks and building societies are significantly different from those in the main Continental economies. Personal debt is proportionately higher, and more of it is at variable interest rates. UK companies are similarly more dependent on floating-rate debt. Also, banks and building societies rely heavily of retail deposits paying variable rates that are closely linked to those set by the Bank of England.

In the UK, only 15 per cent of the outstanding mortgage debt is at fixed rates, which anyway tend to be fixed for less than four years. In Germany, just over 50 per cent of mortgage debt is at rates that are completely fixed; in France, the figure is as much as 90 per cent. The implication is clear:

unless UK balance sheets become more European (inside EMU), the UK would be more sensitive to changes in short-term interest rates than other countries.

Of course, policy could be framed so as to encourage a move to more European-style balance sheets. A switch from variable- to fixed-rate debt could be encouraged, maybe by setting differential capital adequacy requirements for banks and building societies, favouring fixed-rate loans. Policies to help reduce gearing could also be implemented, say through various tax changes which would make debt more expensive. The current tax breaks for mortgages (MIRAS) and companies (full deductibility of interest payments from taxable income, but less generous treatment for equity funding) encourage debt financing.

The labour market

The seriousness of the loss of policy flexibility inside EMU depends, to a large extent, on the structure of the labour market. If nominal wages are inflexible, then exogenous shocks will change real variables (employment and output). In a single currency area, a given degree of labour market inflexibility will become more costly in terms of lost jobs and output. But having flexible labour markets is desirable anyway. Low marginal tax rates and a benefits system that does not discourage job creation are good things for every country. It is not obvious that EMU *per se* raises new policy issues for the UK labour market.

The UK as an 'out': longer term macroeconomic issues

The changing environment

As an 'out', the UK could continue to use all its existing policy instruments. In itself, this may seem an advantage; though the macroeconomic record of the past thirty years provides numerous examples of those instruments being misused. What is certain is that the wider context for macroeconomic management would change: living next door to an EMU with which the bulk of the UK's trade was conducted would have major ramifications.

If EMU works well, the euro would become the key currency for UK business and a large proportion of its trade would be priced and paid for in euros. Similarly, UK investors (and overseas investors holding UK financial assets) would view euro-denominated assets as a natural part of their portfolios. Any perception that the UK would have higher and more variable inflation than the EMU countries, or generally looser fiscal policy, would cause the demand for sterling assets to fall.

Even if EMU works badly, the UK could suffer. EMU members would probably be particularly sensitive to the sterling-euro rate, and prone to accuse the UK of stealing an unfair competitive advantage within the single market by devaluing the pound. The 'common concern' clause of the Maastricht Treaty means that EU countries that do not adopt the single currency are obliged to consider the knock-on effects for EMU members of any change in exchange rates. In a sense there is nothing new in this (EU countries outside the ERM are under a similar obligation), but the context will have changed. If EMU members no longer have their own national monetary policy, they will be even more alert to the behaviour of others.

Perceptions of motive would count for a lot. It would be far better for the UK to be seen as a sympathetic 'out'; 'out' because of its concern over its structural economic idiosyncrasies, but nonetheless committed to greater economic integration in Europe. If the UK were seen as a carper and a blocker, wanting the benefits of the single market without the obligations of the single currency, it would surely suffer increasing discrimination from EMU members.

Policy instruments and targets

As an 'out' the key policy issues will be:

- If an inflation target is to be retained, how tight should it be?

- Does it make sense to assign instruments to targets: having the Bank of England set interest rates to hit the inflation target, and setting tax and spending plans in a long-term context to control debt and deficits (and perhaps using intervention to influence the value of sterling)?

- Should there be a target for the sterling-euro exchange rate?

The ECB will aim to achieve price stability. If this means that there is an explicit inflation target in EMU, it would have implications for the UK. For example, it would be difficult for the UK's inflation target to be higher than the ECB's without some loss of credibility.

Although the precise level of the UK inflation target would matter, the credibility of the means to achieve it would count for much more. The recent move to give the Bank of England operational independence will help in this respect.

We mentioned above the danger of sharp movements in the sterling-euro exchange rate, so some kind of exchange rate stability would certainly be welcome. But if the UK were to adopt and exchange rate target against the euro, would this replace—or be combined with—the inflation target? If the latter, then these two targets would need two policy instruments. For all the reasons demonstrated by ERM experience, the interest rate needed to keep inflation low would not necessarily be consistent with the exchange rate target.

Fiscal policy

As an 'out', the UK would not be subject to the Stability Pact, and so would not be subject to fines if its budget deficit exceeded three per cent of GDP. As the three per cent limit is arbitrary, it is hard to see that not sticking to this limit would seriously endanger credibility. Nonetheless, it already has some symbolic significance. As a result, if any UK government did want to exceed the three per cent limit, it would need to explain why; it would also probably need to stress that the move was temporary; and it would also need a longer-term framework of policies to ensure that the ratio of its total debt/GDP remained on a sustainable path.

The ways ahead

The UK has three possible strategies for EMU:

- Decide soon to join in a few years' time.

- Wait and see.

- Decide in principle not to join.

Decide soon to join in a few years' time

If a decision were made soon to join in a few years' time, then the practical problems of preparing for euro area membership could be eased, or even eliminated. Legislation would have to be introduced in order to make the Bank of England fully independent by the time of joining. It would also be desirable to bring in legislative measures to:

- enhance the fiscal stabilizers so that they have a chance to start working;

- reduce the tax incentive to use debt. This would help make the transmission mechanism of UK monetary policy more like that in other euro area countries.

Such legislative changes could be made in a relatively relaxed manner if several years were allowed for the UK to make its euro preparations.

However, the greater advantages of joining in a few years' time relate to changes in the cyclical economic position of the UK economy. Arguably, by 2002 or 2003, the euro interest rate may well be broadly what the UK needs in the cyclical circumstances it will then find itself; and sterling's value against the euro may be broadly appropriate.

Wait and see

A wait-and-see strategy has the obvious advantage that some of the uncertainty about EMU—on the operation of monetary policy; on the demand for, and value of, the euro; on the strains generated by a single short term interest rate for all the 'ins'—will be reduced. But, in order to keep open the option of joining EMU some way down the road, it would still be desirable to reduce the fiscal deficit and remove tax incentives to use debt. It would also be sensible to draft amendments to the Bank of England Act in a way which allowed it to operate as part of the European Central Bank, if the decision were taken to join.

Staying out

If the UK was to stay out of EMU, the euro-sterling exchange rate would be of great significance: it would be more important for UK business than any bilateral rate now is. Sharp fluctuations could be damaging and because countries inside the single currency area could not independently do much to alter their exchange rate against sterling, the UK could risk discrimination in certain respects. The surest way of avoiding this is to participate actively in the development of the single market. Much will depend on attitude. If the UK is seen as a constructive agnostic, it will be listened to on such subjects as competition policy. If it comes across as a whingeing outsider, it will not.

Notes for Chapter 8

[1]*Bayoumi, T. and Eichengreen, B. 'Operationalizing the Theory of Optimum Currency Areas' CEPR Discussion paper No. 1484, October 1996. Aggregate demand shocks are those which affect demand conditions in the economy and it is assumed that their only long-run effect is on prices. Supply shocks can also affect output in the long run.*

[2]*There are some other minor exceptions.*

Åke Gustafsson
Swedbank, Stockholm

Chapter
9

The Nordic countries and the euro

The Nordic countries (Denmark, Finland, Norway and Sweden) in many ways make up an homogenous market area. All these four countries have for a long time been characterized by political and social stability and relatively high living standards. Common to all countries are also their relatively small population and their high degree of dependence on international trade. Exports, as well as imports, represent a significant share of these countries' aggregate GDP. Trade between the Nordic countries is also relatively extensive.

Following a period of more or less widespread economic imbalance in all the Nordic countries during the early 1990s, all the countries have recovered to the point where their economies are now relatively healthy. The financial and economic crisis at the beginning of the 1990s was most pronounced in Finland and Sweden, which, from 1992 to 1995, showed significant deficits in their public finances coupled with far-reaching problems in the financial sector. The crisis made rather less of an impact in Norway, where problems were in essence limited to the banking sector. Denmark was the country which overcame the Nordic crisis best, since economic policy reforms had been implemented as early as the mid-eighties. Consequently, Denmark remained relatively stable compared with the other Nordic countries.

Following a period of significant austerity, the Nordic countries now have, by international standards, strong or very strong economies. GDP growth is high—except in Sweden, where the growth rate in 1997 was no more than 1.8 per cent. Moreover, all these countries are enjoying a low inflation rate and current account surpluses, and have relatively strong public finances. Despite the fact that central government debt in Denmark and Sweden still exceeds 60 per cent of GDP, both these countries are expected to show budget surpluses during the coming years, which should result in their debt ratios falling relatively quickly. To sum up, strictly on the basis of economic fundamentals, all four countries would probably have qualified for admission to EMU, had they all wished to join.

A snapsot of the Nordic region

FINLAND

Population (million):	5.1
GDP 1997 (Ecu bn):	105.1
GDP growth 1997:	5.9
Inflation (HICP):	1.2
Central government debt (% of GDP):	55.8
Budget deficit/surplus (% of GDP):	0.9
Current account surplus (% of GDP):	5.3

NORWAY

Population (million):	4.4
GDP 1997 (Ecu bn):	135.5
GDP growth 1997:	3.9
Inflation (HICP):	2.5
Central government debt (% of GDP):	40.6
Budget deficit/surplus (% of GDP):	-7.3
Current account surplus (% of GDP):	7.2

SWEDEN

Population (million):	8.9
GDP 1997 (Ecu bn):	210.0
GDP growth 1997:	1.8
Inflation (HICP):	1.8
Central government debt (% of GDP):	76.8
Budget deficit/surplus (% of GDP):	1.1
Current account surplus (% of GDP):	2.8

DENMARK

Population (million):	5.3
GDP 1997 (Ecu bn):	150.2
GDP growth 1997:	3.4
Inflation (HICP):	1.9
Central government debt (% of GDP):	67.9
Budget deficit/surplus (% of GDP):	-0.7
Current account surplus (% of GDP):	0.6

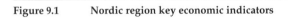

Figure 9.1   **Nordic region key economic indicators**

Different attitudes to the EU and EMU

Attitudes toward the EU and EMU differ relatively widely among the countries, presently as well as historically.

Denmark was the first Nordic country to become a full member of the EU, as long ago as in 1973. Denmark has also participated in some form of European exchange rate co-operation since 1972 when the country tied its currency to the then European currency 'snake', following the collapse of the Bretton-Woods system. Denmark entered the European Monetary System (EMS) in 1979, and since 1982, Denmark's monetary policy has focused on achieving currency stability in relation to the Deutschemark.

Finland and Sweden entered the EU together at the beginning of 1995, after having joined the European Economic Area (EEA) in 1994. In historical terms, Sweden's ties with the rest of Europe have been slightly more established than Finland's. Between 1973 and 1977, Sweden participated in the currency 'snake'. The Swedish krona was also linked to the Ecu between May 1991 and November 1992. Between these periods, the Swedish currency was tied to a trade-weighted index based on the relative significance of Sweden's 15 most important trading partners. Since 1992, Sweden has had a floating exchange rate.

Finland has a long tradition of using monetary policy to stabilize its currency. Between 1977 and June 1991, the Finnish markka was pegged to a trade-weighted index. Since the former Soviet Union was an important trade partner for Finland during this period, the Russian rouble was an important component in the index. Between June 1991 and September 1992, the Finnish markka was tied to the Ecu. When the ERM crisis occurred in 1992, the Finnish markka was allowed to float (in September of that year). Since 14 October 1996, Finland has been a member of the European currency system, the ERM. The central exchange rate in relation to the Ecu is fixed at 6.01125.

Like Denmark and Sweden, Norway also joined the currency snake following the collapse of the Bretton-Woods system. The European currency system meant, however, that the Norwegian krone tended to appreciate, as a result of which Norway withdrew in 1978. Between leaving the currency snake and 1990, Norway's currency policy was based on having a fixed exchange rate in relation to a trade-weighted currency index. In 1990, the Norwegian krone was linked to the Ecu within a band width of ±2.25 per cent. Norway then also abandoned its currency ties with the Ecu in connection with the ERM crisis in 1992. Since then, Norway's policy has been to have a 'managed float' against a basket of European currencies, of which the Ecu is the most important target variable.

To sum up, there are at present three different monetary policy regimes in the Nordic countries. Two countries, Denmark and Finland, are members of the existing ERM system. Norway has currency policy targets outside the ERM. Sweden is the only Nordic country to have a specific inflation target for its monetary policy.

At present, however, it is clear that of the four countries, only Finland will join EMU at the start in January 1999. Initially, the three other countries, for different reasons, will remain outside the monetary union. It was to be expected that Norway would stay outside, this being a direct consequence of Norway's not even being a member of the EU. The Danish and Swedish decisions to remain outside are mainly based on political considerations, as public opinion in both these countries is against membership of EMU. Denmark, like Great Britain, has an opt-out clause.

In contrast to Denmark and Great Britain, Sweden has no formal opt-out clause. However, in the light of strongly negative attitude towards EMU in Sweden, the present government has decided that Sweden should remain outside EMU at the start. The Swedish government's stated position is that participation in the currency union must have strong democratic support as EMU is very much a political project. A further aspect of the government decision, made in December 1997, was that the electorate should be consulted on the issue of Swedish membership before the country joins EMU.

Four countries – four different monetary policy regimes

It appears inevitable that the four Nordic countries will arrive at four different solutions for the formulation of monetary policy during the coming years. By virtue of its membership of the currency union, Finland will be integrated into the single EMU monetary policy which, despite everything, is perhaps the most significant reorientation of monetary policy that any of the Nordic countries will have to carry out in the short term.

The other three countries will hardly make any significant changes to the focus of their monetary policies. Both the Danish government and the country's central bank have declared that Denmark will participate in ERM2, which is only a marginal change from Danish membership of the present ERM regime.

The Norwegian government declared on 6 May 1998 that its monetary policy would continue to be focused on maintaining exchange rate stability, even after EMU had come into effect. Norwegian policy will therefore still be focused on maintaining exchange rate stability in relation to other European currencies. In principle, the Norwegian decision means that the Ecu will be replaced by the euro as the most important counterparty currency in Norwegian currency policy.

As far as Sweden is concerned, it looks as if monetary policy will remain unchanged for the immediate future. Since the Swedish krona was allowed to float, monetary policy has been directed towards maintaining price stability, with the CPI as the only target variable. This monetary policy stance will be retained, at least for the next few years. Since the reform of Sweden's monetary policy at the beginning of 1993, Sweden's central bank, the Riksbank, has established relatively strong credibility for its policies. It must also be noted that the principles of the bank's current monetary policy enjoy solid support in parliament and among the Swedish public.

When will EMU be put back on the agenda?

The positions of the three Nordic countries outside the EMU vary slightly. In the case of Norway, the question appears irrelevant, since Norway has decided not even to join the EU. It will take time before Norway takes action to change this situation. Norway has held referendums on membership of the EU on two previous occasions: the first time being in 1972, when 53.5 per cent of the electorate voted against membership. The second referendum was held as recently as 1994, and 52.2 per cent of the voted against. The question of Norway joining the EU thus appears to be an extremely remote eventuality.

At first sight, the positions of Denmark and Sweden appear to be rather similar. However, upon closer scrutiny, relatively significant differences emerge. Two underlying distinctions may be highlighted. The first is that there is a majority in favour of membership of EMU in the Danish parliament; this is not the case in Sweden. The second difference is that Denmark has a formal opt-out clause. This stipulates that another referendum has to be held before membership can be returned to the agenda.

At present, the Danish government has no plans to hold such a referendum. Public support for membership of both the EU and EMU is still weak in Denmark. According to the EU Commission's *Eurobarometer* (No. 47), 54 per cent of the Danish electorate is against joining EMU, whilst only 32 per cent are in favour. As things stand at present, the Danish government's European policy is best described as seeking to minimize the disadvantages and thus the cost of remaining outside. It will probably be some time before the next, and probably decisive, referendum is held. In terms of domestic policy, the most important factor is the attitude of the electorate. A Danish government is hardly likely to call a referendum on this issue without already being convinced that the result will be positive. The fact that there is a political majority in parliament in favour of membership will probably help to ease the passing of all the laws and regulations that will be needed to minimize the adverse effects on the economy of not belonging to EMU.

The situation in Sweden is slightly more complicated. As already observed, there is at present no support for membership of EMU in the Swedish parliament. This is due, above all, to the fact that the Social Democratic Party has not yet made up its mind on this issue. Furthermore, it may be some time before the Social Democrats do make up their minds, as the party is split into two more or less equal groups, representing opposite viewpoints.

Given that the EMU issue is not a priority on the political agenda, the Social Democrats (assuming they win the September 1998 general election as expected), are hardly likely to want to get their next term of office off to a flying start by putting EMU back at the top of the agenda. The last Social Democratic Party conference, which was held in September 1997, decided that EMU would need to be considered by a further party conference before it could be put to the electorate in a referendum. However, the next regular party conference will not take place until 2001. The minutes from the 1997 party conference state, however, that the party executive board will make regular analyses and assessments of developments with regard to EMU. Should the domestic situation or developments in Europe indicate that the benefits of membership appear to be substantial, the board has been empowered to convene an extraordinary conference before the next regular one is due. However, the fact that EMU will not start until 1999, and that it will take a relatively long time to evaluate and analyze its effects, indicates that EMU will not be given high priority in the short term. All in all, this leads us to conclude that the Swedish government can hardly make a definite decision, either way, on EMU before the end of 1999.

The next important deadline, as far as Sweden is concerned, will occur during the second half of 2000 when Sweden's first tenure of the presidency of the EU starts drawing close (Sweden holds the presidency for the first half of 2001). As the time to take over presidency gets nearer, international and domestic political pressure will likely intensify for Sweden to clarify exactly where it stands in relation to EMU. If the start of the monetary union has been characterized by stability and the government therefore decides to put EMU onto the agenda for the party conference in 2001, there is a fairly high probability of the Social Democratic Party taking a clearer stance on the issue of membership.

A Swedish link with the ERM

The lukewarm interest in early membership of EMU makes the probability of the Swedish krona becoming linked to ERM2 in the near future very low. However, the issue will in all probability assume growing importance during the course of 1999, especially towards the end of the year. This view is based on the wording highlighted by the EU Commission in its case for why Sweden failed to qualify to participate in EMU from the start. In its reasoning, the EU Commission applied a strict interpretation of the exchange rate criterion, an approach it could continue to adopt in the future. At the same time, it should be borne in mind that a strict interpretation of the exchange rate criterion is at present not necessarily absolutely binding under an ERM2 regime. What is essentially emerging is an entirely new type of fixed exchange rate regime within Europe.

The introduction of a new exchange rate regime also represents a reorientation of monetary policy: from the present position of having an inflation target, with the CPI as the target variable, to having an exchange rate target with the euro/krona rate as the target variable. Such a change can hardly come about before a high degree of mutual understanding has been reached with regard to EMU or, alternatively, confidence in Sweden's low inflation policy has been further consolidated. From today's perspective, continued high volatility in the krona's exchange rate *vis-à-vis* the euro and the dollar would probably be regarded by the Riksbank as relatively strong grounds for wishing to introduce a new exchange rate regime. Excessive fluctuations in the currency could put the credibility of its monetary policy at risk.

All in all, this means that the krona will not be linked to the ERM until the year 2000 at the earliest. The exchange rate and stability of the krona will probably be one of the most important parameters determining how soon the Swedish currency can be brought within the ERM2 system.

International developments will play a decisive role

In the case of both Sweden and Denmark, external developments—not only political, but also commercial—will play a decisive role. Politically, the ongoing evaluation of the EMU project will, in all probability, focus on a couple of specific fields. Firstly, the progress of the monetary union as such will naturally be very important. Day-to-day developments and fiscal policy co-operation within the framework of the growth and stabilization pact in particular will be watched closely, since one of the most critical reasons for the hesitant attitude of both countries is their fiscal policy autonomy, or rather the risk of excessive supranational involvement in the fiscal policy field. The other very important factor is development of, and effects on, the labour market. Measures to retain the favorable trend in employment are currently the most important features in the economic policy of the two countries. A further question of the utmost political importance to both Denmark and Sweden is the development of the UK stance towards EMU. Should the UK show clear and unambiguous signs of moving closer to membership of EMU, pressure on the Nordic countries will build up markedly. This is due partly to the expansion of EMU and partly to the UK's significance as a trading partner of both countries. There is also considerable mutual dependence between the two Nordic countries. For example, should Denmark announce plans to join EMU, the pressure on Sweden to join would increase, and vice versa.

To sum up, it looks as if it will be some time before the three Nordic non-members join EMU. In Norway's case, the most likely outcome is that if and when the country joins EMU, this would take place at the same time as Norway joins the EU. However, this is still a remote eventuality, and Norwegian membership of the EU is not to be expected in the foreseeable future. Denmark and/or Sweden appear more likely to become members of EMU, even though this would probably also be a relatively drawn-out process. The main obstacles are the negative public opinion in both countries. In the short-term perspective, this will tie the hands of politicians in the two countries as they will not wish to challenge public opinion. This situation also means that developments in other countries will have a very important effect on the timing of an application to join the currency union. The factor which currently appears to be most important is what attitude the UK will adopt. If Great Britain were to join this would probably result in the two Nordic countries following suit within a relatively short period of time. This would mean that Denmark and Sweden could join EMU in, say, 2003 or 2004.

Consequences of remaining outside EMU

As far as the three Nordic countries are concerned, remaining outside EMU would probably involve certain general political costs. The most obvious is that, by remaining outside EMU, the Nordic countries would, in all likelihood, have slightly higher interest rates than those applying in Euroland. At present, the spread between the Danish and Swedish bond yields, on the one hand, and German yields on the other, is around 20 basis points. Provided the economic development of the two countries show continued stability, coupled with inflation rates that do not deviate from inflation within Euroland, and as long as public finances in the two

Nordic interest rates...

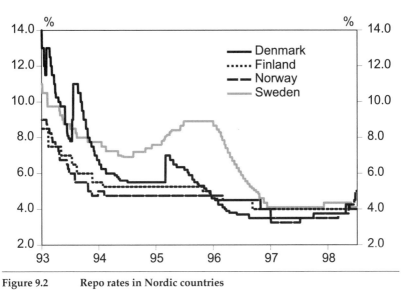

Figure 9.2   Repo rates in Nordic countries

...and yield convergence

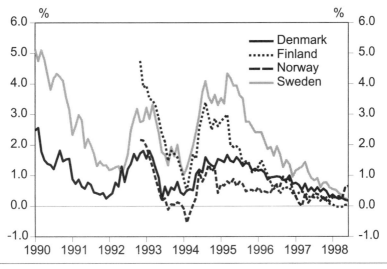

Figure 9.3   Nordic 10-year yield differentials with Germany

countries continue to strengthen, the yield spread could remain at its present level or even diminish slightly. In this context, it is important to observe that both Denmark and Sweden have more ambitious fiscal policy goals than those stipulated in the Stability and Growth Pact. The Swedish government has declared that its goal is to have an average budget surplus corresponding to 1.5 per cent of GDP over an economic cycle. Ambitious indeed! Denmark's economic policy is also focused on maintaining a budget surplus between now and 2005, by when the aim is to have reduced the central government debt to 40 per cent of GDP (67.9 per cent in 1997). There will also be a political price to pay, although quantifying this will be difficult. This is the cost of seeing the country's political voice marginalized, not least because the countries will remain outside the euro-11 group. Moreover, this political voice could become further muted in connection with other pan-European issues, such as labour market and environmental issues, both of them policy areas to which both Denmark and Sweden attach great political importance.

The increased currency risk also suggests that there will still be a modest risk premium in relation to Euroland. In this connection, Sweden's monetary policy, with its floating exchange rate, appears to represent a slightly greater threat than Denmark, which aims to maintain a fixed exchange rate in relation to the euro. Moreover, as things are, Denmark will probably enjoy somewhat greater confidence as Danish economic policy has been consistent for a far longer period than that of Sweden.

The slightly higher interest rate level that can be expected in these countries if they remain outside EMU will primarily affect consumers and small- and medium-sized companies, which make relatively greater use of the domestic loan market. Large multinational enterprises, by contrast, will probably hardly be affected at all as they already have full access to international capital markets. This situation will not be changed by EMU.

Of the Nordic countries, it is only Finland which can fully enjoy any advantages that membership of EMU will bring in the form of low interest rates, for example, and lower transaction costs for cross-border payments as a result of full access to the European TARGET payment system. The adverse effects caused by restrictions on access to TARGET should, however, not be exaggerated. The leading banks in non-member countries have subsidiaries or branches in EMU, which will offset the adverse consequences of any discrimination within the TARGET system.

However, the major banks will have to be prepared to provide the euro-based services which their major clients, in particular, will start demanding once EMU gets off the ground in 1999. Most of the major corporate clients of these banks are already internationally-orientated with significant commercial activities in Euroland. Consequently, these companies already have complementary banking connections in the EMU zone. Euro-based services could also experience relatively rapidly expanding demand from small- and medium-sized firms. Some of these companies are already highly dependent on international markets, due to their export and/or import activities, or because they are sub-contractors to one or a few multinational enterprises in their own country. Naturally, having to make significant parts of their range of financial services available in two separate currencies will involve higher costs for banks and other financial institutions.

Discrimination within TARGET will have a more serious effect on small, regionally-orientated banks in Denmark, Norway and Sweden. However, these effects will probably also be limited, at least in the short term, as banks of this type mainly serve private clients and small local firms. The demand for euro-based products and services among customers in these categories will probably be relatively modest during the next few years, not least on account of the small interest rate spread. In time, however, the situation is expected to change and an increasingly specific demand for euro-based services will also emerge among customers of this type. As far as private clients are concerned, demand for euro-based services will probably emerge mainly in the saving and asset management segments, where the significantly larger and deeper European market, coupled with diversifying saving tendencies, will have a considerable appeal. The demand for financial services among private clients will probably not expand so rapidly. However, should it start becoming evident that one or both countries will join EMU in the relatively near future, demand would probably accelerate rather fast.

Entry by the back door?

There is no doubt that the implementation of the currency union will have a significant impact on all the Nordic countries—especially in the light of the very extensive international trade among all the Nordic countries and between them and the countries in Euroland. Furthermore, the political ties are clear-cut because of Denmark's and Sweden's membership of the EU. Consequently, both Denmark and Sweden are subject to the rules in the Stability and Growth Pact, even though their non-membership of EMU prevents sanctions from being imposed on the two countries. The political ties between Norway and the rest of Europe are also very strong, even though Norway has opted to remain outside the EU. These ties are reflected, for example, in Norway's membership of the EEA.

The very extensive trade between the Nordic countries and Euroland, coupled with the fact that many Nordic companies are already well established in Euroland, creates additional direct and very strong financial links between these two blocs. Naturally, the direct ties are most evident in the case of cross-border transactions and payments. Financial integration is already very far reaching and includes all aspects of the financial markets. One obvious example of this is that both Denmark and Sweden are currently investigating the effects on the local stock markets of the introduction of the single currency. (Incidentally, it should be mentioned that, in January 1998, the stock exchanges in Copenhagen and Stockholm entered into an alliance in an effort to create a platform for a co-ordinated Nordic market.)

In Sweden, the government presented the results of an investigation in the middle of December 1997, one recommendation of which is that it should become possible for Swedish companies to make up their profit income statements and balance sheets in euros and redenominate their share capital in euros. A good deal of study still remains, as well as the work involved in adapting and amending all the relevant laws and regulations. However, the government's intention is to ensure that the necessary changes are implemented before the end of 1998. Given the extent of the work remaining to be done in Sweden, however, it is unlikely that all the legal amendments necessary will be completed by then. The Danish government is also reviewing and amending the relevant legislation. According to the Danish Ministry of Finance, this work will be completed before the of 1998.

This does not, however, mean that all leading Danish and Swedish enterprises will suddenly change over to using the euro as their group currency. According to surveys carried out in Sweden, around 30 per cent of Sweden's leading enterprises plan to start using the euro as a group currency at some point during the course of 1999. At the same time, there is much to suggest that companies could derive considerable benefits from making this change, which suggests that more companies will probably follow their example relatively promptly. An important point for those companies whose attitude is more hesitant is that they would like all the legislative amendments to be completed before they change their group currency. It is also important to bear in mind that, if a company's share capital is to be redenominated, the key decision will—in the final analysis—be made by its shareholders.

Once large domestic enterprises start using the euro as their group currency, the euro is likely to come into markedly more widespread use in the economy generally. Dispersion effects could be considerable as domestic suppliers will probably change into line with their major customers and start using the euro for quoting and invoicing. Many small firms could find that the euro will simplify their everyday lives, not least those which already supply companies in their own country and export to one or more countries in the planned currency zone. This could represent a further force that would contribute to making the use of the euro more widespread also in countries which decide to remain outside the monetary union.

Alongside amendments to laws which regulate the right of companies to use the euro as a group currency, the stock market in Sweden is planning to enable Swedish companies to have their shares listed in euros with effect from 4 January 1999. Several interrelated factors will influence decisions on whether or not to quote Swedish equities in euros. The first is the wish to benefit from the dynamic developments which will probably be a consequence of the start of the new, enlarged single currency zone. Another reason is that issuers of Swedish equities should be able to issue shares on the same terms as their competitors in Euroland. In the final analysis, however, it is largely a matter of enabling Stockholm to survive and develop as a competitive financial market. The risks associated with retaining the present arrangements is that large Swedish companies will prefer to have their shares listed on stock markets in Euroland, which would have adverse consequences on the liquidity of the Stockholm market.

According to the Stockholm Stock Exchange's original proposal, the 30 largest Swedish companies will be listed solely in euros, while other companies would continue to be quoted in Swedish kronor. In this context, it is worth noting that the 30 largest companies on the Stockholm market account for some 77 per cent of its turnover. However, representatives of small shareholders have protested against these plans and, moreover, they have attracted some support from political quarters. The point currently being examined is a system of dual pricing of shares in the leading Swedish companies. However, the technical problems associated with this are not insignificant, not least because the currency market is a spread market.

Whatever proposal emerges in the end, it may be observed that investors on the Swedish stock market, both domestic and foreign, will be able to buy Swedish shares denominated in euros as of 1999—if that is what they want. This is another means, along with the use of the euro by companies as their group and invoicing currency, whereby the new currency will naturally come into increasingly widespread use in the economy. Given the extent to which the Swedish public has taken up the habit of owning shares, trading on the stock market could also lead private individuals to take up the practice of opening accounts and equity deposit accounts in euros. However, this is a development that will probably initially only emerge relatively slowly, although it may be expected to accelerate as it becomes increasingly evident that Swedish membership of EMU has been brought back on the political agenda.

Section

III

The
euro

The institutions of the euro

Darren Williams &
Richard Reid
UBS Limited

A central bank for Europe

The European Central Bank will assume control of European monetary policy in 1999. On paper, it is a strong replacement for the Bundesbank. In practice, it could be handicapped if the German central bank's low inflation constituency is not mirrored elsewhere in Europe. The statute of the European Central Bank attempts to create an independent central bank with a firm mandate for low inflation. The ECB's primary goal is to ensure price stability; it is prohibited from financing government deficits and is protected from political influence and interference. Indeed, on most relevant factors, the ECB scores as well as, if not higher than, the Bundesbank. But the Bundesbank's position amongst the world's most credible central banks is not due simply to the statute book. Rather, it reflects a domestic consensus in favour of low inflation which might not be shared by Europe as a whole. Without such a constituency, the ECB's ability to resist political pressure—which would surely arise should Europe fail to answer its unemployment problems—might be greatly reduced. Some European governments have already expressed their reservations about the blueprint for monetary union signed at Maastricht. The French government's insistence on the establishment of Euro-X, an upgrading of the commitment to growth and employment, and a downgrading of the commitment to budgetary discipline, all represent potential threats to the independence of the central bank. The ECB will be a new central bank operating in a new monetary area and, as such, it is impossible to know exactly how it will perform. It is clear that, on paper, it is a fitting replacement for the German central bank. However, if the current institutional setting is changed, there might come a day when the passing of the Bundesbank is widely lamented.

The Bundesbank will be subsumed by the ECB

From 1 January 1999, the Bundesbank will cease to be the dominant force in European monetary affairs. Instead, as a constituent member of the European System of Central Banks (ESCB) which will govern European monetary policy during Stage Three, the Bundesbank will be just one voice amongst many, and its influence will be much reduced. Despite an almost impeccable track-record in forty years since it came into existence, the German central bank is likely to have little more say over the course of European monetary policy than its less-credible counterparts from southern Europe.

Fortunately, this is not the whole story. Although we will lose the Bundesbank as we currently know it, the central bank's work has not been in vain. Throughout the 1980s and 1990s, the Germanic model of central banking has been exported to most other European countries. So much so, that it is hard to believe that the Bundesbank could have been any tougher on inflation than either the Bank of France or Bank of Italy have been in recent years.

But the Bundesbank's greatest legacy is that the future guardian of European monetary stability, the European Central Bank (ECB), has been designed along German central banking lines. Indeed, on paper, the ECB might even represent an improvement on the Bundesbank. Where there are ambiguities in the division of responsibilities between the central bank and the government in the Bundesbank Act, the Maastricht Treaty makes these explicit, mainly to the advantage of the central bank. In theory, the ECB is a form of 'super-Bundesbank'.

Theory is, of course, very different from practice. The Bundesbank's reputation for hard-nosed anti-inflation policies was not bestowed upon it by the Bundesbank Act. Rather, it was earned over a period of time, and through a series of tough battles with the federal government, some of which the Bundesbank lost, but most of which it won.

In this respect, the dispute between the Bundesbank and the government in 1997 about the revaluation of Germany's gold reserves is instructive. When the central bank decided that Mr Waigel's plans for revaluation posed a threat to its independence, it objected in a very public manner, and popular support for the Bundesbank caused the government to abandon its plans.[1] It has been suggested that this represents an early victory for the ECB, although we are more sceptical. The Bundesbank's ability successfully to confront its own government owes much to the special position it holds within German society. Would the ECB be able to rely on such support?

Bundesbank Council

ECB Council?

Figure 10.1   Will the ECB be a good replacement for the Bundesbank?

If the ECB is successfully to take the place of the Bundesbank, it will have to earn its spurs. Unfortunately, it is impossible to know today precisely how the ECB will perform in practice. But there are several important clues and, in this chapter, we intend to explore them. We start by taking a closer look at issues related to central bank independence, move on to consider how these are likely to apply to the ECB, before finally drawing some conclusions.

Assessing central bank independence

The benefits of independence

Central bank independence has been the subject of considerable debate in recent years. Although many different methods have been used to quantify the degree of independence, most point to an inverse relationship between independence and inflation (see Figure 10.2). In other words, the more independent a central bank, the lower inflation tends to be. In addition, there has been little conclusive evidence of any relationship between the independence of a central bank and either the strength or volatility of economic growth.

It is the evidence suggesting that central bank independence delivers lower rates of inflation without any identifiable cost in terms of growth which lies behind the move towards greater independence in recent years. However, some caution is necessary, as there is little evidence to suggest a causal link between independence and low inflation. Rather, it can be argued that independent central banks are more likely to be established in countries where there is an existing consensus in favour of low inflation. Germany is a case in point.

Central bank independence in the European Union

Historically, European countries have had very different approaches to central bank independence. Figure 10.2 suggests that the northern European countries such as Germany, Switzerland and, to a lesser extent, the Netherlands, have histories of strongly-independent central banks, but that countries such as France, Italy, Spain and the UK do not. (Note: while Figure 10.2 shows the results of just one study, the findings of alternative approaches are very similar.)

Of course, the last few years have seen significant changes in this latter group of countries, with even the Bank of England now 'operationally' independent of government control (this is not the same as full independence, as the government retains the right to set the key inflation target). Meanwhile, the central banks in France, Italy and Spain have all

Central bank independence brings lower inflation

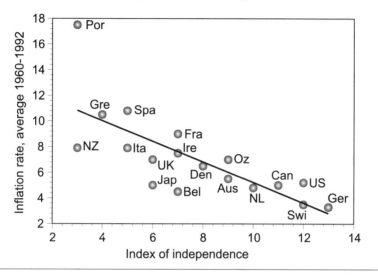

Figure 10.2   Central bank independence and inflation performance
Source: Bank of England, drawing on data in Cukierman, 1992. The index is a weighted average of data from 1950-89 of legal provisions regarding; (1) appointment and dismissal of the governor; (2) procedures for the formation of monetary policy; (3) objectives of central bank policy; (4) limitations on lending by the central bank. The minimum score (least independent) is zero and the maximum score (most independent) is 1.00. Note that independence has recently improved in many European countries.

been granted independence during the 1990s. It is, however, instructive that in none of these cases did the granting of independence pre-date the signing of the Maastricht Treaty (which committed EU governments to independent central banks).

Hence, it is not clear that France's move to grant independence to its central bank means that society has been fully converted to the concept of Germanic central banking. Rather, as the French move to establish Euro-X (see Chapter 11) as a political counterweight to the ECB might suggest, it might simply have been seen as a necessity for France to qualify for monetary union. Put another way, it is still not clear that the low-inflation consensus which allows the Bundesbank to conduct a strong anti-inflation policy in Germany exists on a wider European scale.

Functional independence

We shall return to the political dimension of EMU later. For now, we shall focus on the ECB as proposed in the Maastricht Treaty. As mentioned earlier, the need to soothe German concerns about giving up the Deutschemark were critical to the success of the Maastricht negotiations and, consequently, the ECB has been constructed largely upon German central banking lines. Indeed, in some respects, one might argue that the ECB has been given an even stronger mandate than the Bundesbank:

- According to the Maastricht Treaty, the main responsibility of the ECB 'shall be to maintain price stability'. This is more explicit than the Bundesbank Act which states that the main function of the central bank is 'safeguarding the currency'. It is the Bundesbank, reacting to the deep-rooted fear of inflation in Germany, which has interpreted this clause in the strictest of fashions.

- The Maastricht Treaty forbids the ECB from granting 'overdrafts or any other type of credit facility' to EU or national government bodies. The Bundesbank Act was changed to bring it into line with this, having previously allowed the government to have minor credit facilities with the central bank.

In reality, these are relatively minor differences. However, that the ECB compares favourably with a central bank which is widely regarded as being amongst the most independent and inflation-averse in the world must count as a strong point in its favour.

Institutional independence

Although the economic literature differs in the methods used to quantify central bank independence, there is considerable agreement over the importance of the institutional setting. How central bank officials are appointed, the length of their mandates, the security of their tenure and the government's ability to influence or interfere in central bank decisions are all regarded as important determinants of a central bank's independence.

Monetary policy decisions of the ECB will be made by the Governing Council, which comprises the Executive Board together with the Governors of the eleven National Central Banks (NCBs) in the euro area. This is a mirror image of the Bundesbank, where interest rate decisions are made by the Central Bank Council, which comprises the Directorate of the Bundesbank and the presidents of the Land Central Banks.

The appointment of members to the Executive Board has been the cause of some consternation, as they will be made 'by common accord of the

The ECB: an anatomical view

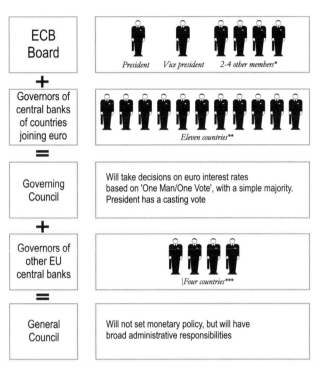

Figure 10.3   Structure of the European Central Bank
initially (from 1999) four other members
**initially (from 1999) eleven countries*
***initially (from 1999) four countries*

member states'. In other words, they will be appointed by politicians. This alone, however, is not sufficient reason for alarm. After all, the members of the Bundesbank Directorate are also appointed by the government. In addition, some comfort can be drawn from the fact that all appointees to the Executive Board must be experts in either monetary or banking matters. The first members of the ECB Board, together with their terms of reference, are set out in Figure 10.4; the national central bank governors are listed in Figure 10.5.

Once nominated to these positions, members of the Executive Board will have a mandate of four to eight years and this will not be renewable. Such a period compares favourably with existing central bank practice (it is the same as for the Bundesbank). Moreover, single terms are thought to remove at least some of the incentives for central bank members to bow to

The ECB: Bundesbank Mark II?

ECB	Bundesbank
Primary goal/function	
'The primary objective of the ESCB shall be to maintain price stability'	'The Deutsche Bundesbank regulates the amount of money in the economy ... with the aim of safeguarding the currency'
Relationship with government	
'Without prejudice to the objective of price stability, the ESCB shall support the general economic policies of the Community.' 'When exercising the powers and carrying out the tasks and duties conferred upon them by this Treaty, neither the ECB, nor a national central bank, nor any members of their decision-making bodies shall seek or take instructions from Community institutions or bodies, from any government of a Member State or from any other body.'	'Without prejudice to the performance of its functions, the Deutsche Bundesbank is required to support the general economic policy of the Federal Cabinet. In exercising the powers conferred upon it by this Act, the Bank is independent of instructions from the Federal Cabinet.'
Decision-making body	
The Governing Council, which comprises the members of the Executive Board (president, vice-president and between 2 and 4 other members) and the governors of the National Central Banks of the euro area (up to 15 at present, depending on the number of initial members of the single currency).	The Central Bank Council, which comprises the members of the Directorate (president, vice-president and up to 6 other members) and the presidents of the 9 Land Central Banks.

Cont.

ECB	Bundesbank

(cont.)

How members are chosen

'Members of the Executive Board shall be appointed from among persons of recognized standing and professional experience in monetary and banking matters and by common accord of the member states at the level of the heads of state or of government, on a recommendation from the Council after it has consulted the European Parliament and the Governing Council (of the ECB).' National Central Bank governors are appointed according to relevant domestic procedures.

'Members of the Directorate must have special professional qualifications.' 'The president and vice-president and the other members of the Directorate are nominated by the Federal Cabinet and appointed by the president of the Federal Republic. When making such nominations, the Federal Cabinet shall consult the Central Bank Council.' The above also applies to presidents of the Land Central Banks, except that they are nominated by the Bundesrat.

Term of office

For the Executive Board, this is normally for eight years and is non-renewable. (Note that some of the initial appointments will be for shorter periods to allow for continuity.)

Members can only be removed if they no longer fulfil the conditions required to carry out their duties, or for gross misconduct, and then only on application from the Governing Council or Executive Board.

The Treaty requires that NCB governors have a mandate of at least five years and that similar provisions as above apply for removal.

Directorate members and the presidents of the Land Central Banks are normally appointed for a period of eight years. These are renewable.

There are no provisions in the Bundesbank Act for removing a member of the Directorate or a president of a Land Central Bank.

Voting procedure

For the purposes of monetary policy decisions, the Governing Council makes its decisions by simple majority, with the president having the casting vote in the event of a tie.

Central Bank Council decisions are made by simple majority, with the president having the casting vote in the event of a tie.

Figure 10.4   Comparing the ECB and the Bundesbank
All quotations are taken from the relevant sections of the Maastricht Treaty and the Bundesbank Act

political pressure. Finally, while members of the Executive Board can be removed or dismissed, this is only possible in exceptional circumstances and only at the request of either the Executive Board itself, or of the Governing Council of the ECB.

The Executive Board will initially comprise six members (strictly-speaking, there can be between four and six members). In the eleven-country euro area, this means they will be outweighed on the General Council by the governors of the NCBs.

Voting behaviour of the ECB

On balance, the overall institutional setting of the ECB can be said to be on a par with, if not superior to, that of the Bundesbank. One area where the ECB is perhaps at a disadvantage, however, is that the Executive Board is likely to have a weaker weighting in Governing Council interest rate decisions than its counterpart, the Directorate, currently has in Bundesbank decisions (see Figure 10.6).

There have been several attempts to determine the likely voting behaviour of the ECB. A useful starting point is to assume that the six members of the Executive Board are professional central bankers, and that they will thus adopt conservative voting habits. The unanimity required to elect members to the Executive Board, the length and security of their tenure and the requirement of technical expertise, all suggest this is a reasonable assumption.

Although this might be a reasonable assumption, it is also quite clearly a best-case scenario. This can be at least partially offset by assuming that the NCB members of the Governing Council vote according to their own government's preferences. This is clearly a worst-case scenario.

However, even with the initial eleven members, it would require only two other NCBs to join the Bundesbank for the conservative central bankers to hold a majority on the Governing Council. As Figure 10.6 highlights, longer-term track-records suggest that three other central banks could probably be relied upon—Austria and, to a lesser extent, the Netherlands and Luxembourg.

There are two potential problems with this analysis. The most obvious is that the ability of a 'hard-core' of conservative central bankers to determine ECB policy decisions would clearly be at risk in an even wider monetary union (if, say, Greece, the UK, Sweden and Denmark eventually joined). However, this should not be a major concern as the behaviour and reputation of the ECB are likely to be established in the very early years of its existence, when membership should be limited to the initial eleven countries.

The assumption that all Executive Board members will be 'hawks' might also be questionable. Admittedly, the first EMI president, Wim Duisenberg, is a professional central banker, but disputes surrounding his appointment show that some EU countries see advantages in securing an ECB president of their choosing.

The real threats to independence

Even allowing for some of the points raised in the last section, the Maastricht Treaty lays out a blueprint for a central bank which is at least the equal of the Bundesbank. Mr Issing (formerly the chief economist of the Bundesbank, who now holds a similar position at the ECB) is in little doubt of this when he says, 'in terms of providing institutional protection to a monetary policy geared towards price stability, as much as can realistically be expected has been achieved'. However, Mr Issing goes on to say that 'the possibility of a dispute over the monetary policy stance of the European Central Bank remains'.

There are three areas in which a dispute between European governments and the ECB could emerge—exchange rate policy, employment policy and fiscal policy.

The exchange rate

'Among the criticisms frequently raised over the statute of the European Central Bank, the exchange rate problem vis-à-vis non-EU currencies has no doubt to be taken most seriously.'

Otmar Issing

The most likely area of dispute between the ECB and governments is over the appropriate level of the exchange rate. The Maastricht Treaty allows the European Council to enter exchange rate systems and agreements and, most importantly, to 'formulate general orientations for exchange-rate policy' (article 109.2).

This represents a departure from the situation in Germany. Although the federal government reserves the right to choose the appropriate exchange rate regime for the Deutschemark (i.e. Bretton Woods, the ERM), the Bundesbank is in active control of exchange rate policy. This is one of the strengths of the Bundesbank Act, which charges the German central bank with 'safeguarding the currency'. If this is interpreted as applying to the external (as well as the internal) value of the currency, the Bundesbank has a direct responsibility for exchange rate policy.

Keeping the NCBs Independent

Institutional independence

The rights of third parties to:

- give instructions to NCBs or their decision-making bodies;

- approve, suspend, annul or defer decisions of NCBs;

- participate in the decision-making bodies of an NCB with a right to vote; or

- be consulted (ex-ante) on an NCB's decisions

...are incompatible with the Maastricht Treaty.

Personal independence

The statutes of the NCBs should ensure that:

- governors of NCBs have a minimum term of five years;

- a governor of an NCB may not be dismissed for reasons other than that he/she no longer fulfils the conditions required for the performance of his/her duties or if he/she is guilty of gross misconduct;

- other members of the decision-making process of NCBs have the same security of tenure as governors;

Functional independence

Requires the statutory objectives of NCBs to be in line with the ESCB's objective (i.e. price stability).

Figure 10.5   Ensuring the independence of national central banks
Source: Progress Towards Convergence 1996, European Monetary Institute.

The ECB was given greater authority over exchange rate matters at the Mondorf informal Ecofin summit in 1997 and the Maastricht Treaty does state that any exchange rate decisions or orientations of the European Council must be 'without prejudice to the primary objective of the ESCB to maintain price stability'. However, there is still clearly room for dispute between the various EU institutions, should adverse exchange rates develop.

Governing councils: ECB cf. Bundesbank

ECB Governing Council	Bundesbank Central Bank Council
Executive Board:	**Directorate:**
President, vice-president, between 2 and 4 other members	President, vice president, up to 6 other members
Normal representation: 6	Normal representation: 8
National central bank governors:	**Land central bank presidents**
Representation: 11 members[1]	Representation: 9
Total members: 17	**Total members: 17**

Figure 10.6   **Comparing the ECB and Bundesbank Governing Councils**
[1]*This depends upon the membership of the single currency. At present, there are 15 National Central Banks within the EU. The 11 members shown above reflects UBS's view that EMU will take place in 1999 and on a broad basis (i.e. including all EU countries except for Greece and the political 'opt-outs'—the UK, Denmark and Sweden).*

The key question is who decides whether or not a given orientation for exchange rate policy is consistent with price stability. In practice, the ECB is likely to decide for itself, but this could lead to a direct and damaging conflict with the European Council. Moreover, it is not clear that the ECB would win such a stand-off.

Employment policy

The Maastricht Treaty calls upon the ECB to 'support the general economic policies of the Community with a view to contributing to the achievement of the objectives of the Community'. Among other things, the latter include a 'high level of employment and social protection'. Again, the treaty makes it clear that this should be secondary to the primary goal of price stability and, it should be noted, there is a very similar clause in the Bundesbank Act. However, as with exchange rate management, there is a potential conflict of interests here, particularly if France is successful in its attempts to gain greater recognition for the social aspects of the Maastricht Treaty.

Independence & inflation:
the EU league table

	Independence rating[1]	Inflation rating[2]	Total rating[3]
Germany	4	4	8
Austria	4	4	8
Netherlands	3	3	6
Luxembourg	2	4	6
Belgium	2	3	5
Denmark	3	2	5
Ireland	3	1	4
France	2	2	4
Finland	2	2	4
Sweden	2	2	4
Greece	3	1	4
UK	2	1	3
Italy	2	1	3
Spain	1	1	2
Portugal	n/a	1	n/a

Figure 10.7   Central bank independence & inflation ratings of EU central banks

[1]*The independence rating is based on the findings of several studies, over varying time-spans pre-dating the Maastricht Treaty. A score of 4 represents the most independent type of central bank.*

[2]*The inflation rating is based on annual average inflation between 1960 and 1990. A score of 4 represents the most inflation-averse country.*

[3]*The total rating is the sum of the first two columns.*

Fiscal policy

'If, even with the threat of non-participation, a member state is neither willing nor able to observe the limits for budget deficits and indebtedness, it is hardly likely that it will make increased efforts when such a strict sanction is no longer available.'

Otmar Issing

The Maastricht Treaty expressly forbids central bank financing of government deficits. In addition, the Stability and Growth Pact signed at the Amsterdam summit aims to place severe constraints upon the ability of governments to run 'excessive' budget deficits. However, the liberal interpretation of the EMU entry criteria and continued watering-down of the stability pact raise serious question marks over just how binding these constraints are likely to be.

Should European governments run excessive budget deficits within EMU, and allow debt ratios to rise, then the independence of the central bank could be impaired. There are number of mechanisms through which this could work. First, in highly-indebted countries, political pressure for lower interest rates is immense and there is also a greater tolerance for high inflation. Second, it is difficult for a central bank in such countries to completely ignore the impact on government solvency of unrestrained interest rate hikes.

However, let us assume that the ECB refuses to finance an excessive deficit—as the Maastricht Treaty requires. The result would be higher interest rates and the crowding-out of domestic spending. This would be compounded if the resultant policy-mix led to an appreciating currency. The ECB would then be 'responsible' for weak growth (perhaps a recession) and a dramatic rise in unemployment, which would lead to enormous tensions. In these circumstances, the temptation to resort to indirect financing of deficits by intervention on the domestic money market (to prevent interest rates from rising), or the foreign exchange market (to prevent the currency from rising), is easy to see. Hence, Mr Issing's statement that 'regardless of the degree of independence, monetary policy will remain an integral part of the economic process'.

Conclusions

We have established that, on paper, the European Central Bank ought to be a fitting replacement for the Bundesbank. On most counts it scores as well, if not better than, the German central bank. In addition, it has the advantage of having its statutes enshrined in an international treaty which would require the unanimous agreement of all EU member states to change.

However, it is equally clear that the Bundesbank's position as the world's most credible central bank is not due simply to the Bundesbank Act. Rather, it reflects a domestic consensus in favour of low inflation which might not yet be shared by Europe as a whole. If not, then the ECB's ability to resist political pressures could be much reduced. That is the real strength of the Bundesbank.

Moreover, there are worrying signs. Having seen the consequences of a rigid commitment to fiscal rules and Bundesbank-style interest and exchange rate policies, the French government is beginning to shy away from the blueprint for monetary union signed at Maastricht. The insistence on the establishment of Euro-X, on an upgrading of the commitment to growth and employment, and on a downgrading of the commitment to fiscal discipline, all represent potential threats to the independence of the central bank.

As the legislation stands, it is probably fair to say that the ECB will be a fitting substitute for the Bundesbank. However, if France succeeds in weakening the stability pact yet further, and in obtaining real powers for Euro-X, then there might come a day when many lament the passing of the Bundesbank.

The role of Euro-X is discussed in greater detail in the next chapter.

Notes for Chapter 10

[1]*The revaluation would have had the effect of reducing Germany's budget deficit, helping it to meet the Maastricht requirement.*

Chapter
10

The Maastricht Treaty and ECB independence

General objectives of the European Union

Article 2*

The Community shall have its tasks, by establishing a common market and an economic and monetary union and by implementing the common policies or activities referred to in Articles 3 and 3a, to promote throughout the Community a harmonious and balanced development of economic activities, sustainable and non-inflationary growth respecting the environment, a high degree of convergence of economic performance, a high level of employment and social protection, the raising of the standard living and quality of life, and economic and social cohesion amp solidarity among member states.

Objectives and tasks of the European System of Central Banks

Article 105

1.   The primary objective of the ESCB shall be to maintain price stability. Without prejudice to the objective of price stability, the ESCB shall support the general economic policies of the Community with a view to contributing to the achievement of the objectives of the

---

Note that, to maintain consistency throughout this book, certain typographical changes have been made to the extracts from original Community texts. These changes have no material affect on either the meaning or sense of the texts.

Community as laid down in Article 2. The ESCB shall act in accordance with the principle of an open market economy with free competition, favouring an efficient allocation of resources, and in compliance with the principles set out in Article 3a.

2. The basic tasks to be carried out through the ESCB shall be:

-   to define the monetary policy of the Community;
-   to conduct foreign exchange operations consistent with the provisions of Article 109;
-   to hold and manage the official reserves of the member states;
-   to promote the smooth operations of payment systems.

Independence of the European System of Central Banks

Article 107

When exercising the powers and carrying out the tasks and duties conferred upon them by this Treaty and the Statute of the ESCB, neither the ECB, nor a national central bank, nor any members of their decision-making bodies shall seek or take instructions from Community institutions or bodies, from any government of a member state or from any other body. The Community institutions and bodies and the governments of the member states undertake to respect this principle and not to seek to influence the members of the decision-making bodies of the ECB or of the national central banks in the performance of their tasks

Financing of government deficits

Article 104

2. Overdraft facilities of any other type of credit facility with the ECB or with the central banks of the member states in favour of Community institutions or bodies, central governments, regional, local or other public authorities, other bodies governed by public law, or public undertakings of member states shall be prohibited, as shall the purchase directly from them by the ECB or national central banks of debt instruments.

Exchange rate policy

Article 109

1. By way of derogation from Article 228, the Council may, acting unanimously on a recommendation from the ECB or from the Commission, and after consulting the ECB in an endeavour to reach a consensus consistent with the objective of price stability, after consulting the European Parliament, in accordance with the procedure in paragraph 3 for determining the arrangements, conclude formal agreements on an exchange rate system for the Ecu in relation to non-Community currencies. The Council may acting by a qualified majority on a recommendation from the ECB or from the Commission, and after consulting the ECB in an endeavour to reach a consensus consistent with the objective of price stability, adopt, adjust or abandon the central rates of the Ecu within the exchange rate system. The President of the Council shall inform the European Parliament of the adoption, adjustment or abandonment of the Ecu central rates.

2. In the absence of an exchange rate system in relation to one or more non-Community currencies as referred to in paragraph 1, the Council, acting by a qualified majority either on a recommendation from the Commission and after consulting the ECB or on a recommendation from the ECB, may formulate general orientations for exchange-rate policy in relation to these currencies. These general orientations shall be without prejudice to the primary objective of the ECB to maintain price stability.

3. By way of derogation from Article 228, where agreements concerning monetary or foreign exchange regime matters need to be negotiated by the Community with one or more States or international organizations, the Council, acting by a qualified majority on a recommendation from the Commission and after consulting the ECB, shall decide the arrangements for the negotiation and the conclusion of such agreements. These arrangements shall ensure that the Community expresses a single position. The Commission shall be fully associated with the negotiations. Agreements concluded in accordance with this paragraph shall be binding on the institutions of the Community, on the ECB and on member states.

Structure of the European System of Central Banks

Article 106

1.   The ESCB shall be composed of the ECB and of the national central banks.

3.   The ESCB shall be governed by the decision-making bodies of the ECB which shall be the Governing Council and the Executive Board.

Article 109a

1.   The Governing Council of the ECB shall comprise the members of the Executive Board of the ECB and the Governors of the national central banks.

2.   The Executive Board shall comprise the President, the Vice-President and four other members. The President, the Vice-President and the other members of the Executive Board shall be appointed from among the persons of recognized standing and professional experience in monetary and banking matters by common accord of the Governments of the member states at the level of Heads of State or of Government, on a recommendation from the Council, after it has consulted the European Parliament and the Governing Council of the ECB. Their term of office shall be eight years and shall not be renewable. Only nationals of member states may be members of the Executive Board.

Article 109b

1.   The President of the Council and a member of the Commission may participate, without having the right to vote, in meetings of the Governing Council of the ECB. The President of the Council may submit a motion for deliberation to the Governing Council of the ECB.

Protocol on the Statute of the European System of Central Banks

Article 10

2.   Subject to Articles 10.3 and 11.3 each member of the Governing Council shall have one vote. Save as otherwise provided for in this

Statute, the Governing Council shall act by a simple majority. In the event of a tie the President shall have the casting vote.

4. The proceedings of the meetings shall be confidential. The Governing Council may decide to make the outcome of its deliberations public.

5. The Governing Council shall meet at least ten times a year.

Article 12

1. The Governing Council shall adopt the guidelines and take the decisions necessary to ensure the performance of the tasks entrusted to the ESCB under this Treaty and this Statute. The Governing Council shall formulate the monetary policy of the Community, including, as appropriate, decisions relating to the intermediate monetary objectives, key interest rates and the supply of reserves in the ESCB and shall establish the necessary guidelines for their implementation.

   The Executive Board shall implement monetary policy in accordance with the guidelines and decisions laid down by the Governing Council. In doing so the Executive Board shall give the necessary instructions to national central banks. In addition the Executive Board may have certain powers delegated to it where the Governing Council so decides.

   To the extent deemed possible and appropriate and without prejudice to the provisions of this Article, the ECB shall have recourse to the national central banks to carry out operations which form part of the tasks of the ESCB.

Article 14

2. The statutes of the national central banks shall, in particular, provide that the term of office of a Governor of a national central bank is no less than 5 years. A Governor may only be relieved from his office only if he no longer fulfils the conditions required for the performance of his duties or if he has been guilty of serious misconduct.

Paul Temperton
The Independent Economic Research Company (TIER)

Chapter 11

Euro-X

In this chapter we look at the likely role of Euro-X, the title given to the group of finance ministers of the eleven euro-area countries. We can only look at its *likely* role because the group itself is relatively new, having held its first meeting in June 1998. Nevertheless, we assess:

- the link between Euro-X and Ecofin, the Council of Economic and Finance Ministers;

- the relationship that Euro-X will have with national governments in the management of fiscal policy;

- the provisions of the Stability and Growth Pact;

- the relationship with the ECB, the European Central Bank.

Euro-X and Ecofin

Euro-X is a sub-group of Ecofin, the Council of Economic and Finance Ministers of the fifteen EU members. It excludes (hence the 'X') the 'out' countries: UK, Greece, Sweden and Denmark. The desire to create an institution along the lines of Euro-X has been clear, especially on the part of the French, for some time. The plans became more concrete towards the end of 1997 but, at that time, it was not known for certain which countries would be 'in' the euro area. It *was* known that the UK would be 'out'. Nevertheless, the UK chancellor of the Exchequer, Gordon Brown, argued that, despite this, the UK would still like to be a full member of Euro-X. Dominique Strauss Kahn, the French finance minister and key supporter of the need for Euro-X, responded to Brown's request by saying that 'if you are getting married, you do not want other people in the bedroom'.

The basic idea behind Euro-X is that it is a counterweight to the European Central Bank (ECB). The ECB has control over euro-area monetary policy. In theory, Euro-X could have control over fiscal policy. In nationalistic terms, Euro-X is a French-inspired check on the Bundesbank-modelled ECB.

Euro-X and national government's fiscal policies

Although, in theory, Euro-X could exert control over euro-area fiscal policy, national governments will, in practice, retain control over their own country's fiscal policy. Furthermore, Euro-X's room for manoeuvre is limited by: the operation of the Stability and Growth Pact; the general need to reduce budget deficits further; and the views and actions of the European Central Bank. We consider each of these in turn.

The Stability and Growth Pact

At the Dublin EU summit in December 1996, governments agreed the Stability and Growth Pact which has, as its main objective, that there should be budget balance. That is, governments should aim to run no budget deficit at all. The pact places a limit on budget deficits of three per cent of GDP (i.e. the same threshold countries had to come under in order to qualify for EMU membership in the first place) and sanctions countries for any transgression. Initially, the country has to make a non-interest bearing deposit, based on a sliding scale according to the extent to which the three per cent limit is breached (see Figure 11.1). The country has two years in which to correct the situation. If it is corrected, then the deposit is returned. If it is not corrected within that period, the non-interest bearing deposit becomes a 'fine', and is shared out amongst the other euro area countries.

Stability Pact fines

DEFICIT	FINE	
3%	0.2%	
4%	0.3%	
5%	0.4%	
6%	0.5%	*(maximum)*

Country is not fined if GDP falls by 2% or more

For falls in GDP of 0.75% to 2.0%, fines are discretionary

Figure 11.1   Stability Pact fines for exceeding budget deficits*
*all figures as a percentage of GDP

The arrangements seem stringent, but there is a certain degree of flexibility. First, the fines are not imposed if the country is in a deep recession, with GDP falling by two per cent or more. If GDP is falling by between 0.75 per cent and two per cent, the fines are discretionary. Second, the fines are not automatic. The decision on whether an excessive deficit exists is voted on by a qualified majority of all 15 member states including the country under examination and even including euro 'outs' (see Figure 11.2).

How the votes are allocated

Country	Votes
Germany	10
France	10
Italy	10
UK	10
Spain	8
Belgium	5
Greece	5
Netherlands	5
Portugal	5
Austria	4
Sweden	4
Denmark	3
Ireland	3
Finland	3
Luxembourg	2
Total votes	**87**
Qualified majority	*62*

Figure 11.2   Qualified majority voting in the EU

A more fundamental issue is that, given the close relationships between the different euro area countries, it is quite unlikely that one country in isolation will be running an excessive budget deficit. For example, if an external shock slows economic growth in all eleven countries, budget deficits could breach the three per cent limit in several countries simultaneously. In those circumstances, the euro area countries could be split fairly evenly between those with and those without excessive deficits and the sanctions could, in practice, prove difficult to apply.

Thus, at the outset, there is concern about whether the fines will be imposed at all. But there is a more benign, and quite plausible, interpretation of how the Stability Pact might work in practice. With all eleven countries redenominating their government debt into euro at the launch of the euro area, yield differentials in the bond market will be determined solely by an assessment of a country's credit risk. Arguably, this credit risk could rise sharply once a country moved close to the three per cent limit and this could bring a potentially sharp rise in the yield differential with other euro-area government borrowers. The threat of that yield divergence may itself, be an important inducement to an early correction of a potentially excessive budget deficit.

Budget deficits near the threshold

Given the risk of fines and/or an increase in a government's yield spread over other euro-area borrowers, it would seem prudent to aim for a deficit some way below the three per cent threshold. But there is, as yet, little sign of countries behaving in this way. There are two reasons. First, to some extent, countries used accounting 'tricks' in order to come under the three per cent limit in 1997. These 'one-off measures' amounted to between 0.1 per cent and one per cent of GDP, according to the EMI.[1] The absence of further special measures will automatically tend to inflate the budget deficit in later years. Second, after the strenuous efforts that were made to reduce budget deficits in 1996 and 1997, many governments may now be suffering from 'austerity fatigue'. In Italy, for example, very little further progress is expected in reducing the budget deficit in 1999 (see Figure 11.3). In France, Lionel Jospin made clear shortly after the eleven countries had been selected that 'my central objective is not the euro but France'.[2] Subsequently, large increases in social security spending were announced and the budget deficit in France is expected by the OECD to amount to 2.6 of GDP in 1999, only marginally under the threshold. As far as current projected budget deficits are concerned, there is no room for manoeuvre. If unexpected events were to lead to slower economic growth, with a resultant increase in the budget deficit, there is a clear risk in many

Euroland: still in the red...

% of GDP	1996	1997	1998[e]	1999[f]
Austria	-0.4	-2.5	-2.2	-2.3
Belgium	-3.2	-2.1	-1.7	-1.6
Finland	-3.4	-1.0	0.6	1.1
France	-4.0	-3.0	-3.0	-2.6
Germany	-3.4	-2.6	-2.3	-2.4
Ireland	-0.9	0.9	1.5	1.6
Italy	-6.7	-2.7	-2.6	-2.5
Luxembourg	2.5	1.7	1.0	n/a
Netherlands	-2.3	-1.4	-1.7	-1.6
Portugal	-3.3	-2.5	-2.3	-2.0
Spain	-4.7	-2.6	-2.2	-1.8
Average euro-11	*-4.1*	*-2.5*	*-2.3*	*-2.2*

Figure 11.3   **Euro-11 government's budget surplus (+) or deficit (-)**

Sources: EMI Convergence Report, March 1998 and OECD Economic Outlook, June 1998
The average for the euro-11 is GDP weighted.
Estimates for 1998 and forecasts for 1999 are taken from the OECD publication.

...and repaying debt only slowly

% of GDP	1996	1997	1998[e]	1999[f]
Austria	69.5	65.2	64.8	64.4
Belgium	126.9	122.4	118.4	115.4
Finland	57.6	55.8	53.4	54.6
France	55.4	57.7	58.9	59.5
Germany	60.4	61.3	60.7	60.5
Ireland	72.7	65.3	57.0	50.3
Italy	124.0	121.6	118.5	116.0
Luxembourg	6.5	6.7	7.1	n/a
Netherlands	76.6	71.4	69.5	68.9
Portugal	68.7	65.3	63.4	61.9
Spain	70.6	69.3	68.5	67.5
Average euro-11	*76.2*	*75.7*	*74.6*	*73.9*

Figure 11.4   **Euro-11 government's gross public debt**

Sources: EMI Convergence Report, March 1998 and OECD Economic Outlook, June 1998
The average for the euro-11 is GDP weighted.
Estimates for 1998 and forecasts for 1999 are taken from the OECD publication.

countries of the three per cent limit being breached at an early stage in the euro's life.

How much leeway is needed?

But how much leeway is needed? Estimates by the IMF[3] show that, on average in the EU, a one per cent drop in output will increase the budget deficit by 0.6 per cent of GDP, with most of the effect coming through relatively quickly. In some countries the impact of the cycle is bigger—in three of the 'outs' (Denmark, Sweden and the UK) as well as the Netherlands. Thus, suppose a government was planning to run a budget deficit of 2.5 per cent of GDP and its forecasts for revenue and expenditure were drawn up on the basis of a forecast of 2.5 per cent economic growth. If growth turned out to be zero, then this slower-than-expected growth would increase the budget deficit by 1.5 per cent of GDP (i.e. 0.6, the average response in the EU, multiplied by 2.5 per cent) taking it clearly above the three per cent limit. Note that zero growth would not be weak enough to allow the country off the Stability Pact hook.

A more prudent government, planning for budget balance on the basis of 2.5 per cent economic growth could tolerate growth turning out five per cent lower than that before it reached the three per cent limit.

The view of the ECB

The view of the ECB on the need to cut budget deficits further has been made clear. When launching its Convergence Report in March 1997, the European Monetary Institute (the ECB's predecessor) commented that 'further substantial fiscal consolidation is required in most member states' and that in Belgium and Italy (two countries where debt/GDP ratios are above 100 per cent), 'the case for sustained consolidation over an extended period of time, requiring substantial fiscal surpluses, is particularly strong'.

Since then, there has been no let-up in the pressure. After the second meeting of the ECB's Governing Council on 8 July 1998, Duisenberg, the president of the ECB noted that 'it is with some concern that we observe that in a number of member countries the prospects for continued fiscal consolidation to actually develop seem to be, to put it mildly, rather subdued' and that 'most member states need to go a step further as they are not yet in compliance with the obligations under the Stability and Growth Pact'.

In other words, the ECB seems to be taking very seriously the Stability Pact's aim of a balanced budget in normal circumstances. Furthermore, it adds to this the requirement that budget surpluses are needed in the countries which still have a high level of debt, so that their debt levels can be placed on a firmly declining trend.

Conclusion

Where does this leave Euro-X? Clearly, if the prudent arithmetic outlined above, the Stability Pact, and the warnings of the ECB, are all taken into account Euro-X is left with the rather limited function of cajoling national governments into further fiscal tightening: that is, singing the same tune as the ECB.

As it is unlikely to do that—the preliminary indications, discussed above, are not encouraging—then the stage is already set for an unpleasant conflict between Euro-X and the ECB. The issue then becomes whether the ECB will raise interest rates purely as a way of signalling its displeasure with Euro-X and loose national fiscal policy. These tensions look set to dominate the first few years of the euro's existence.

Notes for Chapter 11

[1]*See EMI, Convergence Report, March 1998.*

[2]*See Financial Times, Monday 27 April 1998.*

[3]*IMF, 'World Economic Outlook', October 1997 pages 58-59.*

Section

IV

The
euro

Legal issues

Clifford R. Dammers
Secretary General, International Primary Market Association

Chapter
12

The euro: eliminating legal uncertainty

The voluntary adoption by a significant number of sovereign states of a single, new currency is unprecedented and has caused bankers, businessmen and lawyers to ask whether this momentous step poses legal problems. Few, if any, initiatives in European history have attracted so much interest in the legal aspects of a change in financial relationships.

The short answer is that for the vast majority of financial contracts and obligations—mortgages, bills of exchange, loan agreements, bonds, cheques—the substitution of a single currency for the national currencies of the EU member states which participate in the monetary union will not raise any legal problems. An obligation to pay in a national currency will be converted into euros calculated in accordance with the official conversion rates which will be set on 31 December 1998. For example, a corporation which borrowed 10 million French francs from a bank on 5 January 1998 and promised to repay it on 5 January 2002, together with interest at 6 per cent p.a., will be required to repay the bank a sum in euros calculated at the official conversion rate. The term of the loan and the rate of interest—and all other terms and conditions—will remain unchanged.

Lex monetae

This result follows from the general principle of law that every country has the power to change its currency and all other countries must recognize and give effect to any such change. After unification the Ostmark was replaced by the Deutschemark and the change was recognized all over the world. Similarly, when France changed from the *ancien franc* to the *nouveau franc*, all other countries recognized the change. This legal principle is referred to in legal shorthand as *lex monetae*.

EMU is slightly different in at least two regards. First, the euro will be a new currency to be adopted by a group of sovereign states on a voluntary basis. It is not the imposition of an existing currency on a country which was absorbed by another. For example, Nazi Germany absorbed Luxembourg into the Third Reich and replaced the pre-1939 Luxembourg currency with the Reichsmark. Second, the euro will substitute on a one for one basis for the Ecu, which is not strictly a currency but a currency basket.

The basic principle of *lex monetae*, however, does apply to financial obligations and the single European currency.

Early in the preparation for EMU legal experts became concerned that these two problems might lead to disputes and possible litigation. Particularly in complicated financial contracts, it could be argued that the purpose of the contract had ceased to exist or that it was no longer possible to perform the contract in a meaningful way because one of the essential terms had disappeared, such as a pricing source. Those concerns were heightened by the confusion in the law of frustration of contract and impossibility in many countries.

These concerns led the European Commission to prepare European legislation which would provide a firm legal framework for the euro. The legislation takes the form of two European Regulations (based on Articles 235 and 109l(4) of the Maastricht Treaty) which were approved by the Dublin and Amsterdam summits, respectively, and national implementing legislation.

The Article 235 Regulation

The first Regulation, which was adopted on 17 June 1997 pursuant to Article 235 of the Maastricht Treaty creating the European Community, resolves most of the legal uncertainty referred to above. It was adopted as early as possible so that the treatment of Ecu obligations and the issue of continuity of contract would be dealt with long before 1999.[1]

Article 2 of the Regulation provides for the conversion of the Ecu into the euro. The Ecu is to be converted into the euro, on a one for one basis, on 1 January 1999. By Ecu is meant the Official Ecu (as defined in Council Regulation 3320/94) and used by the European Union as its unit of account and the private Ecu if it is defined to be equal to or the same as the Official Ecu (as is the case in most Ecu-denominated bond issues and loan agreements). If a contract provides for payment in the private Ecu and does not contain such a definition, the Regulation provides a presumption that the Ecu was meant to be the same as the Official Ecu but this presumption 'is rebuttable taking into account the intention of the parties'. There do not seem to be very many, if any, contracts involving the private Ecu where the parties intended not to follow the Official Ecu.

Article 3 of the Regulation preserves the continuity of contracts. It is intended to ensure that neither party to a financial contract, such as a loan agreement or a derivative contract, has the right to terminate or amend the contract just because the national currency in which the payment obligations are denominated is converted into the euro or because of the introduction of the euro more generally. It reads as follows: 'The introduction of the euro shall not have the effect of altering any term of a legal instrument, nor give a party the right unilaterally to alter or terminate a legal instrument'. 'Legal instrument' is given the broadest possible definition and includes all contracts and agreements, whether in writing or oral, unilateral legal acts and payment instructions.

The Article goes on to provide that if both parties to a legal instrument—a contract—agree otherwise, either at the time the contract was entered into or subsequently, they are free to amend or terminate the contract.

In addition to resolving any doubts about the status of the Ecu and continuity of contract, the Regulation sets the framework for the introduction of the euro in those areas where advance notice, with legal certainty, is necessary so that work on changes which require a long lead time can be started.

Article 4 provides that the conversion rates (as one euro expressed in terms of each of the national currencies) shall be adopted on 1 January 1999 with six significant figures counting from the left.

The Regulation also establishes rounding rules for conversions and cash payments and accounting.

Continuity clauses

Transition periods can be especially difficult for legal relationships which span the transition period. The period leading up to 1 January 1999 is no exception.

In addition to legislation, what can be done to ensure that contracts which are entered into before the introduction of the euro and require performance after 1 January 1999 are not subject to legal doubt? One solution is to include in new contracts provisions setting forth the parties' considered agreement as to what they want to happen after 1 January 1999. If the parties want the contract to continue unchanged in every respect except for the currency of payment, they can provide for that result. Alternatively, they can decide that the contract should terminate once the euro is substituted for the national currency or they can decide that some of the terms of the contract should be modified.

Most banks have decided that it is not necessary to insert continuity of contract clauses in their contracts. The approval of the Euro Regulations encouraged those banks which had adopted this course of action.

A few banks and securities firms in New York, London and Frankfurt have decided to include continuity of contract clauses in certain types of contracts—e.g., derivatives contracts and bond issues. In some cases the banks only do so if their customer is from outside the European Union, reasoning that such customers are less likely to be bound by the Euro Regulations or to be aware of the imminence of EMU.

Such clauses are usually disclosure clauses rather than operative clauses. In other words, they inform the investors or the bank's customer/counterparty that EMU may happen and that it could result in the conversion of the currency of payment.

The International Swaps and Derivatives Association published on 8 July, 1997 an EMU Continuity Provision for use in existing and future ISDA Master Agreements where the parties wish to document their intention that EMU should not affect the continuity of their contract.

The International Primary Market Association Working Group on Currency Continuity concluded that continuity of contract clauses are not necessary or desirable for bond issues or medium-term notes, at least where they are governed by the law of one of the 15 member states of the European Union—as is the case for almost all bond issues and medium-term notes which are denominated in European Union national currencies.

Successor price sources

One of the remaining areas of legal (and economic) risk is successor price sources. When the euro is substituted for national currencies interest rates for the national currencies will disappear. If the Deutschemark disappears, the Frankfurt interbank offered rate for deposits in Deutschemarks (FIBOR) will no longer exist. Long-term contracts, such as revolving bank credits, floating-rate notes and fixed/floating swaps, which provide for payments to be determined by reference to such price sources may be called into question.

Most such contracts have fallback provisions which direct the parties how to calculate the reference rate if the originally intended reference rate disappears. However, until recently such provisions were drafted without reference to EMU.

Article 3 of the Article 235 Regulation sets forth the policy that such contracts are to continue but the Regulation does not and could not direct the parties as to how to calculate payments when the original price source disappears.

The international and national trade associations have worked with the sponsors of the price sources and the data vendors such as Reuters and Telerate, who publish the reference rates, to provide for successor price sources. It is essential that these successor price sources are clearly identified as such and that the market accepts them without dispute as the proper successor to the original price sources.

The question, then, is whether a successor rate exists at all and whether it can be used in the context of a specific bond issue, bank loan or derivative contract. The terms of each relevant transaction will have to be reviewed in order to follow the specified fallback procedures, which in some cases may present their own difficulties. They may, for example, require reference to a source which has already ceased to exist independently of EMU, or which has become unsuitable in market terms. Moreover, any fallback may fail to match the successor price source in a swap or other hedge.

BBA LIBOR

The British Bankers' Association currently sponsors LIBOR fixings in thirteen currencies including six of the major 'in' currencies and the Ecu, which are made available by electronic screen providers.

On 13 October 1997, the BBA published a paper setting out the details of how BBA rates for the euro will be fixed using a panel of sixteen major banks active in the euro market at 11.00 London time on all TARGET business days. The rate will be fixed for two days forward value and will be on an actual/360 basis.

The BBA will cease to provide a LIBOR fixing for Ecu and replace it with a LIBOR fixing for the euro.

For the 'in' currencies for which it currently calculates LIBOR, the BBA will continue to 'calculate' a LIBOR rate which will be the same as the euro rate. This is designed to ensure the fewest differences possible between the old LIBORs and the new euro LIBOR and thus maximize the acceptance of euro LIBOR as a successor rate to the old LIBORs.

It is expected that the new BBA euro LIBOR will be accepted as the successor rate to the current BBA LIBORs.

The majority of floating rate notes issued in 1998 and denominated in euros or providing for redenomination into euros have opted for the BBA euro LIBOR as the specified successor price source. However, a number of issuers, mainly large European entities, have indicated their intention to use EURIBOR as the reference rate for future issues.

EURIBOR

On 15 December 1997 the European Banking Federation and the ACI published a paper setting out their proposal for a new European reference rate for euros, EURIBOR. There will be a start-up phase of one year, during which the panel will be composed of 47 banks based in the participating countries, four banks from the United Kingdom, Denmark and Sweden and up to six international (non EU) banks which are expected to be active in the euro market. After this time the panel will be revised in the light of actual market activity. Quotations will be posted at 11.00 a.m. Brussels time on an actual/360 day basis for two day settlement, on TARGET business days.

EURIBOR differs from existing rate fixing methods in a number of ways. The panel, for instance, is larger than any existing panel and contains banks which may not be particularly active in these markets, though perhaps in relatively small numbers. It differs also in this way from the new BBA euro LIBOR. EURIBOR is clearly not a national rate in the sense that the pre-1999 national rates were because the panel is not located in one national centre. It does reflect conceptually the move from the national currencies to the euro.

It is expected that, despite these considerations, EURIBOR will be accepted by the markets as the successor rate in the case of existing provisions relating to the national rates. These are relatively few in number for bond issues but there are large numbers of bank loans which use national rates as the reference rate for setting interest rates.

French franc-denominated FRNs and MTNs seem to be the only case where significant numbers of bond issuers chose the national rate (PIBOR) as opposed to the BBA LIBOR rate for French francs.

The French legislation on the introduction of the euro contains a provision designating EURIBOR as the successor rate to PIBOR. The euro legislation in Germany, Spain and Italy also contains similar provisions designating or empowering the Government to designate EURIBOR as the successor price source.

PIBOR uses a one day rate fixing convention. The French Bankers' Association has decided that French banks will continue to use the one day convention although they will use the EURIBOR rates which will use a two day convention.

Reuters, Telerate and Bloomberg will publish the new BBA euro LIBOR and EURIBOR.

Many floating-rate note issues and loans are swapped or otherwise hedged. It is desirable that the successor price source for the FRN or loan be the same as that for the related swap or hedge.

The International Swaps and Derivatives Association has developed a multilateral protocol which will enable individual institutions to agree amendments to their outstanding contracts. Participants will select from a list those provisions which they wish to adopt. Once two parties have made their selections and submitted an Adherence Letter to ISDA, any Master Agreement between them will be amended by the terms of their selected provisions to the extent that both parties have made matching elections. Adherence to the Protocol therefore enables amendment of existing contracts between all adhering parties without the need for individually negotiated bilateral amendment agreements. As a result, outstanding contracts will be affected as soon as both counterparties to a specific contract make the same election in their Adherence Letter.

The ISDA Protocol includes an election which addresses the successor price source issue. If a party to the Protocol makes the successor price source election, it will be confirming that:

a) the new rate appearing on the existing screen page will be used in place of the old rate;

b) if there is no new rate on the existing screen page, it will use the officially designated successor rate;

c) if there is no officially designated successor rate, it will use EURIBOR;

d) if EURIBOR is not available, it will use reference banks; and

e) existing day count conventions and fixing periods will continue to apply.

Fallback provisions

Even where a successor rate is satisfactorily identified it is necessary to look at the fallback provision for existing issues to see if they can be effectively implemented in the event that the first choice of rate is not available for any reason. Existing fallback provisions vary widely in their wording and it would be undesirable to have to interpret each one separately. Accordingly, the International Primary Market Association and the International Paying Agents Association intend to produce standardized interpretations of such provisions, taking into account the factual circumstances of the single currency, which will satisfy both legal and market demands.

The Article 109l(4) Regulation

The second Regulation will come into force on 1 January 1999 and was approved pursuant to Article 109l(4) of the Treaty creating the European Community as amended by the Maastricht Treaty.[2] Unlike the first Regulation, the Article 109l(4) Regulation will not apply to the United Kingdom until and unless it joins EMU. Protocol No. 11 of the Treaty explicitly precludes application of Article 109l(4) to the United Kingdom. (Paragraph 5).

However, most lawyers are of the view that much of the Article 109l(4) Regulation will be incorporated into English law by *lex monetae*. This will almost certainly be the case for the first seven articles but opinion is sharply divided about Article 8.

The Regulation provides for the introduction of the euro on 1st January 1999 and states that 'the currency of the participating member states shall be the euro' (Article 2). Article 3 provides: 'The euro shall be substituted for the currency of each participating member state at the conversion rate'. In other words, the old national currencies will become non-decimal sub-units of the euro and will cease to have any legal existence except as such sub-units.

Article 4 provides that the euro will be the unit of account of the European Central Bank and of the national central banks of the 'in' countries.

It would be impossible as a practical matter to effect a complete changeover from the old currencies to the euro on a single day. For example, coins and banknotes will not have been prepared in sufficient quantities on time and withdrawing old coins and notes in exchange for euro coins and banknotes will inevitably take considerable time

Articles 5 through 9 are transitional provisions for the period from 1 January 1999 through 31 December 2001.

For example, Article 9 provides that banknotes and coins in each national currency will remain legal tender within that currency's territorial limits. Austrian schillings will continue to be legal tender in Austria (but not elsewhere) until Austrian banknotes and coins are withdrawn and replaced by euro banknotes and coins during the first half of 2002.

The most controversial article in the Regulation is Article 8. Clauses 1 and 2 have not provoked any serious debate. They provide that parties to legal instruments which provide for payment in a national currency (or the euro) or are denominated in a national currency (or the euro) shall perform their payment obligations in the currency so specified. This reflects the 'no compulsion, no prohibition principle'. Of course, the parties may agree to perform and accept performance in the euro if the legal instrument originally stipulated payment in a national currency, and vice versa. This reflects the principle of freedom of contract.

Article 8 (3), however, creates an exception to Article 8 (1) by imposing a conversion duty on banks in the participating countries. It reads as follows:

Notwithstanding the provisions of paragraph 1, any amount denominated either in the euro unit or in the national currency unit of a given participating member state and payable within that member state by crediting an account of the creditor, can be paid by the debtor either in the euro unit or in that national currency unit. The amount shall be credited to the account of the creditor in the denomination of his account, with any conversion being effected at the conversion rates.

For example, a debtor can repay his French franc debt to a creditor by transferring euros to the creditor's bank account in France. If the creditor maintains its account in French francs, the bank is required to credit the account in French francs, using the official conversion rate.

The Regulation is silent as to whether banks may charge for making the conversion. The European Commission has strongly recommended that banks not charge for such conversions and most national banking associations have announced that their members will not be charging.

Article 8(4) authorizes participating member states to redenominate their own general government debt 'denominated in its national currency unit and issued under its own law.' It goes on to provide that other issuers may redenominate their outstanding debt which is denominated in the currency of a member state which has redenominated its debt 'unless redenomination is expressly excluded by the term of the contract'.

Debt is defined as (i) debt issued by the general government of a member state and, in the case of other debtors, (ii) bonds and other forms of securitized debt negotiable in the capital markets, and (iii) money market instruments.

Article 8(4) also authorizes organized markets and clearing and settlement systems to change their unit of account from the national currency to the euro. All of the stock exchanges, national securities clearing organizations and wholesale payment systems in the participating countries have announced that they will trade, settle and clear only in euros from 4 January 1999. Euroclear and Cedel Bank will also convert to the euro at the same time but they have announced that they will continue to accept and make payments in the old national currencies throughout the transition period, if a participant prefers.

At the end of the transition period, there will be countless laws and regulations which refer to the national currency units; for example, schedules of fines for violations of the criminal law. While many debt instruments will be redenominated and still more will mature and be repaid, many will remain outstanding and denominated in the old national currencies. Article 8(14) addresses this problem. Anywhere any law, regulation, instrument or contract refers to a national currency, the reference will after 31 December 1999 be deemed to be a reference to the euro at the conversion rate. The rounding rules specified in the Article 235 Regulation will apply.

Issuers, therefore, will not have to redenominate their debt and may simply rely on redenomination by operation of law as of the end of the transition period.

Article 15 provides that coins and banknotes in the old national currency will remain legal tender until 30 June 2002 but authorizes each participating country to shorten the period. Several countries have indicated that they intend to avail themselves of this power.

The Euro Regulations are of necessity very general in their terms and are open to conflicting interpretations in a few places.

The European Commission published a very useful question and answer document entitled *The Legal Framework for the Use of the Euro* in November 1997. It should be the first point of reference for anyone seeking a detailed explanation of the Regulations.

Redenomination

Redenomination can mean any of three things: (i) simple currency conversion, (ii) renominalization or (iii) reconventioning.

i)   **Simple currency conversion** means that the interest and principal payable in respect of a bond denominated in a participating currency is re-stated as an exact amount in euro at the conversion rate. This amount is then rounded to the nearest euro cent so that the securities can be held in nominal amounts to two places of decimals. All payments of interest and principal after the redenomination date will be made in euro.

For example, if the conversion rate were to be 1 euro = DM1.87848, a DM bond with a face amount of DM1000 would be converted into a euro denominated bond of 532.35 euros (i.e. DM1000/1.87848 = 532.345 euros, rounded to 532.35 euros).

Euroclear and Cedel Bank and the national clearing organizations have announced that they are or will be able to handle nominal positions in euro.

ii) **Renominalization** means a change in the minimum nominal amount in which a bond is held and traded, carried out in order to facilitate trading, following simple currency conversion. For example, in the Deutschemark bond above, the issuer could reduce the minimum nominal amount of its bonds to one euro cent—in which case, the holder would have 53,235 bonds of one cent denomination.

If the issuer were to round up, it would increase the amount of debt outstanding with no compensatory gain to it. If the issuer rounds down, the investors must be compensated for their loss. This would normally be done by the issuer making a cash payment to the investors.

iii) **Reconventioning** means changing the terms of the outstanding bonds to reflect the different market conventions which will be used for bonds redenominated in euro after 1 January 1999. For example, the euro markets will use a different definition of business days and the day count fraction for the calculation of accrued interest will change from the 30/360 method to the actual over actual method.

The question of the currency in which bonds are quoted, traded and settled, whether or not they are redenominated in any of the above senses, is a separate matter.

All of the participating member states have announced that they will redenominate their publicly traded central government debt over the conversion weekend (31 December 1998 to 4 January 1999). They will use several different methods.

Relatively few private sector issuers are expected to redenominate their outstanding bond issues or certificates of deposit. The only significant exceptions are (a) in France, where it is expected that almost all French domestic bonds issued by corporations and banks will be redenominated during the first three or four months of 1999, using the same method as the French government, (b) Dresdner Bank, which announced on 3 February 1998 that it will redenominate all of its outstanding Deutschemark denominated bonds over the conversion weekend and (c) the German mortgage banks which intend to redenominate their outstanding jumbo and global *Pfandbriefe*—asset-backed bonds.

Redenomination (beyond simple currency conversion) will entail significant costs if bondholders' consent is required or if bonds in definitive form in the national currency must be exchanged for new definitive bonds in euro. Unless otherwise specifically provided for in the terms and conditions, bondholders' consent must be obtained for any form of redenomination if the bonds are governed by New York or English law.

French law required bondholder consent but the French legislation on the introduction of the euro abolished that requirement.

German law does not have any provision for bondholder consent but the German legislation on the introduction of the euro gives issuers the unilateral power to redenominate, renominalize (to one euro cent) and reconvention.

National changeover legislation

Each of the member states has enacted or will shortly enact legislation relating to the introduction of the euro. Typically the legislation provides for redenomination of government and private sector debt, elimination of certain currency based restrictions on the issuance of various kinds of debt instruments, designation of EURIBOR as the successor to national price sources such as FIBOR, PIBOR and MIBOR, provision for no par value shares, a general clean up of company law to reflect the substitution of the euro for the national currency (e.g., minimum share capital) and authorization for companies to prepare their accounts in euros or the national currency.

The provisions on redenomination have received the most attention.

The redenomination article in the Article 1091(4) Regulation does not enter into any of the detail of redenomination, leaving it to each member state to decide such matters. The national legislation prescribes the mechanics of redenomination for government debt and in most cases authorizes other issuers to use the same method. The national legislation overrides any existing requirement of bondholder consent. This step only applies where the bonds are denominated in the currency of the country in question and are governed by the law of that country.

For example, the German legislation, the *Euro-Einführungsgesetz*, authorizes issuers of Deutschemark denominated debt instruments which are governed by German law to redenominate without having to obtain bondholders' consent (Article 6(3)). The German legislation also authorizes issuers to redenominate bonds which are denominated in the currency of another participating member state provided such bonds are tradable on a securities market and are governed by German law and the member state has itself redenominated its own government bonds.

Legal certainty beyond Europe

The Article 235 Regulation applies in all member states, whether or not they participate in monetary union. Many international financial contracts are governed by English law, even when the currency in question is not sterling.

Articles 2 and 3 of the Regulation will resolve most questions involving the conversion of Ecu into the euro and continuity of contract for such contracts.

The question is less clear-cut if the parties have chosen the law of a non-EU member to govern their contract. For example, many master swap agreements are government by New York law and private placements and lease financings in Japan are frequently governed by Japanese law.

Lex monetae will provide for continuity of the vast majority of such contracts even though the Article 235 Regulation does not apply outside the European Union directly. However, under the principle of lex monetae the courts of New York and Japan will recognize the effect of the two Regulations. In fact, the Regulations will be helpful because they clarify the legal framework and make it easier for a foreign court to know exactly what the monetary law of the European Union is.

However, the more difficult cases, such as disappearing price sources and basis swaps, may prove to be more problematic where the contracts are governed by the law of a non-EU jurisdiction. The problem is probably most acute in the case of the law of the State of New York because many financial contracts are governed by New York law, the courts appear never to have referred expressly to *lex monetae* in their reported decisions and the judicial decisions applying the doctrines of frustration of contract and impossibility are relatively numerous and sometimes difficult to reconcile.

In order to resolve the potential legal uncertainty in New York and other jurisdictions, international and national trade associations[3] and legal working groups drafted and introduced bills in the New York, Illinois and California state legislatures which provide for continuity of contract and the recognition of the conversion of the Ecu into the euro on terms very similar to the language of the Article 235 Regulation. The legislation has been passed by all these States.[4]

Legal working groups have reviewed the existing law of money and continuity of contracts in several other countries. In Australia it has been decided that continuity of contract legislation, while not necessary, would be helpful to avoid disputes and uncertainty. The Australian banking and securities trade associations are working with the Australian legislature to prepare continuity legislation.

Working groups in Japan and Switzerland have also concluded that there is no necessity for such legislation.

The Euro Legislation Working Group of the Canadian Bankers Association concluded that Canadian law is sufficiently clear that legislation is not necessary and recommended that no continuity of contract legislation be sought.

EMU break-up

The Maastricht Treaty does not provide a mechanism for the break-up of economic and monetary union, or the withdrawal of a participating country. The Treaty does not even contemplate break-up or withdrawal; Article 109l(4) refers to the *fixed* rates at which the euro will be substituted for participating currencies.

On 1 January 1999 the individual national currencies will cease to exist and will be converted into the euro at fixed conversion rates. Notes and coins in the national currencies will continue to circulate until the end of the transition period in 2002, but they will, from a legal point of view, merely be non-decimal sub-units of the euro.

It is impossible to predict what the legal position of the national currency of a participating state would be if it were to withdraw from monetary union, either on a negotiated basis or unilaterally, or if EMU were to break up. A withdrawing country would have to create a new currency; it could not simply recall to life its pre-1999 national currency. It is impossible to predict with legal certainty the parameters of such a new currency.[5]

Conclusion

The legal framework for the introduction of the euro is in good shape. The most important areas of legal uncertainty have been resolved and the remaining problems are much less difficult and more manageable. The work of the European Commission and the European Council and the international trade associations is to be commended.

Notes for Chapter 12

[1]*For the full text of this Regulation, see Appendix 1 on page 367.*

[2]*For the full text of this Regulation, see Appendix 2 on page 373.*

[3]*International Swaps and Derivatives Association, International Primary Market Association, the Securities Industry Association and The Bond Market Association.*

[4]*New York Continuity of Contract legislation is set out in Appendix 3 on page 383.*

[5]*For a more detailed analysis of the legal aspects of a break-up, see Economic and Monetary Union: Thinking the Unthinkable—The Break Up of Economic and Monetary Union, C. Proctor and G. Thieffrey, Norton Rose, 1998.*

Section

V

The
euro

Problems ahead?

Paul Mortimer-Lee
Paribas

Chapter	The	euro
13		

Could EMU break up?

The launch of EMU has been compared to putting a space ship into orbit. As recently as the mid-1990s, EMU was regarded as an ambitious plan and many were sceptical that the rocket would even get to the launch pad. Only 48 per cent or respondents in a survey in November 1995 (see Figure 13.1) thought EMU would be launched on time on 1 January 1999. Now that the rocket is on the launch pad and ready for blast-off, virtually no one expects the project to be delayed. But sceptics now point to two risks, Either that it will crash back to earth before it reaches its final orbit (i.e. before 2002). Or that once it is in orbit problems will arise. Either bits start falling off the spaceship (some countries leave) or the entire thing falls to pieces.

According to a recent survey by Paribas, 13 per cent of financial market participants thought that EMU would break up at some stage, with the most likely timing being after 2002 (see Figure 13.2).

Financial markets clearly see a realistic possibility of break-up risk and it is the purpose of this chapter to assess: the forces which could drive EMU apart; possible leading indicators of such crises; and the potential impact on financial markets. We conclude that the probability of EMU break-up is relatively low, and suggest the risks will not be significantly greater during the 'transition period' from 1999 to 2002.

Break-up pressure points

The forces which, in theory, could break the currency union can be divided into three principal areas.

- First, speculative pressures, both before and after 1 January 1999. Regarding the former—speculation against exchange rates ahead of EMU—we expect that the adoption of ERM central parities as bilateral exchange rates, combined with the commitment to unlimited intervention, will preclude any such pressures. The period from 1999, once exchange rates have been irrevocably fixed, will be

Markets expect EMU to be launched on time...

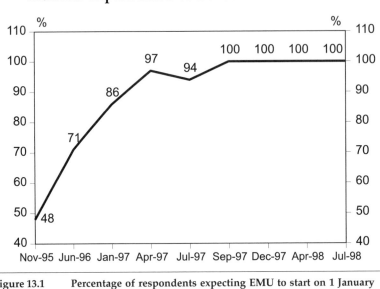

Figure 13.1   Percentage of respondents expecting EMU to start on 1 January
1999
Source: Paribas Survey

..but with a 13% chance of subsequent break-up

Survey month	Overall risk of break up	Pre-2002	Post-2002
September-97	23	6	17
December-97	39	17	22
April-98	26	13	13
July-98	13	2	11

Figure 13.2   Percentage of respondents expecting EMU to break up
Source: Paribas Survey

rather different, as pressures would translate into strains in national banking systems and greater volatility in long-term interest rates. However, this too looks to be relatively unlikely.

- Second, there is the potential damage wrought by economic shocks, manifested via demand- or supply-side problems. On this issue, there are significant concerns as to whether the convergence amongst the EMU participants has been deep enough to absorb possible shock waves.

- Finally, there is the political risk to membership. In the short term, with so much political will invested in the EMU project, the chances of a politically-induced rupture are extremely low. Nonetheless, the well-publicized difficulties over the ECB presidency and the role of Euro-X, for example, highlight the divisions over the way in which Euroland policy should move forward. Adverse economic conditions could push these tensions to breaking point.

Risk I: Speculation

With Euroland short rates set to converge before the beginning of 1999, this effectively offers a window of opportunity to speculate virtually free of charge against the EMU currencies. But in all probability, the period up to the irrevocable locking of those exchange rates at the turn of the year should be crisis-free. The markets' confidence that ERM central parities have become sustainable is a clear advantage in their adoption as bilateral rates. Moreover, even in the event of an attack on bilateral rates, it seems almost certain that any such defence would involve co-ordinated intervention—in theory, unlimited—between EU central banks, given the common interest in maintaining stability.

1999 to 2002: In transition

The monetary framework of the EMU members will, of course, change radically over the 'transition period'. Although the former national currencies will still be used, in a legal sense they will cease to exist as a currency in their own right and will become a sub-denomination of the euro. Speculative tensions, however, will still be a theoretical possibility. This relates to the ability to switch financial assets from one nation's banking system to another, i.e. in anticipation of a member country leaving the monetary union. A common example is the perceived preference of those holding assets in Italy to switch those assets to Germany in order to protect themselves in the event of the domestic currency being reintroduced—and simultaneously devalued—should Italy leave the currency union. This could bring severe liquidity problems to the Italian banking system as the outflow of assets erodes the monetary base. But why should it break the monetary union? As long as the central banks concerned are confident that EMU is here to stay, they should be content to balance out the flows of assets and liabilities.

The nature of speculation post-1999 will clearly differ radically to that in previous crises in Europe. The ERM crises of the early 1990s, for example, were characterized by aggressive position taking against the exchange rate parities of the ERM. But once exchange rates have been subsumed into the euro, this will no longer be an option. With regard to the Italian-German example, assets could still be shifted from one country to another in the expectation of future break-up—at minimal cost and with potentially huge returns. However, whilst large-scale speculation of this kind could cause problems for an individual country's banking system, it is unlikely to break EMU unless there is a simultaneous economic or political disruption. Speculators, therefore, stand to benefit from a break-up, but they are unlikely to be able to force the issue as they did in previous crises.

In theory, the EU could also take some legal steps to address the break-up issue. A clear legal framework, for example, could be put in place detailing the consequences should a member country depart from EMU. However, the counter argument (adopted by the EU) is that the incorporation of an 'exit clause' into EMU legislation might in fact invite it to happen. In this context, the biggest obstacle to break-up is the absolute commitment of the EMU participants to the concept of irrevocability—at any price.

A number of issues with regard to the status of the euro during the 'transition' period are worthy of clarification at this stage.

First, EMU is not a fixed exchange rate regime. On 1 January 1999, the euro will become the legal currency in Euroland, while local currencies turn into mere sub-denominations of the euro. After the launch of the single currency, EMU member states cannot: either modify the conversion rate between the national currency and the euro, which is set irrevocably on the start of Stage Three of EMU; or revert back to their 'old' currency should EMU break apart. Though existing national currency notes and coins could still be used prior to 2002 in the event of break-up, a 'new' currency would still have to be legally established.

Second, between 1 January 1999 and 30 June 2002, national currencies remain legal tender in their origin country alone. However, it is important to note that this does not affect the legal relationship between the national currencies and the euro.

Third, payment obligations, which arise from financial contracts stipulated under the law of a member states, usually refer to the 'lawful currency'. Therefore, in Euroland, monetary obligations will refer to the euro, despite the fact that national currencies remain legal tender until 2002.

The legal status of the national currencies after the launch of EMU has important implications for break-up scenarios. A key issue is the fact that the transition period does not embed any supplementary risk to EMU. It has been argued that, because national currencies are still in circulation during the transition period, a nation's incentive to leave EMU is greater before 2002. We do not share this view. First, as mentioned before, the legal relationship between the national currencies and the euro does not change before and after the transition period. The euro becomes the lawful currency in the member states on 1 January 1999. Second, if a country wished to leave EMU between 1999 and 2002, it could not simply revert to its former currency. Although the existing notes and coins could still be used, and the previous moniker adopted, a 'new' currency would still have to be legally established.

This has important consequences for the use of traditional financial instruments in the case of break-up risk. In particular, the use of swaps and futures, which involve national currencies, are not necessarily effective in a euro context. Because national currencies become sub-denominations of the euro on 1 January 1999, a swap involving only Deutschemarks and French francs loses its fundamental economic rationale, becoming equivalent to a euro-euro swap agreement.

Risk II: Economic shock

What if a member country had no alternative but to leave EMU due to economic circumstances? Severe economic shocks, for example, seem to carry a greater long-term risk of breaking EMU apart. Think of the havoc which a sharp downturn in demand could wreak on Europe's already poorly performing labour markets—and the political consequences. And what of the potential for asymmetric shocks, via prices or labour markets, for example? By definition, shocks are swift and sudden, and it is fair to say that there are still question marks as to whether economic convergence in the EU has been sufficiently deep to absorb the potential shock waves. These issues are discussed in more detail in Chapter 7.

Risk III: Political pressures

It is this political context of EMU membership which arguably represents the greatest threat of break-up. The probability of political turbulence is high: the application of the Stability and Growth Pact; the role and responsibilities of the euro-11; and foreign exchange policy under EMU, for example, will all have be to be tackled in the coming years. The performance of Europe's labour markets will also be crucial from the perspective of public support for the single currency. Severe political tensions have already been evident in some economies and the point of maximum risk for EMU could well rest with the onset of the next economic downturn in Europe.

Therefore, whilst the debate over break-up in EMU has tended to focus on the 'peripheral' member states—i.e. those perceived to exhibit unsustainable convergence in terms of inflation and wage growth, but who will now be unable to devalue their way out of trouble—the political risks would appear to be greater at the 'core', where the cost-benefit analysis of EMU participation is less compelling.

On the positive side though, public opinion with regard to EMU will clearly be closely correlated to the authorities' record on economic growth and employment creation. Hence the fact that the cyclical improvement in Europe will become more forcibly established over the next couple of years should help to boost sentiment over the single currency and, therefore, reduce the risk of domestic tension. Having shrugged off sluggish growth, with clear regional disparities, and unemployment levels rising to pre-war levels, EU governments can presumably look forward to the next few years with less trepidation. The labour markets of France and Germany, for example, have already begun to take a decisive, if unspectacular, turn for the better. Governments' support for EMU has proved incredibility resilient in Europe, having survived numerous changes of administration, and the impending upswing in growth should not be underestimated as a potential source for a turnaround in public sentiment.

Cost constraints

Moreover, the severe consequences were a country to leave EMU—both in terms of the financial and political fall-out—remain the biggest obstacle to break-up. The financial costs would be huge, both in terms of the sunk start-up costs and the potential for serious disruption to the economy and the financial system. With a national currency to be reintroduced, but all contracts between residents and foreigners in euro left open, the impact on business and the banking sector of a subsequent devaluation could be devastating. The more a country has exploited the financial markets under the euro, the greater the exposure to any financial crisis—and the financial crisis would clearly spill over to the currency union as a whole. The longer EMU lasts, therefore, and the further it evolves, the greater ultimately the financial crisis in the event of a member state departing.

Economic chaos and financial crisis would, in turn, have serious political repercussions. It is difficult to envisage a post-EMU Europe, racked by economic and financial turmoil, going back to an ERM-style environment. One way of limiting the risk of break-up, therefore, is to integrate financial markets to such an extent as to make going back to national currencies so painful as to make it unthinkable. In simple terms, it is the potentially disastrous consequences of an EMU exit which makes the occurrence of such an event so unlikely.

Leading indicators of a crisis

In this section we will draw on historical experience to address two additional issues relating to break-up risk. First, we will briefly examine whether economic fundamentals and financial markets offer any accurate leading indicators of a crisis. Second, we analyse the possible evolution of a crisis in EMU and its potential effects on financial markets.

There is an abundance of academic research on the subject of whether economic and financial market variables can be used as leading indicators of crises; we will principally draw on IMF research. As a detailed analysis lies beyond the scope of this chapter, we will therefore limit ourselves to a brief description of the leading variables to provide a basic framework of how financial crises can be monitored.

Economic indicators

Despite the different nature and origins of different types of crises—be it a currency, banking or foreign debt crisis—empirical evidence shows that common economic indicators of vulnerability do exist. Three principal leading indicators are identified:

- the real exchange rate;

- domestic credit growth; and

- the M2-to-reserves ratio.

Based on empirical evidence, the overvaluation of the real exchange rate has consistently been among the earliest and most reliable indicators of a crisis. On average, the real exchange rate begins to 'over-appreciate' thirteen months before a crisis begins and remains above its medium-term trend as the crisis builds up. Furthermore, the combined use of this variable with credit growth and the M2-to-reserves ratio is found consistently to signal the likelihood of a crisis, without sounding frequent false alarms.

The growth of the M2-to-reserves ratio, in particular, is a direct consequence of the fact that gross capital inflow declines as the crisis gathers momentum. The capability of the banking system to withstand the pressures on the currency depends on the extent to which domestic liabilities are backed by foreign reserves. Obviously, as foreign reserves decline in defence of a currency, the ratio of M2-to-reserves increases. Often, such indicators are combined with declining equity prices, low real interest rates and terms-of-trade deterioration, although these are less reliable indicators.

Financial market indicators

Studies into the use of financial variables as leading indicators of crises are less common, although options in particular are seen as a useful monitoring tool, as they incorporate information about the entire probability distribution of future events. Recent studies relating to the ERM crisis, for example, suggest that option prices did predict the ERM crises.[1] Unlike economic variables, however, the warning signals were only flashing a matter of days before the crisis. Thus, options and financial variables in general, are only short-term indicators of vulnerability. In addition, their use as leading indicators of a crises tends to be less consistent than the economic variables to which we referred earlier.

In the case of EMU, the monitoring of these leading financial variables will prove less useful. As the introduction of the euro will unify both the exchange rate and monetary policy, indicators like the real exchange rate and the M2-to-reserves ratio will not differentiate between the individual member states of EMU. However, other indicators may do a similar job: a comparison of non-tradable and tradable goods prices between economies, for example, could be used as a proxy for the real exchange rate. Furthermore, financial market indicators could still be efficient in forecasting a crisis, as they provide information on the entire spectrum of likely events.

The composition of crisis

In general, the development of a crisis in one country or area gives rise to three main patterns:

- A deterioration of the credit rating and the consequent widening of the credit spreads;

- a devaluation of the currency; and

- a flight to quality into traditionally stable currencies.

Deterioration of credit spreads

As European debt gradually redenominates into euro, the main driver behind yield spread will become credit, coupled with the liquidity and the depth of the market. Therefore, given the central role of credit in EMU, we believe that, in the case of break-up risk, the deterioration of credit ratings will be a key development.

Interestingly enough, rating agencies do account for the 'secession' risk of a country when analysing its credit rating. In a document published by S&P in November 1996, the rating agency pointed to the fact that economic shocks and the high adjustment costs needed to complete convergence might lead to tensions in Euroland. In particular, 'public opinion in some countries may come to question the wisdom of discarding the exchange rate adjustment option'. Political, social and/or economic tensions might lead to the secession of one or more member states of EMU. Secession risk is therefore a variable which rating agencies do account for when valuing the credit of EMU member states.

A lesson from Canada

The performance of Quebec, a Canadian province which has repeatedly called for independence, provides some insight into how break-up risk might be priced in Euroland. Figure 13.3 highlights the crucial dates in Quebec's struggle for independence. Figures 13.4 and 13.5 show the performance of the 10-year spread between Quebec and Canadian government bonds, and Canadian and US Treasuries, respectively, since 1990.

There are two important conclusions to be drawn from the Canadian experience. The first is that, in periods of tension, the spread of Quebec bonds to Canadian government bonds (Figure 13.4) widened, with the yield spread at times rising to more than 100 basis points. Arguably, this

Quebec's independence struggle

Date	Description
1980	Separatists lose dependence referendum by 60-40 margin
1990	Constitutional accord offering recognition of Quebec as a 'distinct society' fails to win ratification
1994	Jacques Parizeau elected Quebec premier on platform promising referendum on independence
1995	Quebec votes against sovereignty, 50.6% to 49.4%

Figure 13.3   The recent history of Quebec
Source: USA Today

reflects the break-up risk premium. It seems reasonable to assume that the impact, should EMU break up, would be much more severe. A second feature is the strong contagion effect between Quebec and Canada. In periods of strong political uncertainty in Quebec, the spread of Canada to US Treasuries also widened. The effects of contagion among European partners should not be underestimated. Tensions could arise in a limited number of countries, only to spread out to a wider area—or to the whole of EMU.

The analysis on the likely effects of break-up risk on credit spreads also provides some useful insights on the kind of financial instruments which should be favoured in case of secession risk. In particular, to hedge from the dramatic widening of credit spreads, investors might turn to a wide range of credit products, including asset swaps and, in particular, credit derivatives. Actually, there has already been evidence of an increased use of these products by institutional investors and hedge funds.

Flight to quality

As soon as financial markets sense that a member state might seek to abandon EMU, or that the whole EMU project is in danger, funds would pour into traditional safe-haven currencies and bond markets. In the case of EMU, an interesting point is whether Germany and the Deutschemark would still play a role as safe haven. If, at the time a crisis develops, the Deutschemark is still in circulation and is perceived as a stable currency, we would be likely to see a shift into Deutschemark-denominated bonds, and particularly German-based, Deutschemark-denominated deposits. Alternatively, if the Deutschemark has been withdrawn from the market

Quebec bond spreads...

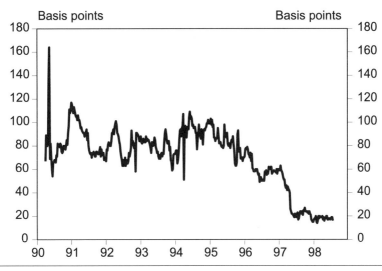

Figure 13.5   Yield spread between Quebec 2003 bond and Canada 2003 bond

... give an indication of break-up risk and contagion

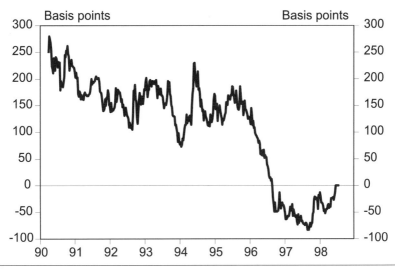

Figure 13.4   Yield spread between Canada 2003 bond and US 2003 bond

and the Deutschemark is no longer legal tender, deposits might still shift into Germany, as investors perceive Germany as the most solid alternative in Europe.

What will be driving these flows is the fact that, if EMU completely breaks apart, and the euro as a currency is abandoned, then Deutschemark-denominated, German-based deposits are likely to be converted into the new German national currency, which investors would expect to be relatively strong. From a non-resident point of view, however, it is worth noting that in the changeover from the euro to the new Deutschemark, they are likely to be treated less favourably than residents, as was the case, for example, when ostmarks were converted into Deutschemarks. On that occasion, credit outstanding by non-residents was converted into Deutschemarks at a ratio of 3:1, compared to a total weighted exchange ratio of 1.8:1.

Conclusions

Concerns over EMU break-up are likely to persist in some quarters, given the question marks over the depth of economic and political convergence across the EU. In the short term, interest rate rises in the 'core' EMU bloc should help to address concerns over economic overheating in some of the 'peripheral' member states. But all the same, the relatively shallow economic convergence in some areas clearly leaves Euroland vulnerable in the event of severe economic shocks. Moreover, the economic reforms which would help Euroland to absorb the impact of the shocks—greater fiscal policy co-ordination and labour market mobility, for example—will be difficult to implement in the current political environment. Still, given the huge financial and political costs which would ensue, the overall risk of EMU break-up remains very low.

Notes for Chapter 13

[1]*The view that option prices predicted the ERM crisis is outlined in Bruce Mizrach, 'Did Option Prices Predict the ERM Crises?', Working Paper, Rutgers University.*

Chapter
14
The euro

Professor Tim Congdon
*Lombard Street Research**

Could EMU be Europe's 'Maoist leap forward'?

The project to introduce a single currency is the most daring step so far in European integration. Indeed, it can be correctly described as revolutionary. It is much more far-reaching than previous moves in this direction over the last 15 years, such as the harmonization of regulations or the ending of exchange controls; it is intended not as an incremental advance, but as a complete transformation of Europe's financial arrangements.

The audacity of the single currency project is the more striking, in that it is a 'revolution from above' rather than a 'revolution from below'. The driving force has not been popular dissatisfaction with the existing currency arrangements, but the integrationist ambition of certain members of the European elite, particularly the German chancellor, the French president and the president of the European Commission. (The integrationist ambition appears to attach to the positions *ex officio* and to be quite unaffected by the particular individuals who currently fill them.) These members of the elite emphasize the political nature of the single currency project, not the economic benefits. For example, Chancellor Kohl has said that European economic and monetary union (EMU) should prevent future wars in Europe.

Does monetary union require political union?

Despite the clarity of this emphasis on EMU's political objectives, some British politicians—such as Mr. Kenneth Clarke, the chancellor of the Exchequer in the last Conservative government—have asserted that

*This chapter is based on a talk given to the Bristol Actuarial Society on 21 May 1998, as part of the Institute of Actuaries' 150th Anniversary celebrations.

monetary union does not imply political union. They have said that Britain could participate in EMU without becoming another state in a newly-created United States of Europe. This paper's theme is that such assertions are wrong. Membership of a successful monetary union is also, as a logical inevitability, membership of a political union. In such a union a central government separate from, and in most essential respects superior to, the state governments would quickly emerge. If it participated in EMU, the British government would therefore cease to be 'sovereign' in the sense now understood. Indeed, a case can be made that the very phrases 'currency system' and 'central bank' make logical sense only if they are attributes of a nation state.

Four arguments on the link between monetary and political union

At least four strands of argument demonstrate the connection between monetary and political union. They are complementary and reinforce each other, with the key element in common being the interdependence of fiscal and monetary policy. A consequence of this interdependence is that the state is necessarily involved in monetary management, both for good and ill.

Argument I: Budget deficits are related to money growth and inflation

The first argument highlights the relationship between budget deficits and money supply growth, and the danger of excessive monetary growth for inflation. If a national government has a large budget deficit which it cannot finance outside the banking system, it may have to borrow from the banks and so increase the quantity of money; and, if the consequent rate of monetary expansion is too high, the result will be inflation. So—in order to prevent inflation—the budget deficit must be restricted. In short, monetary policy can be anti-inflationary only if it is supported by the appropriate fiscal policy.

This theory of money and inflation was termed 'English' by Professor Bresciani-Turroni in his famous study, *The Economics of Inflation*, about the 1923 hyperinflation in Weimar Germany. He chose this label because of the position taken by representatives of the British Treasury at international meetings in the early 1920s.[1] They pointed to the budget deficit as the cause of the hyperinflation, unlike their German counterparts who said that the central bank printed new bank notes in response to customer demand. In a magnificent historical irony this so-called 'English' view of inflation was entirely erased from the institutional memory of the British Treasury over the following 30 years. By contrast, its obvious validity in the hyperinflations of both 1923 and 1946 made a deep impression on the German economics profession. The legislation which established the Bundesbank in 1957 specifically prohibited it from lending to the German government.

This same view of inflation—that it originates in budget deficit and the consequent 'printing of money' (or, in jargon, the 'monetization of deficits')—explains the Maastricht Treaty's insistence that countries can participate in EMU only if they have curbed their budget deficits to a low ratio of national product. The treaty refers to deficits in the period before the single currency. Subsequently, agreement has been reached on a Stability and Growth Pact, which maintains a similar discipline over the size of budget deficits once the new currency has been brought into being. If the deficit limits are breached after EMU has been established, nations are to be fined. The result is plainly a huge erosion of national government's financial independence.

It is sometimes remarked—particularly by enthusiasts for European integration—that the Stability Pact relates to *the size of deficits*, not to *the levels of government spending and taxation*. It is claimed that, because governments can determine how much they spend, they remain very much in control.[2] However, in the real world decisions to spend and decisions to borrow cannot be entirely distinct. A fundamental shift in power is in prospect.

The scale of this shift is readily demonstrated by considering how a government might respond to a sudden change in its financial circumstances after the Stability Pact had become effective. Suppose that the sudden change leads to a large and unexpected imbalance between revenue and expenditure. A deep recession (which hits tax revenues), a commodity-price shock (like a fall in the oil price in the UK) or a systemic crisis in the financial system (which may require an infusion of public money to recapitalize loss-making institutions) are examples. But by far the most drastic case is war. In that event, any government would want to increase defence spending and, almost inevitably, to raise the budget deficit. Under the Stability Pact, the government concerned would have to seek the approval of other European governments before it could react to foreign aggression.

Chancellor Kohl might say that this discussion shows, exactly, the importance of monetary union to the avoidance of intra-European war.

But military threats to the nations of Europe do not nowadays come from each other. Instead they come from delinquent nations in other parts of the world, such as Argentina in its invasion of the Falklands in 1982 or Iraq by its annexation of Kuwait in 1990. Under EMU, Britain would have had to seek the agreement of other European governments for the stand it took in these two conflicts, because of the implications of more defence spending on its budget deficit and so for the Stability Pact.

Chancellor Kohl might claim that the European Union would always support one of its members in such circumstances, but this is far from certain. (Italian public opinion was unsympathetic to Britain during the Falklands conflict.) Perhaps he might also reflect on the difficult situation in which Germany itself would be placed by ethnic turmoil in the Balkans or a renewal of Russian territorial expansionism, with a revanchist military government in Moscow invading the Baltic states. It is quite conceivable that the European Union would be split on the appropriate response, but every nation—including Germany—would have to seek the approval of the Ecofin-Council for any rise in defence spending which led to an excessive deficit.[3]

Evidently, the centralization of the power to issue money has led, via the necessary consequent restrictions on individual governments' ability to run budget deficits, to a situation where these governments are no longer in control of their own diplomatic and military destiny. The term 'sovereignty' is ambiguous and complex, and lends itself to verbal conjuring tricks. But, surely, on any reasonable definition of the term, once a government has to seek other governments' consent to raise finance for a war, it is no longer 'sovereign'.

The argument so far may seem drastic enough, but much more can be said in the same vein. If a government exceeds the deficit ceiling laid down in the Stability Pact, the so-called 'Excessive Deficit Procedure' starts to operate. After receiving a report from the Commission, it is the task of the Ecofin-Council—taking a decision by qualified majority voting—to confirm or deny that the deficit is indeed excessive. If Ecofin decides that the deficit is excessive, it makes recommendations about fiscal policy in the country at fault and 'requires that effective actions have to be taken within four months'.[4] If the country fails to take such actions, Ecofin imposes a fine. The fine takes an unusual form, with the offending government having to lodge a non-interest-bearing deposit at a European banking institution, presumably the ECB. It forfeits the interest until its finances again comply with the Stability Pact.

This sounds tough, but is it credible? It lacks plausibility, for at least two reasons. First and most obviously, the fine would widen the deficit and so aggravate the problem. But, more fundamentally, how would Ecofin react to fiscal transgressions by a number of European countries, where the countries stubbornly refuse to take 'effective actions'? Would it expel them from the monetary union? Perhaps this is the unstated threat, but the treaty says nothing about the mechanics of expulsion. And what happens if the number of European countries with excessive deficits becomes so large that they can block a hostile vote in Ecofin? In the extreme, high-deficit countries might outnumber low-deficit countries, so that the financial delinquents controlled Ecofin. In that event, the incentive for every European government is straightforward: it is to cheat on their public finances and maximize the deficit.

The natural answer—almost certainly the only effective long-run answer—to problems of this kind would be to have a single federal European government, with a centralized Treasury and the undoubted ability to enforce financial sanctions ('rate-capping' and the like) on formerly sovereign national governments. Monetary union would have led to political union.

The proliferation of new bodies involved in European monetary policy—bodies which might be fashionably described as stakeholders in EMU—multiplies the scope for debate and disagreement. There is great uncertainty about the relative powers and responsibilities of Ecofin and the newly-created Euro-X committee, about the operation of the chain of command from the European Central Bank to the national central banks, about the extent of the ECB's accountability to the European parliament, about the political status of the technical input from Eurostat and the EU's 'economic and financial committee', and, indeed, about how each and every one of these bodies is to relate to all the others.[5] There is a clear need for a single over-arching organization, a democratically-elected central government of Europe, to set agenda and arbitrate disputes.

Argument II: The need for political accountability

To mention the multiplicity of stakeholders in EMU demonstrates the importance of a clear assignment of responsibilities between them. This introduces the second argument on the connection between monetary and political union, which turns on the need for the new institutions to be politically accountable. In most nations, the central bank is publicly-owned and part of the state; it is therefore accountable to the legislature. This accountability holds even when the central bank has operational independence to determine interest rates, to conduct banking supervision and so on.

In some countries, such as New Zealand, the central bank's accountability appears to be to the executive branch of government. (Under legislation passed in 1989, the governor of the New Zealand Reserve Bank has to meet inflation targets set by the minister of finance, not the New Zealand parliament.) But since the executive is itself answerable to the legislature, this does not change the essence of the matter. In other countries, the accountability to the legislature is explicit. For example, in the USA, the Senate reviews appointments to the Federal Reserve and routinely takes evidence from the Federal Reserve's governors.

But what is to happen in Euroland? Euroland does not have an executive branch of government in the same sense as the various nation states of Europe, unless the Council of Ministers is thought to perform that role. It does have a proto-legislature of sorts in the form of the European parliament, but the European parliament does not in fact pass legislation. So to which democratically-elected organization (or organizations) should the ECB be accountable? One answer might appear to be the national parliaments of the member states. But Duisenberg, the first president of the ECB, has refused to appear on a regular basis before the French parliament and, by extension, before any national parliament. He could reasonably point out that the Maastricht Treaty does not envisage accountability on national lines, perhaps for the trite practical reason that it would become repetitive. He will attend hearings at the European parliament, even though the European parliament has no sanctions over the ECB if the ECB's performance is unsatisfactory.

The obvious way to introduce the kind of accountability found in the USA, New Zealand and other countries would be for the European parliament to become a genuine, fully-fledged legislature for the European Union. The Maastricht Treaty would have to be revised, with the granting of new powers to the European parliament to discipline the ECB in the event of poor monetary policy, inadequate banking supervision or whatever. However, in that event, the European parliament would have captured powers and responsibilities in relation to the ECB that are now lodged with national parliaments in relation to national central banks. Monetary union would therefore have put Europe further on the path to political union. Once again, the need to make the new arrangements democratically accountable ends in the conclusion that monetary union and political union must be closely linked.

Argument III: 'Seigniorage' accrues to national central banks and governments

The third strand of argument pivots on the similarity of the power of national governments to raise taxes and to issue legal-tender currency. Obviously, tax-raising extracts resources from the private sector and makes them available to the government. But the issue of legal-tender bank notes has much the same effect. If the government borrows from the central bank and the central bank issues new notes, the goods and services purchased with the notes also become available to the government. This power to extract resources comes under the general heading of 'seigniorage'. The *Concise Oxford Dictionary* defines 'seigniorage' as 'profit made by issue of coins rated above intrinsic value' and notes that, historically, it was 'something claimed by sovereign or feudal superior as prerogative'.[6]

The definition involves these awkward words 'sovereign' and 'prerogative'. Despite the many semantic games that can be played in this area, it is clear that the right to extract resources from a particular nation by the issue of money is a right which, over extended historical periods, has belonged only to the sovereign power within that nation. Further, a strong justification can be found for the state's monopolization of this right. Suppose that the right to seigniorage were spread among dozens of private companies. Since each of them could extract resources by printing money, and since each individually maximizes its revenue by printing as much as possible, a widely-dispersed seigniorage right would lead to over-issue and inflation. This danger is avoided when the government restricts the right to issue legal-tender money to itself. In most countries, the history of monetary legislation has been largely the history of the elimination of private note issues and the concentration of the right of issuance in the government's own bank. Indeed, it was very much for this reason that the government's bank became the central bank.[7]

In the context of EMU, this argument creates a serious problem. The European Central Bank is to be the banker, not just to one government, but to a number of governments. The question immediately arises, 'how much seigniorage is to be appropriated by each nation?'. The Maastricht Treaty does in fact have a formula which determines the answer. The formula—in which seigniorage is based on population and gross domestic product—looks fine in principle. So it might also be in practice, if all the governments and central banks of Europe had understood what they were doing. Unfortunately, that does not seem to be the case. Relative to the current situation, the formula implies a large shift in seigniorage from

Shareout of the ECB's profits

	Currency in circulation (US$bn)	% share of euro-11 currency	% share of paid-up ECB capital	Monetary income assuming 3.3% return (US$m)	Share of pool of monetary income (US$m)	Loss/gain from ECB shareout formula (US$m)
France	43.5	13	21	1436	2399.0	963
Italy	59.5	18	19	1963	2127.6	164
Belgium/Luxembourg	7.9	2	4	260	410.8	150
Portugal	4.3	1	2	141	273.7	133
Finland	2.6	1	2	86	199.0	113
Ireland	2.8	1	1	92	119.2	27
Netherlands	19.0	6	5	628	608.6	-20
Austria	11.1	3	3	365	336.5	-28
Spain	53.1	16	11	1752	1255.7	-497
Germany	135.7	40	31	4477	3471.1	-1006
Euro-11 total	**339.4**	**100**	**100**	**11201**	**11201.1**	

Figure 14.1

Source: Central Banking Journal Volume VII No. 4, updated July 1998 with actual ECB shares and currency figures from Datastream.

The 3.3% assumed rate of return corresponds to the Bundesbank's July 1998 repo rate. The ECB's repo rate will almost certainly be higher.

The decision of the ECB to impose uniform reserve requirements probably means monetary income will only be calculated against circulating currency.

Source for Currency outside Banks - IMF IFS Reserve Money:Currency outside Deposits Money Banks (IMF IFS line 14a).

Germany and Spain to France. It seems that—when the German government signed up for the Maastricht deal—neither it, nor the Bundesbank, recognized the scale of the loss. According to the estimates presented in Figure 14.1, the loss to Germany could be $1 billion per year. Not surprisingly, Germany and Spain (the next biggest loser) want the relevant part of the Maastricht Treaty to be reconsidered, and perhaps even renegotiated. According to the journal *Central Banking*, 'Behind the scenes feverish negotiations have been going on to try and reduce these transfers'.[8]

But the problems do not stop there. One question is the distribution of seigniorage between nations; another is the distribution of seigniorage between the government and the central bank in each of the nations; and a further related matter is the extent to which the seigniorage is supposed to cover a particular central bank's own costs. Most European countries have specific legislation to deal with these matters. As EMU approaches, they are all having to change the legislation, sometimes with curious results. In France the government has found considerable resistance in parliament to its proposals. The *Financial Times* of 7 April 1998 reported that the cabinet-approved draft law had 'been altered in commission, making it difficult for the Bank of France to reduce any of its almost 17,000-strong staff'. In other words, the French parliament and government seem to believe that, under EMU, they will have a veto on any decision by the ECB which might affect the Bank of France's staff numbers. The relationship of seigniorage revenue to staff costs, or indeed of any revenue to any costs, is apparently not deemed to be relevant.

Are these details so petty that they do not deserve to be mentioned? Supporters of EMU might insist that the Bundesbank's loss of seigniorage and the Bank of France's staff costs are trifling considerations, particularly when compared with the vast geopolitical benefits of a single European currency. But there is a pressing need—in this whole subject—for the discussion to be brought down from the geopolitical sublime to the logistical nitty-gritty. The size of central bank losses and profits, and the division of such losses and profits between the nations of Euroland, are highly-contentious subjects. National pride and self-respect are at stake. The tensions would be most simply overcome if the national governments were subordinate to a single European government, presumably based in Brussels. Again, EMU inevitably creates pressures for political unification.

All over the modern world, the world of paper money, a particular set of monetary institutions is found. In each nation state, there is one government, one central bank and one legal-tender currency. The central bank is the sole issuer of the legal-tender currency, and it is also the banker to the government and the commercial banking system. Usually, although not invariably, the central bank is owned by the government. There are no examples of the same legal-tender currency being shared by several significant nation states. Each central bank is the central bank in the nation concerned; it does not share its note-issuing power, or its functions as banker to the government and the commercial banking system, with another central bank; indeed, it could not be the central bank if these powers and functions were shared among a number of institutions. The

European System of Central Banks proposed under EMU will be a unique institution, where money-issuing powers and the related functions are to be shared—within a single monetary area—by 11 distinct national organizations. Doubts have to be expressed about whether this can work.

The attempt to distribute seigniorage between nations by an international treaty is—logically and intrinsically—inconsistent with the way that seigniorage is earned, as a by-product of a central bank's monopoly of the note issue within a single nation state. However, the inconsistency is overcome if the separate governments of Europe form a single government. In that case, the normal set of monetary institutions in the modern world is restored and, of course, monetary union is accompanied by political union.

Argument IV: Political union and the protection of bank deposits

The fourth strand of argument originates in the modern conception of bank deposits. When a bank takes deposits of notes from the general public, there is a risk that the bank may not be able to repay them in full. In the 19th century, bank failures were accepted as part of business life. However, in the 20th century—and particularly since the traumatic effect of bank failures in the 1930s on economic activity—public policy has taken a close interest in the security of bank deposits.

The modern view is that public policy should—as far as possible—ensure that bank deposits are always worth their nominal value. (In other words, banks must be able to repay their deposits with notes of the equivalent value.) Various institutional arrangements have therefore developed to protect depositors. The textbooks of money and banking often highlight the role of the central bank as lender of last resort. If one bank (or a small group of banks) is unable to maintain payments, and if this isolated failure casts doubts on other banks and causes depositors to withdraw their cash *en masse*, the central bank must lend to all banks or purchase assets from them. The effect is to replenish their balances at the central bank. These balances can be converted at will into notes and so be used to repay depositors. If depositors are persuaded that there is no point in further withdrawals, the panic is over.

The lender-of-last-resort role is important. Indeed, a serious defect of the Maastricht Treaty is that it says almost nothing about how lender-of-last-resort operations are to be conducted under EMU.[9] One interpretation of the apparent oversight is that, nowadays, central banks are not, in fact, the only—or even the main—organizations responsible for deposit protection. Arguably, lender-of-last-resort assistance is the provision of liquidity to the banking system, but this is merely a temporary palliative. At root, major financial crises in the last 20 or 30 years have been about the insolvency of one or a number of banks; they have been due to a lack of capital, not to a shortage of cash. The lack of capital has typically been a result of imprudent lending and heavy bad debts. If the bad debts are so large as to have exceeded a bank's capital, the depositors risk losing their money.

How are depositors protected in these circumstances? The arrangements vary between countries but, in general terms, a 'chain of security' can be described.[10] If one link in the chain is broken, another link comes into play. Once the capital of the bank in question has been exhausted, four links come into play. First, the capital of other banks may be available, either because the central bank coerces them into supporting the failed bank (as in 'the lifeboat' in Britain in the mid-1970s) or because they see genuine commercial opportunity in absorbing the failed bank's infrastructure. Obviously, this first link is reliable only if most of the banking system is healthy and profitable. If not, the first link in the chain is severed.

The second link is the resources of the deposit insurance agency, if there is one. (Note that some countries do not have a deposit insurance system. The UK did not have one until 1979.) Deposit insurance involves the payment of premiums into a central fund by all banks and a promise by that fund to make good depositors' losses up to a certain figure. Deposit insurance is usually for the benefit of small retail depositors. The fund rarely covers losses incurred by corporate depositors or, indeed, losses on loans between banks. In any case the resources of the deposit insurance agency are in most countries rather small compared with the banking system's capital. In a big crisis—say, of the kind that hit the American savings and loans industry in the early 1990s, or being experienced in Japan today—the deposit insurance agency may itself be threatened with bankruptcy. If so, this second link in the chain of security is also broken.

What, then, about the third link, the capital of the central bank? Plainly, this is a question of the relative size of the capital of the central bank and the commercial banking system, and of the central bank's willingness to shoulder losses. In most developed countries, and certainly in the European Union, the capital of the central bank is a fraction of all commercial banks' capital in combination, while central bankers are reluctant to take on substantial business risks. The Bank of England has sometimes stepped in to support an ailing institution, but its implied investment has been criticized in parliament as 'a waste of taxpayers' money', or something of the sort.[11] In short, the central bank's capital can

Central bank capital: too small in a crisis

(Ecu billion)	Capital of central bank		'Capital accounts' of deposit money banks
	Narrow definition	*Broad definition*	
Germany	11.7	26.0	322.1**
France	2.4	30.8	160.6
Italy	2.1	45.9*	130.7
Spain	9.7	11.7	68.7
Netherlands	1.4	10.4	42.4**
Belgium	1.3	6.6	32.5

Figure 14.2

Notes: *The narrow definition of central bank capital includes capital, reserves and undistributed profit; the broad definition includes the narrow definition, the revaluation surplus on the foreign exchange reserves and gold, provisions and other items of a capital nature. Figures for central bank capital are taken from accounts of the central banks; figure for deposit banks 'capital accounts' come form International Monetary Fund's 'International Financial Statistics'.*

* *Banca d'Italia's wider capital includes Ecu38.5bn of 'sundry provisions'.*

** *These figures described as 'other items (net)' in 'International Financial Statistics'. In the German case, this figure is much above commercial banks' combined equity capital.*

be used to protect depositors only in very exceptional circumstances and, even then, only to a limited extent.

So—if a banking crisis is systemic and deep-seated, and if the resources of the commercial banks, the deposit insurance agency and the central bank have been swept away by a tidal wave of loan losses—who remains to ensure that depositors are paid in full? The answer, of course, is the government. It has tax-raising and note-issuing powers, so that its support for the banking system is theoretically almost limitless. Whatever the formal position, and despite the existence of deposit insurance and central banking, the underlying reality of deposit protection in a modern industrial state is simple. In the final analysis, it is the government that makes sure bank deposits are repaid in full. But this obligation is not without limits. Crucially, the government of a particular nation is most comfortable when it protect deposits made by the citizens of that nation. (The citizens are also voters.) It does not like giving similar protection to deposits from foreigners.

If the single currency proceeds, Europe must, over time, also have an increasingly integrated banking system. The clear expectation, and indeed the official intention, is that banks are to take euro-denominated deposits and make euro-denominated loans in many countries, and to have shareholders across Europe. They are to become—in effect —'transnational'. However, under EMU, deposit protection is to remain a national responsibility, with the concept of 'nationality' determined by the centre in which a bank is registered. In principle, all banks could register in Luxembourg, but conduct their business (including deposit-taking) in every country of Europe.

This is a recipe for chaos. Consider the pattern of incentives on banks, borrowers and depositors. Banks' managements will find it advantageous to register in the nation with the lightest regulation and supervision; depositors will transfer funds to capture the protection of the most generous deposit insurance scheme; borrowers will take out loans in the country with the narrowest bank margins (and, probably, the least adequate deposit insurance, and the sloppiest and cheapest banking supervision); and so on. This statement is an exaggeration, but it is a fair summary of the direction of the likely pressures.

What would happen in the event of a big crisis, in which bad debts had obliterated the capital of several large banks? It was argued earlier that nowadays the last link in the chain of deposit protection is the government of the country in question. But there is no European government, only the governments of the various European nations. No definite prediction can be made about the outcome under EMU, but the tendencies are clear. None of the national governments would quickly and willingly inject capital to overcome a banking crisis; every government would blame bank managements and economic conditions elsewhere in Europe for the bank failures, and try to force other governments to meet the cost. As far as possible, national governments would refuse to bail out 'European banks'. Parliamentary debates would give ample scope for banker-bashing, tinged with nationalism and selfishness. The disturbing conclusion has to be that, from a supervisory standpoint, the safety of bank deposits under EMU would be less than at present.

These comments are admittedly rather lurid. Central bankers could object that the trend towards the internationalization of the banking system is already well-advanced and EMU will only give it extra impetus. But international banking today is mostly about wholesale banking, where depositors are corporate and grown-up, and know they are at risk. The integration envisaged by EMU is different, in that it concerns the retail side of banks' operations. The reference to Luxembourg was deliberate, because it was the country where the notorious Bank of Credit and Commerce International was registered. When BCCI was shut down in 1991, thousands of small depositors in the UK and elsewhere lost large amounts of money. (At the time of BCCI's worst transgressions, Luxembourg had 15 bank examiners.)[12]

At worst, the inconsistency between national responsibility for deposit protection and the increasingly transnational character of European banking could lead to the formation of a number of banks like BCCI. This would be a nightmare for banking supervisors and the national central banks. The obvious way to end the inconsistency, and to restore the traditional chain of security in deposit protection, would be the formation of a European central government. Ideally, both a truly unified central banking system and a single banking supervisor would be answerable to the one central government. As in the conventional modern relationship between government and central bank, this central government would have tax-raising and note-issuing powers. These powers would absorb those which had traditionally been held and exercised by Europe's independent national governments. Monetary union would have culminated in political union.

Conclusion: monetary union can work—with political union

Chancellor Kohl is right: the logical accompaniment of EMU is European political union. However, it is important to understand precisely what is being said. The four strands of argument developed in this paper show that monetary union without a central government cannot work. Monetary union requires a central government to decide fiscal policy, to receive seigniorage and determine its distribution between regional governments and central banks, to make the ECB democratically accountable and to protect depositors in the event of a systemic banking crisis. If monetary union is attempted before such a central government exists, the momentum of events will demonstrate the practical necessity of early political union. Political leaders will soon see that they must form a central government which reduces their still nominally 'national governments' to the status of regional governments in a federal union.

But the analysis has another implication. Without a central government of the kind described here, monetary union will fail. The heart of the problem is that a single authority is essential to set the agenda of fiscal and monetary policy, to carry it out and to be accountable for mistakes. Each of the four lines of argument has the same message. If there are a multiplicity of monetary authorities, areas of responsibility are not demarcated clearly. Where these areas overlap, it is inevitable that muddle and confusion will lead to tension, indecision and disputes on such a scale that the system cannot survive.

None of this might matter, if the governments of Europe had understood the consequences of their decisions. But Europe's leaders have not understood what they have done. Many of them believe that the essence of monetary union is the change from one unit of account to another. They correctly think that the switch from one unit of account to another is a straightforward matter, like decimalization or metrication, and does not necessitate a radical institutional upheaval. They have not seen that for an object to be 'money' it must serve as both a unit of account and a medium of exchange, and that it can serve as a medium of exchange only if it has value. The conferral of value on a monetary medium of exchange—by legislation on legal tender, central banking and deposit protection—is a highly political act and must involve the power of the state. To introduce a new medium of exchange therefore necessitates institutional upheaval on a huge scale.

The key conceptual mistake of Europe's elite—the belief that the essence of monetary union is a change in the unit of account—is evident in the Maastricht Treaty itself and in the sequence of new bodies created since the signing of the treaty. The treaty includes a long period from January 1999 to July 2002 (Phase B of Stage Three) in which the legal unit of account has changed, because the euro is said to exist 'in its own right', and yet in which notes and coin, the actual media of exchange, continue to be the old national-currency notes. It is already clear that this period will at best be awkward and inconvenient and, at worst, could create serious contractual uncertainties.[13] Meanwhile, the passage of the Stability and Growth Pact, the formation of the Euro-X committee and the refurbishment of the EU 'monetary committee'—all of which post-date the Maastricht Treaty—show that EMU was not well-conceived at the start. Instead of being planned well in advance, vital institutions are being cobbled together almost at random.

In this year's Jubilee Lecture, Lord Hurd described the EU's approach to the single currency project as a 'Maoist leap forward'. He was worried by our neighbours' embrace of radical change for its own sake, regardless of the exact consequences. EMU could indeed prove to be a catastrophe for the integrationist project. It can work if it leads quickly to a comprehensive scheme of European political union. But, without European political union, it will prove impractical to the point of impossibility. If so, its failure will be the greatest setback to the cause of European integration since the formation of the European Economic Community in 1957.

Notes for Chapter 14

[1] *Constantio Bresciani-Turroni 'The Economics of Inflation' (London: George Allen & Unwin, 1937), pp.46.)*

[2] *Christopher Johnson 'In with the Euro, Out with the Pound' (London: Penguin Books, 1996), pp.106-27.*

[3] *The Ecofin-Council is the Council of Ministers, when it is attended by finance ministers. The Council of Ministers decides on whether legislative proposals emanating from the European Commission should be submitted to national parliaments. The Council of Ministers consists of foreign ministers when foreign policy is under consideration, of transport ministers when the subject is transport policy and so on.*

Note that Germany is opposed to Russian membership of the European Union. But how can any settlement in Europe guarantee peace if Russia is an outsider? Kohl avoids this difficult subject, although it is fundamental to the security of Germany and Europe.

[4] *The quotation is from K. Regling 'The Stability and Growth Pact', paper given at the Royal Institute of International Affairs' conference on 'European Economic and Monetary Union: the politics and practicalities' in London on 23rd October 1997.*

[5] *The Euro-X committee supplements Ecofin; it consists of finance ministers from the 11 countries destined to participate in Euroland from the start. The 'economic and financial committee' is the successor to the EU monetary committee which prepared Ecofin meetings. See supplement on 'The birth of the Euro' in the 'Financial Times', 30th April 1998.*

[6] *'Concise Oxford Dictionary' (Oxford: Oxford University Press, 1982), p. 953.*

[7] *The claims made in this paragraph are contentious, being opposed by the neo-Austrian school which favours the denationalization of money. For further discussion, see T. G. Congdon 'Is the provision of a sound currency a necessary function of the state?' (National Westminster Bank Review 1981).*

[8] *The subject was discussed in two articles in successive issues of 'Central Banking': "ESC profits: a Bundesbank miscalculation", pp.19-24, in the winter 1996 issue and "Dispute over ESCB profits", pp. 7-10 in the spring 1997 issue. The quotation is from p. 23 of the winter 1996 issue.*

[9] *The subject has also been reflected in the European Monetary Institute's 'Annual Reports'.*

[10] *The following discussion of the chain of security to protect bank deposits was prompted by an exchange with Lord Simon and Mr. Howard Davies, then deputy governor of the Bank of England, at a televised debate held on the Bloomberg television channel in 1997. A short correspondence with Mr. Davies followed. I am grateful to Mr. Davies for his interest, although we hold different views.*

[11] *Stephen Fay 'Portrait of an Old Lady: turmoil at the Bank of England' (Penguin Books: London, 1988), pp. 141-72.*

[12]*James Ring Adams and Douglas Frantz 'A Full Service Bank: How BCCI stole billions' (London, Sydney and New York: Simon & Schuster, 1992), p.29.*

[13]*Walter Eltis 'The Creation and Destruction of the Euro' (London: Centre for Policy Studies, 1997).*

Section

VI

The *euro*

The foreign exchange market

Chapter
15

Avinash Persaud
*J P Morgan Europe**

The international role of the euro

The introduction of the euro is expected to lead to a switch of official reserves out of dollars into euros to the tune of $310bn. A further $300bn-600bn is expected to be switched into euros by investors and corporates. Current patterns in the foreign exchange market are changing: the euro's arrival could push the dollar lower and the euro higher.

Previously, the euro was seen as a 'weak' currency

Between 1996 and 1998, whenever the prospects of a broad EMU have grown, the Deutschemark has weakened within Europe, and the European bloc of currencies weakened against the dollar and, to a lesser extent, the Swiss franc. This behaviour reflected a widely-held view that the euro would not be a fair exchange for the Deutschemark, because the European Central Bank (ECB) would not be a credible replacement for the Bundesbank. This view was a reflection more of instinct or wishful thinking than judgement. In this chapter, we critically assess the potential sources of weakness and strength for the euro and European currencies in the run up to EMU and in the aftermath of EMU-day.

Especially from 1996 until late 1998, the dollar strengthened as financial markets became increasingly optimistic that the euro would be launched on time with a broad number of participants (See Figure 15.1). One of the reasons was the widespread conviction that a motley collection of European central bankers, unaided by an active fiscal centre, overseeing an area of high unemployment and large regional growth disparities, would be biased to an easy monetary policy and a weak exchange rate. Less well discussed has been the impact of EMU on the size and composition of *central bank reserves*, and the use of the euro as a *vehicle currency*. These issues are the focus of this chapter. Our findings challenge the growing

**With assistance from Mark Goddard.*

belief that EMU is good for the dollar and that the future euro could be a weak currency. We uncover structural forces which could strengthen the future euro against the dollar and may even begin to press down on the dollar before EMU-day. By the end of 1999 we expect the Deutschemark to have strengthened to around DM1.55/US$.

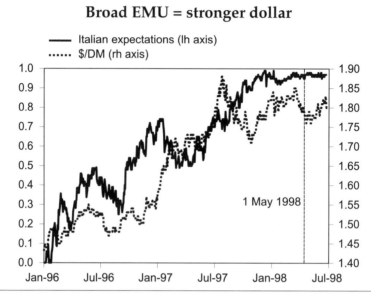

Broad EMU = stronger dollar

Figure 15.1   **$/DM and the probability of Italy participating in EMU, derived from the EMU Calculator**

To analyse whether the euro will become a reserve currency and a vehicle currency, we examine the implications of EMU arriving on 1 January 1999 with 11 countries and with all 15 members of the European Union participating in EMU by 2002. The founding eleven will be: Germany, France, Belgium, Luxembourg, Netherlands, Austria, Spain, Italy, Portugal, Ireland and Finland.

European central banks' reserves

On EMU day, foreign exchange reserves held by one participating country in the currency of another, will become local currency and will not be available for foreign exchange intervention. For example, after 1 January 1999, Deutschemarks held in the coffers of the Bank of France will be converted to euros. You cannot defend the euro on the foreign exchange markets by selling euros, you need foreign currency: dollars and yen. The shrinkage of foreign currency reserves will be significant.

At the end of 1997, the founding 11 countries held approximately $271bn of foreign currency reserves, of which an estimated $45bn was held in euro-zone currencies. Hence, if the level of reserves held roughly constant up until EMU day, the reserves of the eleven would fall by $45bn (17 per cent) to $226bn on EMU day (see Figure 15.2).

Changes in reserves

	Pre-EMU-day		Post-EMU-day	
	Level, $bn	*%*	*Level, $bn*	*%*
US$	186	47.8	186	54.1
JPY	23	6.0	23	6.8
Euro-bloc	45	11.6	-	0.0
Other	17	4.4	17	3.1
Total FX	*271*	*69.8*	*226*	*64.0*
Gold	118	30.2	118	34.2
Total	*389*	*100.0*	*344*	*100.0*

Figure 15.2   **Composition of euro-11 FX and gold reserves**

If the ECB sought to replenish all of the $45bn 'loss' by selling euros for dollars ahead of EMU, this would place substantial upward pressure on the dollar. Indeed, part of the dollar rally in late 1996 and early 1997 may have been fuelled by Deutschemark sales for dollars by European central banks. We estimate that the size of European currency holdings has already shrunk from $90bn in early 1997.

However, the ECB is unlikely to replenish any of the $45bn of 'lost' foreign exchange. Indeed, it will be looking to *reduce* its overall level of dollar reserves. European reserves are too large. Worldwide, there is a strong relationship between the level of a country's foreign currency reserves and the level of its imports (see Figure 15.3). The sum of imports of the Euro-11 today is roughly $1700bn. However, because the 11 countries trade intensively with each other, the amount of imports originating *outside* the core is 40 per cent less, at $1000bn. On EMU day, foreign currency reserves will shrink by around 17 per cent, but imports will fall by 40 per cent.

Reserves linked to imports

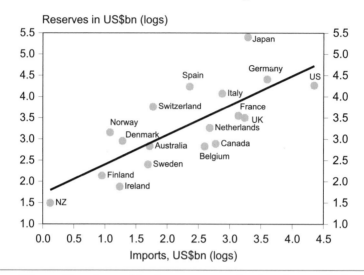

Figure 15.3   Size of central bank reserves are related to the magnitude of imports (end-1997, US$bn)

The average ratio of reserves to imports of 23 industrialized countries implies that a country with imports in the region of $1000bn would have reserves in the region of $115bn. This is a reasonable figure. It is substantially above the level of foreign currency reserves held in the US and is close to the level of reserves held in Germany. It is also some $111bn less than the projected level of reserves after EMU day. Even if the ECB decided to hold 50 per cent more reserves than indicated by the average ratio of reserves to imports, say, $176bn, it would still have $50bn of excess dollar reserves.

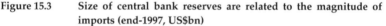

Excess reserves and euro credibility

The ECB will not want to reduce its level of reserves instantly, not just because of the market disruption this would cause, but because a high level of reserves could help to augment the new central bank's credibility. However, excess foreign exchange reserves will be reduced over time and a significant portion may be reduced early. Excess reserves represent an economic loss. Here is capital that fiscally hard-pressed governments will want to put to other, more productive uses.

If $50bn of the excess dollar reserves are sold for euros and added to the $45bn of reserves 'lost' when they converted to euros at the outset, central bankers could offer member governments a fund of $95bn in order to support fiscal consolidation or economic activity. Member governments could use this fund to underwrite borrowing by the European Investment Bank, to help ease regional growth disparities within the union. This could reduce pressure on the European Central Bank to hold interest rates down to the level of the member state with the weakest economy. Whatever is done, the message is that the freeing-up of nearly $95bn of foreign exchange reserves may provide some solution to the credibility problems of an economically-weak monetary union which starts with a liberal interpretation of the Maastricht Treaty and without the support of a fiscally-active central government.

Non-European central bank reserves

Not only will the composition of ECB reserves change by virtue of EMU, so too will the composition of reserves of non-EMU central banks and the use of European currencies as vehicle currencies for trade and investment.

If the level of central bank reserves is related to the total amount of imports, the foreign exchange *composition* of those reserves is largely determined by the proportion of trade and investment invoiced in different currencies (see Figure 15.4). Currently, 21 per cent of world exports outside of the European Union (EU) are invoiced in the 11 European currencies and these currencies make up around 19 per cent of the foreign exchange reserves of countries outside the EU. Central banks would want to increase their allocation of euro reserves if the euro's role as an invoicing currency is greater than the sum of its constituent parts. This is very likely.

Vehicle currencies

The theory...

Exporters and importers choose a currency for invoicing and settlement which can be bought or sold at low transaction costs in the foreign exchange market, or has a high degree of acceptability for other transactions. Exporters or importers have a preference for invoicing in their home-currency, but if there is no home currency preference or agreement between importers and exporters, an already important international currency with a deep and broad foreign exchange market

Trade invoicing and currency holdings

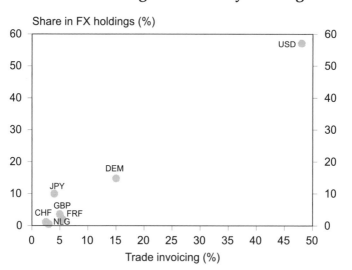

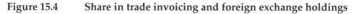

Figure 15.4   **Share in trade invoicing and foreign exchange holdings**

and a high degree of international acceptability is chosen. As a result, there are 'thick externalities' or concentration in the choice of invoicing currencies: the more a currency is used for trade and invoicing the more it will continue to be used.

...and the practice

The currencies of big exporters are used disproportionately to invoice trade. Around 13 per cent of world exports originate from the US but as much as 48 per cent of world exports are invoiced in dollars. Around 10 per cent of world exports originate from Germany, but 15.3 per cent of world exports are invoiced in Deutschemarks, a ratio of 1:1.5. The currencies of small countries are generally avoided as invoicing currencies, even when they are strong currencies. An estimated 3.5 per cent of exports originate from the Netherlands, but only 2.5 per cent of world exports are invoiced in guilder.

After EMU day, 25 per cent of world exports will originate from the Euroland, significantly more than from the US and more than twice the level of exports from Japan. Given the thick externalities mentioned above it would be safe to assume that the ratio of exports-to-invoicing would be greater in the case of the euro than the Deutschemark. If we were to assume, very conservatively, that the ratio would be the same as in the case of the Deutschemark, 38 per cent of world exports might one day be invoiced in euros. An increase in the proportion of exports invoiced in European core currencies from 21 per cent to 38 per cent would lead to an additional demand for euros from non-European central banks of $175bn. The process of invoicing a substantial part of world imports in the euro rather than the dollar will also lead to a fresh demand for euros from importers. Roughly, importers hold cash balances in the invoicing currency of around 10 per cent of the value of imports. Exporters who receive the invoicing currency understandably hold a smaller proportion. If 38 per cent of world imports become invoiced in euros and importers held euro balances to cover 10 per cent of the value of these imports, then there would be a further, one-off, demand for euros worth US$50-75bn.

Perhaps the uncertainty surrounding the change over to a new currency will delay its use as a vehicle currency. But even if the process was spread over five years, the combination of $95bn excess dollar reserves, $175bn new central bank demand for euros and $50bn exporter-importer demand for euros would still leave an average boost to euro demand of almost $65bn per year.

Private portfolio flows

Central bankers are not the only ones that show a preference for large, liquid markets. Private portfolio flows will also respond to the arrival of the euro. Potentially, this could be an even greater flow and a faster moving adjustment than the switch of central bank reserves out of dollars into euros.

The superior depth and width of the US market are some of the reasons why non-residents own a disproportionately large share. Non-resident holdings of Treasuries are a healthy 25 per cent compared with just 17 per cent in other major markets. If this eight per cent gap reflects the dollar's role as a reserve currency and the superior liquidity of US markets then we might expect a similar effect in euro markets. An eight per cent rise in the overseas holdings of euro-denominated government bonds would be in the region of $300bn.

Moreover, European markets will grow. The ratio of marketable euro assets to the size of euro GDP is particularly small; as euro markets become deeper and more liquid, there will be a disintermediation from assets held by the banking system to marketable securities. If there was an eight per cent rise in the overseas holdings of liquid, creditworthy euro assets and the amount of marketable euro assets were to rise to a level where the ratio

Portfolio diversification

	Total outstanding bonds & equities, $ billions	Percentage held by foreigners
Australia	386	16%
Belgium (Dec 94)	392	17%
Canada	781	33%
Denmark	346	16%
France	1,559	20%
Germany	2,855	20%
Italy	1,160	20%
Japan	7,501	8%
Netherlands	642	21%
Spain	373	28%
United Kingdom (Jun 95)	1,901	22%
United States	15,517	9%
Total	*33,413*	*12%*

Figure 15.5   **International portfolio diversification, Dec 1995**

of assets to GDP was similar to that of the United States, then this would imply an increase in overseas holdings of euro assets in the region of $600bn.

These numbers are as uncertain as they are large. One offset to this large net new demand of euro paper from overseas investors is that a liquid market also offers attractions to borrowers. If overseas borrowers are eager suppliers of euro paper, they will help to meet this extra demand for euro assets, ameliorating some of the upward strength on the euro.

Conclusion

During the 1990s, over a dozen new currencies were born in eastern and central Europe. When the euro arrives at the end of the decade, it will not be just one more new currency with an unproven central bank. The economic size and potency of the euro area will mean that the euro will quickly become an 'international currency'. It will play an important role as an intervention currency and as an invoicing currency. As a result, there will

Correlations with the $

Correlation with $/DM

	Correlation with $/DM
$/AUD	-0.299
$/BEF	0.995
$/CAD	-0.312
$/CHF	0.957
$/DEM	1.000
$/DKK	0.994
$/ESP	0.909
$/FRF	0.949
$/GBP	0.454
$/ITL	0.696
$/JPY	0.486
$/NLG	0.996
$/SEK	0.539
Core Europe	**0.980**
Non-core Europe	**0.758**
Non-Europe	**-0.042**

Figure 15.6   Correlation between FX spot rates against US$

be a large demand for euros from central bankers, investors, importers and exporters in the early years. This demand-shock promises to be substantial, in the region of $400bn plus—large enough, perhaps, to offset any euro weakness stemming from perceived policy dilemmas. These dilemmas may be smoothed by the transfer of EMU's hidden booty: nearly $100bn of excess dollar and euro reserves.

Chapter
16

David Abramson
Bank Credit Analyst ForexCast[*]

The euro and central European currencies

In sharp contrast with the obsession in several European Union (EU) countries, there is no government in emerging central Europe whose main focus is on European monetary union. Investors and analysts alike reacted with surprise and amusement in early 1997 when the Polish finance minister remarked out of the blue that the country would be ready for EMU in the year 2006.

Central European countries such as Poland, Hungary and the Czech Republic (CE3) attach much higher priorities to joining Nato and the EU for obvious military, historical and agricultural reasons. However, the importance of monetary union can only grow as the long-standing twin goals of Nato and EU membership are achieved by the early part of the next decade. Nato membership has already been promised for the CE3 countries by April 1999. Negotiations for EU membership have begun in early 1998.

In addition, most central European countries are acting as if they want to satisfy the Maastricht criteria—albeit without the formal commitment made by western European policymakers. The economic orthodoxy and convergence-orientated logic of the Maastricht criteria are less controversial than they were when the western European periphery tried to stabilize their currencies and reduce inflation and budget deficits in the late 1980s. The Czech currency turmoil in May 1997 has further concentrated the minds of central European policymakers on the role of their exchange rate in relation to the Deutschemark and, soon, the euro.

Public attitudes also play a role. It is telling that *Eurobarometer*, the publication that surveys European attitudes, does not even bother to

[*]BCA Publications, Montreal, Canada. Max Tessier, Tom Fahey and Stine Madsen made significant editorial and technical contributions. Special thanks to Mehran Nakhjavani for comments.

question the public behind the former Iron Curtain about EMU. Nevertheless, the central European public has a positive view towards both the European Union and market reforms in general although support has eroded in the past few years (see Figure 16.1 a,b,c). One would expect the pattern to extend to the popularity of the single European currency, as is already evident in the peripheral countries being considered for the first round of EMU, such as Italy, Spain and Portugal.

These trends imply that the central European currencies will eventually be ready to adopt the euro. However, they also imply that exchange rate stability will increasingly be viewed as a policy target—rather than simply a policy tool in the CE3 countries. That leaves room for trouble, and even a 1992-style currency crisis on the path to convergence. The key questions for investors are: When will the CE3 be ready for EMU? What are the preconditions? Will there be bumps along the way and are there reliable early-warning signs of trouble?

This chapter sets out to answer these questions in seven sections. The **first section** maps out the current attitude of central European central bankers to European monetary integration. The **second section** provides a thumbnail sketch of the transition that the CE3 have already made and compares their situation with the western European peripheral countries that are likely to be in the first round of EMU. The conclusion is that the economic transition in central Europe has been impressive and rapid but still has a long way to go; the **third section** underscores this point with comparisons to Finland. The **fourth section** provides a paradigm for anticipating the currency bumps along the way as central Europe tries to converge with western Europe. The **fifth section** provides practical early-warning indicators in line with this paradigm and uses them to compare the 1995 Mexican peso turmoil and the 1997 Czech koruna devaluation. The **sixth section** compares the present central European currency environment with that preceding the 1992 ERM crisis for the western European periphery. The **seventh section** discusses the lessons of the Asian crisis for the CE3 currencies. The **final section** lists the conclusions.

Central Europe's view of the euro

A desire to join the euro club...

A starting point for understanding how the central European currencies will interact with the euro is to examine the attitude of CE central banks towards EMU. The overall impression is of an outsider wanting to 'join the club'. The conclusion is that CE central banks will increasingly view currency stability *vis-à-vis* Europe's core as an end in itself, rather just an instrument of policy.

Czech National Bank governor Josef Tosovsky gave an address in early 1997 at the London School of Economics, entitled 'European Monetary Integration from the Perspective of Central European Countries'. His discussion makes clear that, while CE is not thinking much about EMU, these countries are on a Maastricht-orientated inflation and fiscal convergence path. It also suggests that, while CE central bankers realize the benefits of a floating exchange rate in theory, in practice they usually prefer a stable or strong exchange rate.

Tosovsky emphasizes three points. First, he recognizes the notion of a dynamic optimal currency area as an argument for fixing an exchange rate to a hard money anchor 'early'. An optimal currency area is usually a static concept in which a fixed exchange rate zone makes sense for countries that tend to be affected in the same way by most economic shocks and have a high degree of factor mobility between the member countries. The dynamic version notes that a country can achieve macroeconomic convergence, and trade integration more rapidly, if the exchange rate is used to tie the hands of policymakers. As an example of a dynamic optimal currency area, Tosovsky refers to the Austrian experience which benefited from linking to the Deutschemark before they were strictly ready.

The second point is that the CE has already made a major transition from looking east for its trade in the Communist era, to trading with the European Union. The bulk of this shift was achieved in the late 1980s. This development increases the odds that CE policymakers will believe that a currency link to the euro, possibly an irreversible one, makes sense.

...but much work remains to be done
The final point is that central bankers realize that a lot of work remains to be done on the central European economies before they can consider monetary integration with the euro. In particular, there is a lot of ground to cover in the area of labour market reform and banking system/capital market liberalization.

Institutional exchange rate arrangements are consistent with CE central bankers attempting to reduce currency volatility and link to a European currency anchor wherever possible. Czech authorities have stated that the koruna will shadow the Deutschemark following the 1997 depreciation. Hungary reduced the depreciation rate of their currency basket from 1 per cent per month in early 1997 to 0.8 per cent per month in mid-1998. Estonia

Western Europe's attitude to EMU*

	1990	1991	1992	1993	1994	1995	1996
Italy	61	57	65.5	68	61	62.5	n/a
Spain	n/a	n/a	n/a	n/a	n/a	40	47
Portugal	n/a	n/a	n/a	n/a	n/a	25	30

Figure 16.1a
* Percentage of respondents who are 'positive' minus percentage who are 'negative'
Source: Eurobarometer

Central Europe's attitude to the EU*

	1990	1991	1992	1993	1994	1995
Czech Republic	47	43	42	27	28	19
Poland	43	46	43	28	35	39
Hungary	49	38	28	28	24	21

Figure 16.1b
* Percentage of respondents who are 'positive' minus percentage who are 'negative'
Source: Eurobarometer

Central Europe's attitude to market reform*

	1990	1991	1992	1993	1994	1995
Czech Republic	54	39	24	15	11	6
Poland	47	28	33	29	26	46
Hungary	47	52	39	21	20	5

Figure 16.1c
* Percentage of respondents who are 'positive' minus percentage who are 'negative'
Source: Eurobarometer

and, more recently, Bulgaria have adopted currency boards that tie the hands of their central banks with rigid exchange rate links to the Deutschemark.

Central Europe's economies: a snapshot

CE has made an impressive, rapid transition...

Economic indicators for the three large CE countries confirms that they are on a path that would eventually lead to sustainable EMU membership. Figures 16.2 and 16.3 demonstrate that these countries have come a long way in a relatively short period of time.

Figure 16.2 looks at the CE3 from the narrow Maastricht point of view. The Czech Republic held inflation down to single digits for four consecutive years before the 1997 devaluation pushed inflation up to 14 per cent, and the Czech National Bank is intent on returning inflation to single digits as soon as possible. The Republic also satisfies the Maastricht fiscal criteria, in part because the split with lower-income Slovakia made the adjustment easier. Hungarian inflation is 18 per cent, but the fiscal criteria are not much different than some of the western European countries that will participate in the first round of monetary union. Poland has an inflation rate of 14 per cent and a hawkish central bank. The Polish budget deficit is less than 2 per cent of GDP and the public debt is only 54 per cent of GDP.

This Maastricht scorecard is even more impressive when judged against the transition that these countries had to endure after the Iron Curtain was lifted. Figure 16.3 shows that these countries underwent their most intense reforms in either 1990 or 1991, depending upon the country. The World Bank calculates a summary measure of liberalization for developing countries based on internal, external and private sector criteria. The measure ranges between 0 (minimal liberalization) and 1 (strong liberalization). In each of the CE3 countries, this liberalization measure rose from extremely low levels (between 0.16 and 0.34) in 1990, to quite high levels (between 0.86 and 0.9) only four years later. The private sector in each of the CE3 has mushroomed to account for more than one-half of total production.

Figure 16.3 also illustrates the noticeable payoff in standard economic aggregates as the shock phase of the transition vanishes in the rear-view mirror. Foreign exchange reserves have risen, external debt burdens have shrunk, economic growth has strengthened, inflation has declined and capital spending is booming. The main cost has been higher

Catching up: on Maastricht criteria

CE not so far behind Western periphery on narrow Maastricht view

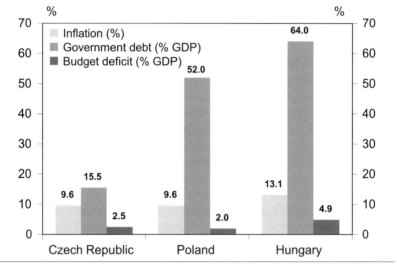

Figure 16.2
Source: OECD forecasts for 1999, apart from debt, 1997 actual data

unemployment, but this comparison may have been distorted by a different definition of an unemployed person under the Communist regime.

...but still has a long way to go

The difficult path already travelled by the CE3 and the ability to endure shock treatment (the exception to shock treatment was the Czech Republic—but they had easier starting conditions), suggest that central European policymakers will set their sights on EU macroeconomic norms in the long term. In fact, such economic goals may occur sooner rather than later once the political goals of Nato and EU membership seem assured. Part of the success of the transition has related to foreign direct investment (FDI) inflows that can only increase as the CE3 become more integrated with western Europe. FDI can help attract portfolio capital inflows, accelerate economic convergence, and stimulate the tradable goods sector of the economy.

Such a strategy should eventually work, but that leaves room for bumps—or even crises—along the way. There are plenty of differences between the CE3 and those peripheral countries of western Europe that are

Catching up: on economic criteria

	Czech Rep.	Hungary	Poland
S&P debt rating	A	BB+	BBB-
Net external debt/exports (%)			
1987-1996	5	161	235
1996	-14	88	55
Reserves/imports (months)			
1987-1996	4.1	4.3	3.5
1996	6.5	6.0	6.8
Real GDP (% change)			
1987-1996	-2.7	-0.8	-0.9
1996	5.5	3.0	5.5
CPI Index (% change)			
1987-1996	13.3	23.8	85.2
1996	8.5	25.0	19.5
Unemployment (% of workforce)			
1987-1996	2.0	6.7	9.3
1996	3.0	10.0	14.0
Real investment (% change)			
1987-1996	0.8	-0.5	3.7
1996	15.0	8.0	14.9
Private sector output/GDP (%)			
1987-1996	5.0	19.0	27.0
1996	69.0	60.0	58.0
% trade with EU			
1989	27.2	26.6	32.9
1996	65.2	62.8	83.5
Year of most intense reform[1]	1991	1990	1990
Prior level of liberalization[2]	0.16	0.34	0.24
Liberalization level in 1994[2]	0.9	0.86	0.86

Figure 16.3

[1] *Source: Åslund, Boone, Johnson, 'How to Stabilize: Lessons from Post-Communist Countries'; Brookings Papers on Economic Activity, no.1, 1996.*

[2] *The World Bank Index of liberalization is a weighted average of change from 0 to 1 along three dimensions: internal prices, external markets, and private sector entry. Prior level refers to the index reading in the year before the most intense reforms were implemented.*

set to participate in EMU. Jeffrey Sachs and Andrew Warner have noted that, even though the CE3 have come a long way, these countries are still far behind in terms of per-capita income levels. Figure 16.4, reproduced from the Sachs/Warner study, shows that CE3 income levels range from one-third to one-half of the EU average. In contrast, 'poor' potential first round EMU participants like Ireland, Portugal and Spain still have income levels ranging from 72 to 84 per cent of the EU average.

From an economic perspective, large income differences make it difficult for a single currency area to function, at least without some mechanism for redistributing income from rich to poor. From a political perspective, the EU would be unwilling to boost structural aid to offset the huge income differential between the CE3 and the rest of the European Union.

It is therefore important to get an idea of at what pace the CE3 will rise towards EU income levels. Figure 16.4 shows some of the variables that determine the pace of development. The CE3 has low tariff levels, although they are still slightly higher than in the European Union. Government spending is also not much greater than for the EU periphery. Savings rates are quite high, but the inadequate pension system stifles the potential for an even greater pool of savings. However, the large tax wedge in central Europe represents a major disincentive to job creation.

All in all, this is not a bad picture. The difficulty is that the CE3 need to have even stronger fundamentals than the 'poor' western European countries in order to catch up. Figure 16.5 provides the Sachs/Warner calculations for when the CE3 would reach 70 per cent of the EU per-capita income (still slightly below Ireland, Portugal and Spain) under three different growth scenarios. Note that a natural tendency for poor countries to converge towards richer neighbours over time is embedded in all the scenarios.

The key factors in each of the scenarios are the degree of economic openness, the domestic savings rate (both public and private) and an Index of Economic Freedom.[1] Of course, these measures are by their nature rough, but they provide a good approximation of why growth rates in differing countries and regions differ over the long term.

The first scenario assumes that the CE3 pursue their current set of policies, the second scenario assumes that they follow policies similar to the EU average and the third scenario assumes that they follow policies similar to eight very fast growing developing economies (VFGE).

Under the optimistic 'harmonize with VFGE' scenario, it will still take between 10 and 21 years for central Europe to achieve the status of the poor western European countries expected to take part in EMU. Moreover, the CE3 are unlikely to imitate the extreme free market, savings-inducing

Catching up: on market reform

	Czech	Hungary	Poland
GDP per capita in PPP prices percent of EU average, 1994 (%)	53	48	36
Average tariff, 1994 (%)	5.0	13	14
Government spending, 1995 (% of GDP)	50.9	54.6	49.4
Tax wedge[1], 1994	128.5	223.8	128.5
Savings, 1995 (% of GDP)	21.2	17.1	18.8
Investment, 1995 (% of GDP)	30.4	21.3	16.9
Index of economic freedom[2]	2.1	2.8	2.9

	Ireland	Portugal	Spain
GDP per capita in PPP prices percent of EU average, 1994 (%)	84	72	81
Average tariff, 1994 (%)	3.6	3.6	3.6
Government spending, 1995 (% of GDP)	45.1	47.3	46.0
Tax wedge[1], 1994	101.6	96.2	114.6
Savings, 1995 (% of GDP)	20.7	20.4	21.0
Investment, 1995 (% of GDP)	17.6	28.5	23.3
Index of economic freedom[2]	2.3	2.3	2.3

Figure 16.4
[1] *Cost of labour to the firm as a percentage of real take-home pay of the average worker*
[2] *EU average*
Source: 'Achieving Rapid Growth in the Transition Economies of Central Europe';
Unpublished paper by Jeffrey Sachs and Andrew M. Warner, July 1996, Harvard Institute for
International Development

Catching up: by when?

	1993 GDP as a % of EU average	'Policy' action	Growth prospects	Years to raise GDP to 70 per cent of EU average
Czech Rep.	53	Keep current policies	3.6	23
		Harmonize with EU	3.5	36
		Harmonize with VFGE	6.6	10
Hungary	48	Keep current policies	1.9	n/a for current prices
		Harmonize with EU	2.8	45
		Harmonize with VFGE	4.6	13
Poland	38	Keep current policies	3.8	104
		Harmonize with EU	4.3	66
		Harmonize with VFGE	6.1	21

Note: VFGE = *very fast growing economies: Chile, Hong Kong, South Korea, Malaysia, Mauritius, Singapore, Taiwan and Thailand*

Figure 16.5

VFGE policies. The central European public already had its share of shock treatment in the early 1990s and the support for market reforms peaked a few years ago, as shown in the polling data in Figure 16.1.

Adopting the norms of EU structural policies is a more realistic scenario given the political, economic and historical tendency of the CE3 to take their cues from Europe's core. It would take the CE3 somewhere between 36 and 65 years to be on a par with Ireland, Spain and Portugal by following the EU model. Carrying on with the status quo, perhaps if the public becomes even more apprehensive of the structural change caused by earlier market reforms, would be a disaster for Poland and Hungary in terms of trying to catch up to 70 per cent of the EU average income. The Czech Republic would require 23 years to reach the 70 per cent barrier.

These estimates confirm that CE3 convergence will be a multi-year process, although they overstate the amount of time that it will take. The earlier examples of Ireland and Portugal demonstrate that EU membership jump-starts FDI inflows and productivity in countries with low labour costs and skilled labour forces. This is also true for the CE3 countries, since they boast relatively literate, well-educated workers and good infrastructure. Of course, EU transfers also helped Ireland and Portugal to get a leg up and this will also be the case for the CE3 once they join the EU.

What does this mean for exchange rate policy? The most likely outcome is that CE policymakers will strive for currency stability relative to the euro in the early part of the next decade. Such a stance would allow for bouts of currency turmoil. The CE3 would be under pressure to achieve a higher growth path than western Europe, but hesitant to let their currencies bear the burden of adjustment as their business cycles overshoot and undershoot Europe's core.

Starting with the Finnish

The Finnish experience supports the notion that central Europe has made an impressive transition, but still has a long way to go. Finland and the CE3 (Poland, Hungary and the Czech Republic) share striking similarities:

Both underwent gut-wrenching monetary and fiscal adjustments as their largest trading partner, the Soviet Union, collapsed in the early 1990s. From 1989 to 1993, real GDP contracted by 11.5 per cent in Finland and by 16.1 per cent in the CE3.

Public sector adjustment in both regions was different, but equally difficult. The priority in Finland was to cut back the welfare state and introduce reforms that would bring public finances into balance and increase market flexibility. In the CE3, there was more emphasis on privatization and deregulation, as well as bringing social transfers in line with the new market reality. However, many of the effects of this adjustment were similar in both regions: rising structural unemployment and declining public sector spending.

Both Finland and the CE3 successfully altered their trade patterns towards western Europe (see Figure 16.6) rather than 'turning inward'. The EFTA was absorbed into the EU and the trading bloc under Soviet influence (COMECON) fell apart, forcing a realignment of trade toward the EU. Figure 16.6 reveals that the CE3 trade shift started two or three years after Finland. The chart also suggests that CE3 trade with the EU may keep rising; it has already reached two-thirds of total trade for Hungary and Poland, and will increase upon accession to the EU.

Despite these similarities, Finland is virtually guaranteed a berth among the first round of EMU participants yet the CE3 will not even be in the running until the latter part of the next decade. Problems of a structural

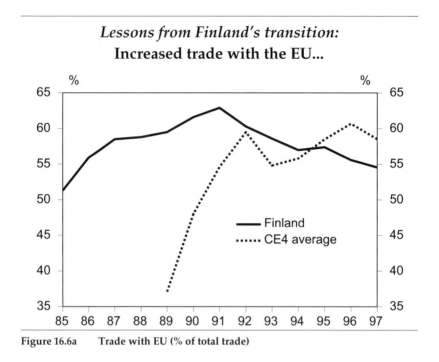

Lessons from Finland's transition:
Increased trade with the EU...

Figure 16.6a   Trade with EU (% of total trade)

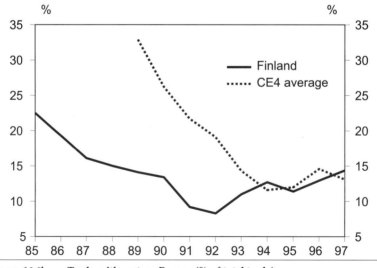

...can quickly replace lost trade with eastern Europe

Figure 16.6b   Trade with eastern Europe (% of total trade)

nature that Finland did not have to deal with in the late 1980s are likely to surface if central European integration is too rapid. Integration hurdles to monitor can be grouped in four categories:

Economic structure: The CE3 economies have not completed the shift away from the industrial sector into services. In Finland, services account for 65 per cent of employment, whereas that number averages less than 50 per cent in the CE3 and is dominated by the public sector.

Investment needs: The ongoing transition requires additional investment for the CE3 economies; fixed capital formation is about 24 per cent of GDP for the region versus 15 per cent in Finland, with the difference explaining much of the current account shortfalls and interest rate differentials.

Wealth difference: Finnish GDP per capita is about 5 times the CE3 average.

Free market institutions: Liberalization and stabilization have done much to put the CE3 on the road to transition. Strong market-orientated institutions and a comprehensive legal framework must be in place before full integration can take place.

Ultimately, the reduction of these four barriers will result in interest rate convergence and greater exchange rate stability for the CE3 *vis-à-vis* the EMU bloc. The CE3 has a much larger labour cost advantage than Finland and relatively-skilled labour supply; both factors have attracted, and will continue to attract, large quantities of FDI to central Europe. Nevertheless, the Finnish markka meltdown of 1992 warns that the integration process will be difficult to manage and that the currency anchor may need to be periodically adjusted.

Currency turmoil: how to anticipate it

Thus far in this chapter, we have argued that CE economic convergence towards the European norm is at least a decade-long process, but that central European policymakers may try to 'put the cart before the horse' and stabilize their currencies *vis-à-vis* the euro. The combination of these two factors is a recipe for occasional bouts of currency turmoil. We now provide some indicators to predict when such turmoil is imminent.

To determine when an emerging currency is heading for trouble, it is important to recognize that successful emerging countries often run large current account deficits. That is because investment opportunities are so prevalent, and the rate of return on capital so high, that foreign capital floods in. The counterpart of massive capital inflows is a current account deficit.

Instead, the emphasis should be on whether a current account deficit is sustainable. The emerging currency paradigm developed by Mehran Nakhjavani lists five criteria to monitor for signs of trouble. The factors shown in Figure 16.7, four domestic and one external, all can be applied to the Polish zloty, Hungarian forint and Czech koruna.

- What is the nature of the **foreign capital** flowing into the country? Is the inflow accelerating at a sustainable rate? Are domestic interest rates competitive in relation to foreign benchmarks, both before and after 'adjusting' for the capital gain/loss of recent exchange rate movements?

- How big is the country's stockpile of **forex reserves** that will help to fend off speculators in case of temporary 'bad news' or a chronic exchange rate misalignment?

- How **competitive** is the currency? Are export profit margins high or low? Is the exchange rate expensive or cheap in real, trade-weighted terms relative to its history? Is productivity in the traded goods sector rising rapidly enough to allow the real exchange rate to appreciate? Has the country been subject to a terms-of-trade shock?

- How rapidly is the **current account deficit** increasing in relation to the growth in income? How big is the current account deficit after adjusting for the fact that foreign direct investment often involves an initial surge in capital goods imports before the export-related benefit shows through?

- Finally, on the **external front**, what is the state of monetary and business cycle conditions in the major developed and developing countries? The Asian turmoil underscores the importance of foreign capital for all emerging market assets, including the eastern European currencies. In the case of the eastern European currencies, the actions of the Bundesbank and Federal Reserve are particularly important because of the importance of the Deutschemark and dollar.

Emerging markets currency paradigm

The 'emerging market' paradigm implies: a rapid increase in inward investment, accelerating GDP growth and globalization and tariff deregulation

↓

Therefore, Current Account Deficits (CADs) are the norm, not the exception

↓

For industrialized countries, this would imply steadily depreciating nominal exchange rates, but in the emerging markets paradigm, CADs can (and indeed *must*) persist for a long time

↓

For the investor in emerging markets, the issue is whether a country's CAD is sustainable. CAD sustainability needs to be monitored from different perspectives

Capital flow	**Reserve management**	**Competitiveness**	**Debt management**
A proxy indicator of overall capital flow measures the aggregate change in the capital and the service accounts	The rate of change in official FX reserves	The rate and scale of recent changes in the real effective exchange rate	Composition of CAD: FDI vs. portfolio flows, export sector vs. consumption
The spread between domestic and foreign interest rates, expressed in nominal terms, in inflation-adjusted terms and in FX-adjusted terms	The size of official FX reserves relative to the volume of imports Efficiency of sterilization, as measured by the size of official FX reserves relative to M1	The rate of productivity growth, factor substitution, labour training issues Micro-reforms affecting labour and other operating costs	CAD vs. GDP growth (i.e. rate of growth of foreign debt) Relative size and servicing requirement of foreign debt

↘ ↘ ↙ ↙

> **The POLICY FILTER**
> How do domestic politics respond to the need for policy change?
> What is the predictability of the policy environment?
> How vulnerable is the system to political shocks?

↑

External shocks
e.g. shrinking Japanese current account surplus
FOMC policy, German re-unification
Asian turmoil and related effects on emerging market assets, including Russia

Figure 16.7

Based on this paradigm, a typical deteriorating picture for an emerging currency would consist of shrinking interest rate spreads, a slowdown in the pace of currency appreciation and foreign exchange reserve accumulation, an overvalued exchange rate, a dramatic deterioration in the current account deficit and a decline in net foreign direct investment inflows. Tightening global monetary conditions would also darken the outlook for an emerging currency already showing signs of wear and tear.

Is the emerging currency paradigm practical for spotting warning signs of trouble in the real world? We have selected two well-known episodes of exchange rate turbulence and compared them to central European currency examples. We examine the warning signs that preceded the 1995 Mexican peso crisis and compare them with the 1997 Czech koruna devaluation. The analysis then proceeds to the 'quest for European convergence' that took place among the western European peripheral countries of Sweden, Italy and Spain that ended in the ERM blow-up of 1992. The comparison here is with the CE3 currencies.

We conclude in both episodes that, while the timing is never perfect, a simple checklist of indicators can alert the investor to when a major depreciation is imminent. This is even the case if the depreciation represents a transitory event on the path to convergence, as is our long-term view for the CE currencies. Note that both the peso and the western European peripheral currencies (WEP) ultimately stabilized after a year or so and no longer exhibit any obvious signs of sustained wear and tear.

Currency turmoil: early warning indicators

The Mexican peso lost 52 per cent of its value against the dollar in only three months after three years of generally stable trading. Likewise, the koruna fell by eight per cent against its targeted Deutschemark and dollar currency basket in less than a month after four years of virtual stability.

Figure 16.8 depicts summary variables for the four domestic criteria in the EM currency paradigm. In the 1994/95, these variables predicted the Mexican devaluation:

- **Capital flows:** The best symptom of a deteriorating capital flow backdrop was the return to dollar-based investors in Mexican short-term assets (Figure 16.8a). This measure peaked in early 1994, nearly a year before the peso meltdown. The reason for this early-warning signal was that Mexican authorities manipulated the peso to stay stable even as the bloom slowly came off the rose for foreign investors in Mexico.

- **Reserve management:** An excellent indicator of the clash between an overvalued currency and a stubborn central bank is the import coverage of forex reserves. Mexican reserves peaked above four months' worth of imports. Mexican authorities then had to eat into their stockpile of dollars, beginning in early 1994, to pay for a rising demand for 'cheap imports' without depreciating the peso. In fact, reserves are such a good indicator that the Mexican authorities hid the deterioration initially by not publishing timely reserve data (this is no longer the case).

- **Competitiveness:** The peso was grossly overvalued more than a year before the turmoil, both on a purchasing power parity basis and judging from four consecutive years of real effective exchange rate appreciation. It does not help that Mexico has a relatively low share of fixed investment versus GDP. Investment can be a proxy for future productivity if used efficiently.

- **Debt management:** Developing countries frequently run current account deficits owing to prevalent investment opportunities but few countries can run external deficits in excess of six per cent of GDP for very long. By mid-1994, it was clear that Mexico's current account deficit-to-GDP ratio was heading for a record eight per cent. Moreover, the dependence on short-term capital increased steadily, judging from the decline in the stock of long-term financial liabilities in the early 1990s. On the surface, the jump in foreign direct investment during 1994 flies in the face of an expensive currency. But this reflects the 'Walmart phenomenon', where foreign firms entered Mexico to sell to the domestic markets and buy real estate, rather than produce for export.

This analysis also predicted the rising strains on the Czech koruna in 1997, but there were several signs that a Mexican-style smash-up was not in the cards:

- The returns to dollar-based investors from Czech short-term assets peaked in the middle of 1995, along with investor euphoria over the 'central Europe turnaround story'. These returns tumbled to new lows only a few months before the devaluation.

- Forex reserve import cover peaked about one year before the koruna devaluation. However, the level of import coverage was still high when contrasted with the Mexican example.

Figure 16.8a   **Short-term returns converted to dollars**

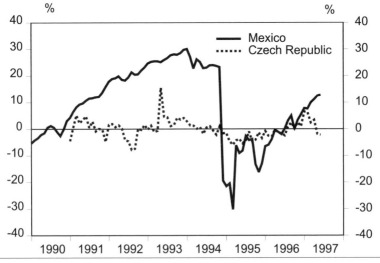

Figure 16.8b   **Purchasing power parity (PPP) valuation***
*koruna versus Deutschemark and peso versus US$.

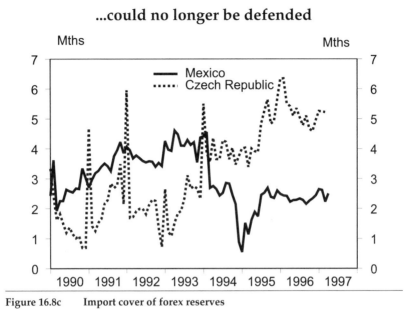

...could no longer be defended

Figure 16.8c   Import cover of forex reserves

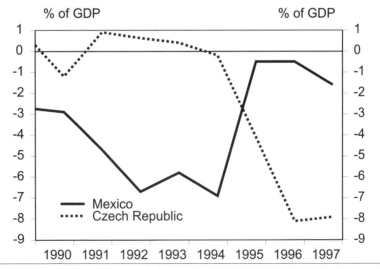

The current account recovered quickly...

Figure 16.8d   Current account balance

...as competitiveness improved...

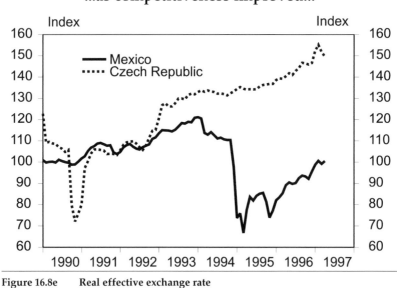

Figure 16.8e   Real effective exchange rate

...and foreign debt declined

Figure 16.8f   Long-term foreign liabilities

Fixed investment has recovered...

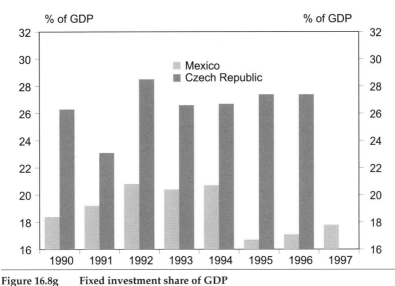

Figure 16.8g   **Fixed investment share of GDP**

...aided by healthy FDI inflows

Figure 16.8h   **Foreign direct investment**

-    Competitiveness had deteriorated to an extreme—whether calculated on the basis of PPP or real, trade-weighted index (TWI) measures. A one-time real exchange rate appreciation was inevitable after the Iron Curtain fell, owing to the low level of labour costs and productivity 'catch up'. But the real TWI had been rising for six consecutive years! Nevertheless, the much higher investment-to-GDP ratio than in Mexico also warned against expecting a meltdown.

-    Neither the size nor the rate of deterioration of the Czech current account deficit was sustainable. Moreover, the rundown of both long-term financial liabilities and FDI pointed to a rising dependence on short-term capital flows.

The external environment in 1997 was more hospitable to overvalued currencies than it was in 1995. Interest rates in western Europe and Japan were much lower in 1997 than two years earlier, at both ends of the yield curve. In addition, the US Federal Reserve was much less intent on tightening liquidity conditions because it perceives inflation to be less of a threat than at the time of the Mexican turmoil.

Lessons from 1992 for the big three CE currencies

We know in retrospect that Italy, Spain and Sweden converged with the Deutschemark-bloc of countries, but there was a confidence-shattering explosion along the way in 1992. The lira, peseta and krona declined by 39 per cent, 32 per cent and 33 per cent, respectively against the Deutschemark from their 1992 peaks, before bottoming in 1995. The current environment for the 'eastern periphery' shares enough similarities with the 'western periphery' in the fall of 1992 to suggest that the convergence path in central Europe will not be smooth even if we are correct that CE policymakers will stay on a convergence path.

Figure 16.9 compares the criteria that got the western European peripheral (WEP) currencies into trouble with the current reading for the zloty, forint and koruna. Figure 16.9 (a-d) depicts an accident waiting to happen among the WEP currencies in 1992: overvalued exchange rates,[2] large current account deficits by developed country standards, industrial production stagnant—or worse—as these countries sacrificed their economies to stick with the Deutschemark anchor, and slowdowns or outright contractions in central bank foreign exchange reserve positions.

Similar indicators are shown for the CE3 in Figure 16.9 (e-h). As with the Mexican comparison earlier, the Czech koruna stuck out like a sore thumb:

Figure 16.9a   Deviation from PPP values

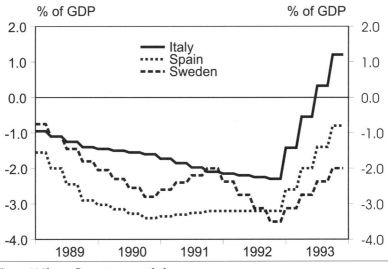

Figure 16.9b   Current account balance

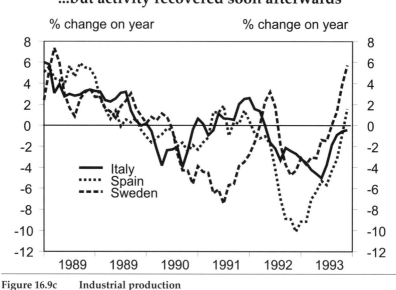

...but activity recovered soon afterwards

Figure 16.9c   Industrial production

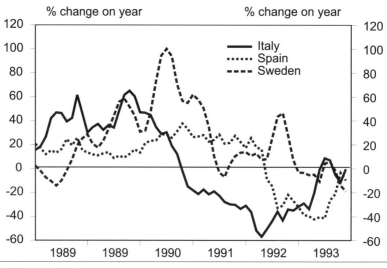

Central banks were unable to defend their currencies

Figure 16.9d   Forex reserves

The CE country with the 'strongest' exchange rate...

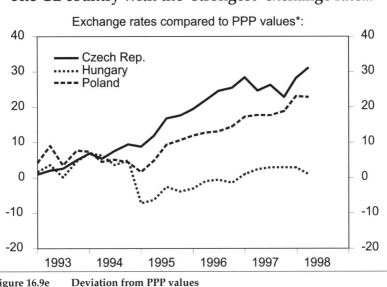

Figure 16.9e   **Deviation from PPP values**
* over (+) or minus (-) valuation compared to TIER estimate of the PPP

...had by far the biggest current account deficit

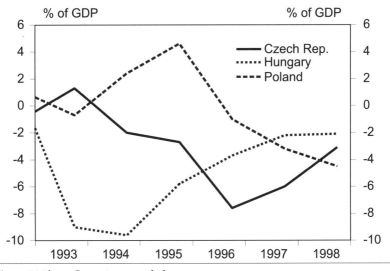

Figure 16.9f   **Current account balance**
Source: JP Morgan; 1998 figures are estimates

The koruna undermined Czech economic health...

Figure 16.9g   Industrial production

...and drained forex reserves

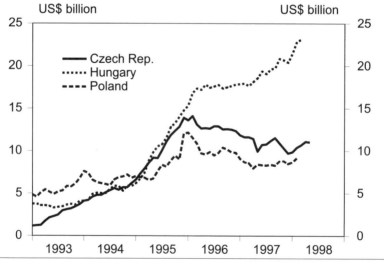

Figure 16.9h   Forex reserves

currency overvaluation, an unsustainable current account deficit—even by developing country standards, falling industrial production, and contracting forex reserves.

The Polish zloty and Hungarian forint give more of a mixed picture based on the comparison with the ERM crisis. Imbalances are slowly building. There would need to be more warning signs before expecting these currencies to deviate from their targeted rates of devaluation. In Poland, the zloty is pricey and the current account deficit is not far from danger levels. Russian turmoil might be enough to spark contagion out of Polish assets. However production is still expanding at a healthy rate and forex reserves continue to rise, even though the National Bank is cutting interest rates. Correspondingly, Hungary has a cheaper currency than Poland or the Czech Republic, but that advantage is eroding.

The desire of the Bundesbank/European Central Bank to keep interest rates low lends some support to the CE3 currencies. Barring an external shock, perhaps emanating from Russia, an erosion in Hungarian or Polish production or worsening current account positions would be necessary before their authorities consider devaluing. In fact, Hungary and Poland are more likely to reduce the prescribed rate of devaluation in the coming years if their economies stay out of recession and the Asian turmoil dies down. That would increase the long-term commitment to an eventual link with the euro, but also boost the chances of periodic episodes of currency turmoil.

The emerging markets currency paradigm and the Asian crisis

Simply placing the Asian crisis under the heading of external factors in the emerging markets paradigm in Figure 16.7 does not do it justice. The need for Asia to export its way out of recession after years of over-investment has three distinct effects on the rest of the emerging markets world, each of which impacts the central European currencies (Figures 16.10 a-c):

- *Commodity prices have dropped sharply.* Asia demands a significant amount of the world's commodities, including energy, because the region is manufacturing intensive. This is a direct positive for the CE3, because these countries are commodity importers, but one must also take into account Russia's dependence upon energy exports to service its foreign debt (see risk premium and contagion factor below).

Declining commodity prices...

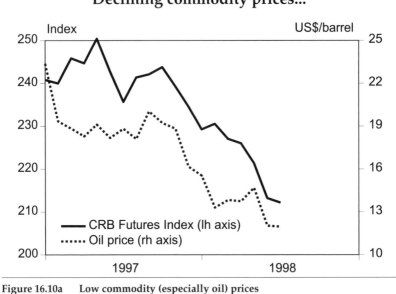

Figure 16.10a   Low commodity (especially oil) prices

...and rising risk premiums...

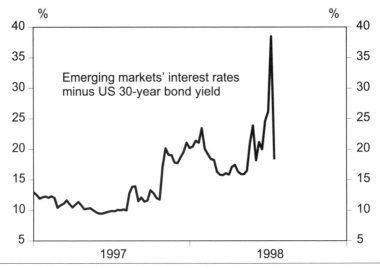

Figure 16.10b   Emerging markets' risk premiums

...have buffeted emerging markets

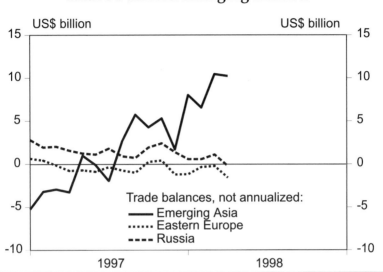

Figure 16.10c   Emerging markets' trade balance deterioration

- *Second, there is the rising risk premium on EM assets and potential for contagion from Russia.* The Asian turmoil revives the time-honoured tradition of feast and famine from developed country investors putting funds into emerging markets. Not only are the CE3 vulnerable on this point, since they have current account deficits, but also because a higher risk premium on Russian assets could feed back on attitudes towards central European assets. The CE3 can therefore be 'guilty by association' if foreign investors reduce overall emerging market exposures. The risk premium on emerging market assets is higher than when the Asian crisis broke but there has also been extreme volatility. One reason is that investors are assuming that several nations, including Russia, are too big or important for the IMF and US to let fail.

- *Finally, there is the effect on trade and FDI as Asian surpluses surge and their competitiveness improves.* The CE3 specialize in low-end manufacturing and have attracted plenty of direct investment, which may shift to cheaper Asian locations. Asia also competes with central Europe in developed country markets. The upshot is that the

CE3 are more exposed to Asian competition than a simply trade-weighted exchange rate calculation would imply. CE3 trade balances can be expected to deteriorate

The CE3 currencies have not yet been noticeably affected by the Asian turmoil. However, one implication of these three effects is that central European current account deficits will be harder to finance. The corollary is that CE3 economic convergence with the EU will be more difficult to achieve without periods of exchange rate pressure.

Conclusions and extensions

Being part of EMU is an inevitable goal of the CE3, now that Nato and EU membership are in their sights. These countries are sufficiently far along in their economic transition to eventually be part of the euro zone, but far enough behind western Europe that it will take at least a decade. There will be plenty of bumps along the way as the uneven convergence path for both macroeconomic criteria and per capita incomes causes the eastern European currencies to ebb and flow relative to the euro.

Simple economic and financial variables can be used to predict when CE currencies are approaching a period of maximum danger. This is the case even though it is likely that the Polish zloty, Hungarian forint and Czech koruna are on a gradual convergence path towards western European norms for per capita income levels, inflation and fiscal accounts.

To evaluate investment risks fully, it is necessary to go beyond the warning signs developed in this chapter. The next step is to gauge how policymakers will react when faced with an unsustainable exchange rate level. Taking the example of the koruna devaluation of 1997, the Czech authorities waited until the forex reserves were plunging and the current account deficit had gone to unreasonable extremes before acting. However, it still seems clear from the koruna devaluation that the Czech National Bank will be more flexible about the exchange rate anchor than Spain, Italy and Sweden were before the 1992 ERM crisis forced their hand.

One can speculate on the implications for the broader range of eastern and central European currencies described in the Appendix at the end of this chapter.[3] There will continue to be a wide variety of arrangements, ranging from a currency board to a 'dirty float'. The tightest arrangements, and therefore the easiest to make the transition to the euro, are the iron-clad Estonian and Bulgarian currency board links to the Deutschemark. However, all of these countries will increasingly view currency stability versus the euro as a goal of policy, as well as an instrument.

Notes for Chapter 16

[1]*According to Sachs and Warner, 'the Index of Economic Freedom (IEF) aims to measure the extent of market distortions in 140 economies focusing on market distortions caused by government intervention and the absence of well-defined property rights ...(t)here are sub-indexes for trade policy, taxation, government consumption, monetary policy, capital flow and FDI restrictions, banking restrictions, wage and price controls, the absence of property rights, regulatory policy, and black market activity.' For details, see 1996 Index of Economic Freedom, The Heritage Foundation, Washington, D.C.*

[2]*The PPP level is measured by using 1987, first quarter, as the base period and then using the average of four cost and price indices (consumer prices, wage costs, export prices and producer prices) from that date to track the PPP path versus the Deutschemark.*

[3]*The Appendix gives details of various eastern and central European currency agreements which are beyond the scope of this chapter.*

Chapter

16

APPENDIX

the euro

Institutional exchange rate arrangements

ESTONIA

Estonian kroon

Estonia was the first of the 15 ex-Soviet Republics to leave the rouble zone and circulate its own currency. The Estonian kroon was first circulated on 12 June 1992. The kroon is pegged to the Deutschemark in the framework of a currency board system. The kroon is fully convertible at the fixed rate of EEK 8.00 = DEM 1. There are no major foreign exchange restrictions. The government and the central bank remain committed to the currency board and no major policy changes are expected in this area of policy for the time being.

Estonia: selected indicators for 1996:

Growth of real GDP (ann. % chg.):	4
Consumer prices (ann. % chg.):	15
Unemployment (%):	6
Fiscal balance (% of GDP):	-2
Current account (% of GDP):	-10.2
Forex reserve import cover (months):	2.5
External debt (% of exports):	16.8
External debt service (% of exports):	1.2
Total public debt (% of GDP):	6.2

LATVIA

Latvian lats

The exchange rate of the lats, introduced on 5 March 1993, is a managed floating currency. Occasionally, the central bank intervenes so that the lats generally moves with the SDR rate. The Latvijas Banka sells foreign currency unconditionally to any commercial bank in Latvia to ensure full convertibility. No major changes in Latvia's foreign exchange policy are expected for the time being.

Latvia: selected indicators for 1996:

Growth of real GDP (ann. % chg.):	3
Consumer prices (ann. % chg.):	13
Unemployment (%):	7
Fiscal balance (% of GDP):	-2
Current account (% of GDP):	-9
Forex reserve import cover (months):	3.8
External debt (% of exports):	32.4
External debt service (% of exports):	4.5
Total public debt (% of GDP):	13.4

LITHUANIA

Lithuanian litas

The litas was first introduced on 25 June 1993. As of 1 April 1994, the litas has been pegged to the US dollar at the rate of LVL 4 = US$1 in a currency board arrangement. ·Eventually, the currency board will be dismantled in favour of a basket more closely linked to the euro. The litas is fully convertible.

Lithuania: selected indicators for 1996:

Growth of real GDP (ann. % chg.):	4
Consumer prices (ann. % chg.):	13
Unemployment (%):	6
Fiscal balance (% of GDP):	-1
Current account (% of GDP):	-8.2
Forex reserve import cover (months):	2.1
External debt (% of exports):	34.1
External debt service (% of exports):	4.3
Total public debt (% of GDP):	17.1

BULGARIA

Bulgarian lev

The lev was a free-floating currency, but the conventional monetary policy was pre-empted by a currency board mechanism in July, 1997. The currency board is being introduced as a cornerstone of the new governments stabilization program The lev is pegged to the Deutschemark at a rate of BGL 1000 = DM1. The lev has certain current and capital account payments restrictions.

Bulgaria: selected indicators for 1996:

Growth of real GDP (ann. % chg.):	-10.9
Consumer prices (ann. % chg.):	311
Unemployment (%):	12.5
Fiscal balance (% of GDP):	-11
Current account (% of GDP):	-2
Forex reserve import cover (months):	1
External debt (% of exports):	159
External debt service (% of exports):	17.9
Total public debt (% of GDP):	175

SLOVENIA

Slovenian tolar

The free-floating tolar was introduced on 8 October 1991. The central bank intervenes occasionally. The tolar is fully convertible for current account transactions, but payment restrictions exist on the capital account.

Slovenia: selected indicators for 1996:

Growth of real GDP (ann. % chg.):	3.5
Consumer prices (ann. % chg.):	8.8
Unemployment (%):	7.3
Fiscal balance (% of GDP):	0
Current account (% of GDP):	0
Forex reserve import cover (months):	3
External debt (% of exports):	38.3
External debt service (% of exports):	9.1
Total public debt (% of GDP):	28.5

ROMANIA

Romanian leu

The leu is a free-floating currency, but the central bank intervenes regularly. Current and capital account restrictions exist. The exchange of foreign currency was liberalized in February 1997, with the view of full currency convertibility. One option under consideration for the stabilization of the exchange rate is to switch to a crawling-peg.

Romania: selected indicators for 1996:

Growth of real GDP (ann. % chg.):	4.1
Consumer prices (ann. % chg.):	57
Unemployment (%):	8.5
Fiscal balance (% of GDP):	-6
Current account (% of GDP):	-6.6
Forex reserve import cover (months):	0.8
External debt (% of exports):	85
External debt service (% of exports):	14.5
Total public debt (% of GDP):	23.6

SLOVAKIA

Slovak koruna

The Slovak koruna was first issued on 8 February 1993, following the dissolution of the currency union with the Czech Republic. Since 14 July 1994, the koruna has been pegged to a trade-weighted basket of currencies consisting of the Deutschemark (60 per cent) and the US$ (40 per cent). The koruna is convertible for current account transactions, but restrictions remain on capital account transactions. The index against the DM/US$ basket is allowed to float +/- 7 per cent against the central parity.

Slovakia: selected indicators for 1996:

Growth of real GDP (ann. % chg.):	6.9
Consumer prices (ann. % chg.):	5.4
Unemployment (%):	12.5
Fiscal balance (% of GDP):	-1.3
Current account (% of GDP):	-10.2
Forex reserve import cover (months):	3.8
External debt (% of exports):	71.5
External debt service (% of exports):	10.2
Total public debt (% of GDP):	32.4

HUNGARY

Hungarian forint

The Hungarian forint is managed as a crawling-peg. The peg is to a basket of currencies that includes the Deutschemark (70 per cent) and the US dollar (30 per cent) and the monthly devaluation is 0.8 per cent. The high Deutschemark weighting is a reflection of the successful redirection of trade flows from the former CMEA members to the EU countries, which now represent almost two-thirds of Hungary's export market.

The exchange rate regime is determined by the central bank in agreement with the government. Exchange rate adjustments of up to 5 per cent can be made independently by the central bank. More dramatic changes require the government's consent.

Hungary has full convertibility of the current account, but capital account restrictions still apply.

Hungary: selected indicators for 1996:

Growth of real GDP (ann. % chg.):	1
Consumer prices (ann. % chg.):	20
Unemployment (%):	11
Fiscal balance (% of GDP):	-3.3
Current account (% of GDP):	-3.7
Forex reserve import cover (months):	7.1
External debt (% of exports):	144
External debt service (% of exports):	28.9
Total public debt (% of GDP):	69

CZECH REPUBLIC

Czech koruna

Following its devaluation in June 1997, the koruna now operates as a managed float. The new exchange rate policy under consideration is an ill-defined 'shadowing' of the Deutschemark. From 1993, the Czech koruna was pegged to a currency basket consisting of the Deutschemark and the dollar, which were weighted at 65 per cent and 35 per cent, respectively. The central bank used to allow the koruna to fluctuate within a +/- 7.5 per cent band. Current account transactions are fully convertible, but capital account restrictions still apply.

The move to the two currency basket, from a five currency basket, reflects the growing importance of the Czech Republic's trading partner's in the DM-bloc.

Czech Republic: selected indicators for 1996:

Growth of real GDP (ann. % chg.):	4.4
Consumer prices (ann. % chg.):	8.6
Unemployment (%):	3.5
Fiscal balance (% of GDP):	0
Current account (% of GDP):	-8.6
Forex reserve import cover (months):	4.1
External debt (% of exports):	68.7
External debt service (% of exports):	13.7
Total public debt (% of GDP):	15.5

POLAND

Polish zloty

The Polish zloty is managed as a crawling-peg, which targets a basket of currencies and devalues by 12.7 per cent per annum. The basket includes the dollar (45 per cent), the Deutschemark (35 per cent), pound sterling (10 per cent), French franc (5 per cent) and Swiss franc (5 per cent). The authorities are moving to liberalize foreign exchange transactions.

The zloty is a fully-convertible currency for all current account transactions, but some capital account restrictions remain.

Poland: selected indicators for 1996:

Growth of real GDP (ann. % chg.):	6
Consumer prices (ann. % chg.):	18.6
Unemployment (%):	13.5
Fiscal balance (% of GDP):	-3.7
Current account (% of GDP):	-1
Forex reserve import cover (months):	6
External debt (% of exports):	139
External debt service (% of exports):	8.1
Total public debt (% of GDP):	54

Sources

Euromoney, 'The 1996 Guide to Emerging Market Currencies', supplement to the June 1996 issue.

Union Bank of Switzerland, *Exchange Rate Arrangements and Regulations*, ed. H. Theiler, November 1994.

The Economist Intelligence Unit.

Section
VII
The
euro

Financial markets

Chapter
17

Paul Temperton
*The Independent Economic Research
Company (TIER)*

The euro and the money market

This chapter looks at the impact of the euro on the functioning of the money market in Europe. Specifically, we examine:

- the new operating environment for setting euro-area interest rates;

- a comparison of EURIBOR, a new reference interest rate, and euro LIBOR;

- the new benchmark overnight rate, EONIA.

A new operating environment

For many years, the Bundesbank's interest rates have been the 'reference' or 'benchmark' interest rates for other European countries. Financial markets have become used to looking at the spread of a country's short-term interest rates over Germany. The interest rate spread has been closely related to the stability of a country's currency versus the Deutschemark. For example, as France successfully pursued a *franc fort* policy in the 1980s and 1990s, the short-term interest rate differential with Germany steadily declined. During the ERM crisis of 1992-1993, very high short-term interest rate differentials with Germany were needed at times in an attempt (sometimes successful, sometimes not) to maintain currency stability.

All of that changes from 1 January 1999. The ECB will set a common level of short-term interest rates for all euro area countries. Money market reference interest rates will also be determined in a new way that ensures interbank rates are the same in all euro area countries out to a maturity of one year. Longer-term interest rate differentials will still exist but these are expected to be small (see Chapter 18).

The pattern of interest rates in Europe...

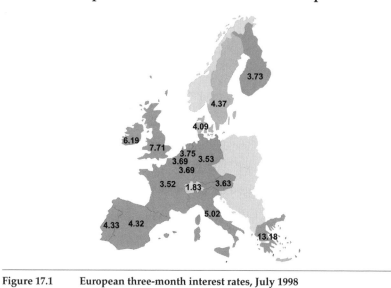

Figure 17.1   European three-month interest rates, July 1998

...will radically alter when the euro is launched

Figure 17.2   Forecast three-month interest rates, January 1999

ECB interest rates

The European Central Bank will set key short-term interest rates. More precisely, the Governing Council of the European System of Central Banks will determine these rates. That Governing Council consists of the Executive Board of the European Central Bank and the governors of the national central banks of the eleven countries in EMU (see Chapter 5). It currently meets once a month. The interest rates which are determined will be common to all countries in the euro area. Within the euro area, interest rate differentials with Germany will be a thing of the past.

However, national central banks will still be responsible for administering the common level of short-term interest rates. Financial institutions will not deal directly with the ECB in Frankfurt.

The three key rates set by the ECB will be:

Marginal lending rate

This will be the rate at which banks which are short of liquidity can borrow from their national central bank. All national central banks in the euro area will set the same marginal lending rate. Banks can borrow during the course of the day, but normally such operations would take place at the end of the day. Liquidity will be provided on an overnight basis. In normal circumstances, the rate on the marginal lending facility will provide a ceiling for overnight interest rates The rate will normally only be altered at the regular ECB Governing Council meetings. It will be analogous to the current lombard rate set by The Bundesbank.

Deposit facility rate

A deposit facility will be available for banks with excess liquidity. They will be able to make overnight deposits with their national central bank at the deposit facility rate. In normal circumstances, this deposit facility will set the floor for the overnight rate.

Repo rate

Together, the marginal lending rate and the deposit facility rate set a corridor within which short-term interest rates will, in normal circumstances, fluctuate. In particular, the ECB will conduct a weekly tender for two-week liquidity. This will be on a purchase and resale (repo) basis. The ESCB will have the option of conducting either fixed-rate (volume) or variable-rate (interest) tenders. In a fixed-rate tender, the ECB will specify the interest rate in advance and participating counterparties bid the amount of money they want to transact at the fixed interest rate. In a variable-rate tender, counterparties will bid the amount of money and the interest rate at which they want to enter into a transaction with the national central banks.

In this way, the ECB will have a key role in determining short-term interest rates in the euro area. A schematic presentation of the ECB's interest rate structure is shown in Figure 17.3. In practice, the structure will be very similar to the structure currently used by the Bundesbank. The main difference from the German system is that the ECB has no discount mechanism—a fixed allocation of cheap money available to eligible banks and savings institutions.

The ECB: instruments

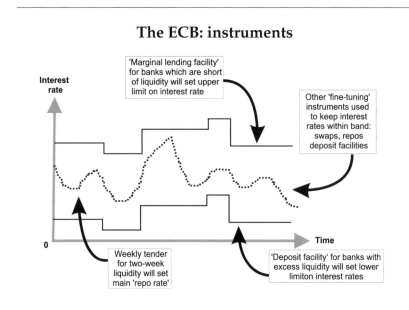

Figure 17.3   Key interest rates of the ECB

EURIBOR versus euro LIBOR

These reference rates determined by the ECB will clearly be highly influential rates in the money market. However, the vast majority of financial market contracts will be linked not to these rates, but to interbank rates. A new reference rate for euro-area interbank rates, known as EURIBOR, is being established. It will replace the national interbank rates (FIBOR, PIBOR, etc.) of euro area countries and will be a measure of the average cost of funds over the whole euro area based on a large sample of banks.

The main competitor to EURIBOR is euro LIBOR. Euro LIBOR will be a measure of the cost of euro funds based on the offer rates quoted by 16 of the most active banks in the London market. Euro LIBOR will replace the LIBOR rates of the national currencies joining in the euro area, as well as Ecu LIBOR. National currency LIBOR rates will still be quoted after 1 January 1999. However, they will not be determined independently. There will be one panel of banks determining euro LIBOR rates and the rates displayed (for example by the various screen-based information service providers) for national currency LIBOR rates will simply be equivalent to these euro LIBOR rates.

Figure 17.4 sets out a comparison of EURIBOR and euro LIBOR.

Euro LIBOR vs. EURIBOR

	euro LIBOR	EURIBOR
Panel	16 major banks active in the euro market in London	57 banks: 47 selected by national banking associations to represent the euro markets in the participating member states; 10 international or 'pre-in' banks active in the euro market with an office in the euro area.
Calculation basis	Discard top and bottom 4 Average remainder	Discard top and bottom 15% Average remainder
Time of fixing	11.00 London time daily	11.00 Brussels time daily
Fixing days	All TARGET days	
For value	Second TARGET day after fixing	
Fixing periods	1 week, 1 month to 12 months	

Figure 17.4   Main characteristics of euro LIBOR and EURIBOR
Source: Bank of England, 'Practical Issues Arising from the Introduction of the Euro', June 1998, page 40.

With both euro LIBOR and EURIBOR there will be no scope for any national differences in interest rates to emerge.

A range of factors will determine whether euro LIBOR or EURIBOR comes to be the most widely-used reference rate in the financial markets.

Reserve requirements

The ECB has already announced that reserve requirements will be imposed on euro area banks. London banks are not subject to reserve requirements. Reserve requirements in the euro area will therefore raise the average cost of funds of banks in the euro area and this will tend to make EURIBOR rates higher than euro LIBOR rates. The difference between the two will depend on the rate at which the reserve requirements of euro area banks are remunerated. If, as seems likely, that rate will be very close to market interest rates, the difference between euro LIBOR and EURIBOR rate should be small.

Familiarity

Use of euro LIBOR in the international markets will benefit from familiarity and from the liquidity that derives from the current weight of contracts based on current national currency and Ecu LIBOR. The notional principal of outstanding interest rate swaps in euro area currencies in 1995 was $3,767 billion, second only to US dollar outstandings of $4,372 billion.

Use in international markets

International market participants, who have existing assets or liabilities linked to LIBOR rates may prefer to have new positions also linked to LIBOR. Linking to EURIBOR instead would expose them to the risk of any change in the spread between EURIBOR and euro LIBOR. The spread could change, for example, if there were a change in reserve requirements (or their degree of remuneration) in the euro area.

Use in euro-area markets

Domestic participants in the euro area might, however, prefer to use EURIBOR, as it will replace their previous domestic rates.

Use in futures markets

MATIF has announced that EURIBOR will replace PIBOR in futures contracts. DTB has announced that it will offer the market a choice, during the transition period, of EURIBOR and euro LIBOR.

EONIA

A new overnight reference rate for the euro area will also be constructed. This is termed EONIA, European Overnight Indexed Average. It will be determined by the same panel of banks that determine EURIBOR. Overnight rates will be weighted according to the volume of business conducted at that rate. The weighting of the individual banks' rates, and the publication of the rate, will be conducted by the ECB.

Mary Pieterse-Bloem
& Paola Lamedica
*Paribas**

The euro and government bond markets

Introduction

The introduction of the single currency marks a significant change for European and financial markets world-wide. On 1 January 1999, the domestic markets of the EMU member states will merge into the second biggest bond market in the world. Its weight in global government bond indices will represent more than 30 per cent, compared to 40 per cent for the US-bloc and 16 per cent for Japan. The newly-born euro market will continue to reflect the characteristics of the individual domestic bond markets, at least initially. However, the prompt redenomination of government debt and the harmonization of market conventions in Euroland will considerably boost the achievement of an efficient euro bond market.

In this chapter, we will take a detailed look at the implications of the euro for European government bond markets. For ease of reference, the sections are numbered. In Section 1, we discuss the features of this new market in terms of both size and liquidity. Understanding the credit implications of the euro, as outlined in Section 2, is necessary for analysing the type of debt which will become the benchmark, which is covered in Section 3. Section 4 discusses the implications of the euro for futures contracts on both short-term and long-term interest rates. The implications for investors and borrowers are reviewed in Sections 5 and 6, respectively, while Section 7 contains our concluding remarks.

*Mary Pieterse-Bloem and Paola Lamedica are Euro Bond Strategists in the Fixed Income Department of Paribas. Mary is also chairman of the Euro Committee, sub-committee of the EFFAS European Bond Commission. The chapter draws heavily from the research conducted by Paribas' research department on the implications of EMU on capital markets and published in the EMU Countdown document.

1. Features of the new market

Currently, the US dollar market is the largest government bond market in the world, with a total amount of US$4.8 trillion outstanding in US public debt (marketable federal debt and municipal securities) as at the end of 1997. Disregarding eurobonds—but including corporate bonds and bonds issued by the financial sector—the size of this market is US$8.3 trillion. The Japanese market follows in second place. The public debt sector in this market accounted for ¥281 trillion (US$3.1 trillion) as at the end of September 1997 and, if one includes the domestic and corporate sectors, the size rises to ¥417 trillion (US$3.4 trillion).

Strictly speaking, the largest government bond market in Europe is that of Italy, with the total amount of government bonds outstanding being ITL1,963 trillion (US$1.1 trillion). In Germany, however, where the size of the domestic sector (which incorporates all bank bonds) is larger than the total amount of outstanding German government bonds, the overall size of the market is larger than the lira market, at US$1.9 trillion. The French market is the third-largest in Europe, with an amount outstanding of FRF4,903bn (US$816bn) in public debt instruments and domestic bonds.

The euro debt market: #2 in the world

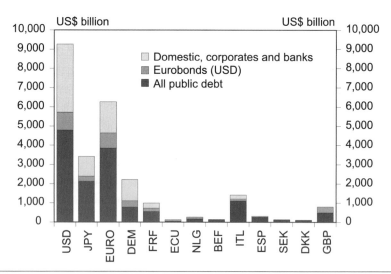

Figure 18.1   Amounts outstanding in the international bond markets
Source: Monetary authorities in the various countries for public and domestic debt, Capital Data Bondware for Eurobonds

The other EMU in markets are all relatively small, with none of them exceeding US$350bn.

The creation of the euro merges all the markets of the participating currencies into one large domestic 'euro' bond market. Judging from the current size of the eleven prospective EMU-entrants, it can be seen that the euro will create a market which will be the second largest in the world. This can be seen in Figure 18.1, where including the relatively large markets of Italy and Spain, the euro creates a market with a total size of US$6.3 trillion including eurobonds and domestic bonds, and a sovereign sector of US$3.8 trillion.

The same picture is revealed by the swaps market. According to a survey conducted by the International Swaps and Derivatives Association (ISDA) for the end of 1996, the largest swap amounts outstanding in any currency were in US$, accounting for US$5.8 trillion of all interest rate swaps and US$559bn currency swaps outstanding (see Figures 18.2 and 18.3). However, in the swaps market the euro will be following closely on the heels of the US$. On the basis of a simple summation of the underlying markets, euro interest rate swaps would amount to only US$30bn less than the amount outstanding in US dollars. In currency swaps, the difference is bigger, with the euro accounting for US$314bn worth of business.

The development of a transparent and homogenous euro market will take some time, as the composition of each domestic market differs and as domestic participants all inherit their own unique characteristics from the past. Two crucial steps towards the creation of a liquid and deep euro bond market are the redenomination of financial instruments from national currencies into euro and the harmonization of market conventions. Harmonization and redenomination are often mentioned in one breath. However, it is worth noting that they involve different processes. Harmonization seeks to standardize the market rules and conventions of the various bond markets which participate in the euro. redenomination, on the other hand, relies on the decision of an issuer to change the denomination of its existing debt from a participating national currency to the euro.

With regard to harmonization, the desirability of harmonizing conventions in EMU has been agreed upon by several working groups, including the major financial associations and a group sponsored by the European Commission. In particular, it has been argued that modifying the conventions for newly-issued debt will prove beneficial for the liquidity and the transparency of the euro market. If left unchanged, the maintenance of different market conventions would undermine the euro market, encouraging fragmentation. Harmonized conventions will allow a straightforward comparison among issues, as the price will reflect

Interest rate swaps in euro: nearly as large as in US$...

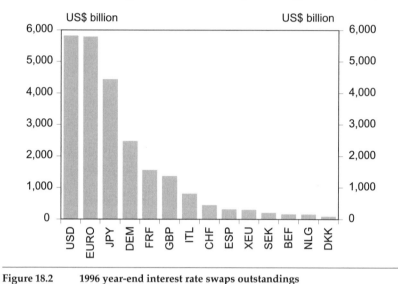

Figure 18.2   1996 year-end interest rate swaps outstandings
Source: ISDA

...currency swaps also possibly #2

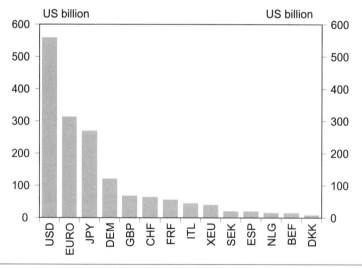

Figure 18.3   1996 year-end currency swaps outstandings
Source: ISDA

fundamental, rather than technical, factors. This element should prove attractive to less sophisticated investors, as harmonization simplifies the understanding of new markets and the implementation of diversification strategies across Europe. New business opportunities are likely to arise from the enhanced transparency of European markets, as new borrowers, including corporates, agencies and other public entities, decide to tap financial markets more often in search of alternative financing sources. In addition, from a practical point of view, harmonization will reduce trading and settlement costs, by minimizing settlement errors and disputes. Figure 18.4 summarizes the new conventions. New conventions will be adopted for debt issued after January 1999. Most member states have also decided to reconvention old, tradable government debt. The reconventioning will usually take place on the first coupon date after January 1999, except for Belgium, which has opted for a 'Big Bang' approach.

Harmonized conventions

Conventions for euro money market	
Day count basis	Actual/360
Settlement basis	Spot/two-day standard
Fixing period for derivatives contracts	Two-day rate fixing convention
Business days	TARGET operating days

Conventions for euro bond market	
Day count basis	Actual/actual
Quotation basis	Decimals
Business days	TARGET operating days
Coupon frequency	No recommendation
Settlement dates	T+3

Conventions for foreign exchange market	
Settlement timing	Spot conventions
Foreign exchange quotation	Rule 'Certain for Uncertain'
Reference rate	ECB responsible for publishing daily reference rate

Figure 18.4   **Harmonized conventions for securities and forex trading**
Source: Association of the Banking and Financial Industry

As far as redenomination is concerned, all member states have decided to convert all or most of their tradable government debt from national currencies into euro on the first weekend in January 1999. This ensures that a large and liquid pool of euro assets is available from the start of monetary union. The redenomination methodologies adopted by the eleven EMU member states differ. Most European countries have opted for the so called 'bottom-up' method, which starts with each individual holding being converted into euro using the fixed conversion rates and rounded to two decimal places (i.e. to the nearest cent). France and the Netherlands have adopted the 'bottom-up' approach. They will however round the redenominated amount down to one euro and settle the difference in cash. Italy and Austria favour the 'top-down' approach, which applies the conversion to the minimum denomination of the bond specified in the terms of issue. Details on the various methods of redenomination that different countries will employ are provided in the annex.

As to the redenomination of existing corporate debt, it is expected to be a continuous process as opposed to a 'Big Bang' approach. Most private issuers will probably prefer to leave their issues denominated in their legacy currency until maturity, as the redenomination process can prove quite expensive, as well as a lengthy and laborious process. In any case, however, cash conversion (nominal maintained in the currency of denomination, but proceeds expressed in euro) will become compulsory by the end of the transition period on 31 December 2001.

To summarize, the euro implies the creation of a domestic European bond market that will rival the US dollar and Japanese yen market in size. Initially, as the participating markets all bring their own unique characteristics to the party, the euro bond market will maintain a segmented character. However, both the redenomination of tradable government debt and the harmonization of market conventions across the euro zone will enable the rapid creation of a liquid and deep bond market. Indeed, governments have strongly committed to convert their debt into the single currency as soon as the conversion weekend. The stance of private borrowers is more uncertain, especially because of the costs implied by the redenomination process. Although only few corporate borrowers will opt for the redenomination of their outstanding debt, most new issues will be in euro.

2. Credit aspects

The elimination of currency risk within the EMU zone means that the valuation of securities in the euro bond market will largely be determined by credit considerations, liquidity, and a residual set of factors such as name recognition and investors' preferences. Presently, government bond yields in Europe are, in the main, determined by a country's exchange rate, short- and long-term interest rates, and the direction of German government bond yields, a fact which is borne out by various econometric studies. The remaining influence on government bond yields reflects the market's perception of a sovereign's creditworthiness.

Ratings assigned by rating agencies like Moody's and Standard & Poor's reflect the probability of default, i.e. failure of timely repayment of debt obligations. But to the credit rating agencies, EMU represents a unique case. The closest comparison of an EMU member state is perhaps a Canadian provincial government. However, the absence in Europe of a supranational power like the Canadian federal government clearly makes the two very different. There are at least two other distinguishing features of EMU. Firstly, the individual member states will continue to have extensive tax raising powers—within the boundaries of the recently-agreed stability pact. Secondly, the member states are subject to the 'no bail-out' clause of the Maastricht Treaty (Article 104b) which stipulates that neither the Community, nor a member state, will be liable for the debts of either a member government or its public authorities. The approach of the major international credit rating agencies to sovereign risk analysis is changing in the light of EMU to incorporate a larger focus on the 'financial flexibility' of a member state as measured by, say, its tax competitiveness, indebtedness, unfunded pension liabilities, etc.

The two leading credit rating agencies, Moody's and Standard & Poor's, have both outlined their approach in analysing credit risk of EMU sovereigns. Both rating agencies have established a Triple-A ceiling for the EMU zone. A critical assumption in this is that EMU is irreversible. A residual foreign currency risk brought about by the possibility of partial break-up of EMU would justify a lower overall rating for the EMU area. Another fact to take into account with respect to the sovereign ceiling is that it will no longer be determined by the foreign currency rating of individual member states. Normally, the country ceiling is set at the same level as the rating for foreign currency obligations of the sovereign. However, under EMU, there are effectively no foreign currency constraints on an entity domiciled within the EMU zone, even if the sovereign rating of the country within which the issuer is domiciled is below Triple-A. Thus the Triple-A sovereign ceiling applies to the entire EMU bloc.

As far as their approach to sovereign ratings are concerned, however, the leading agencies do not have similar views. Standard & Poor's is of the opinion that the euro should be considered as a foreign currency debt obligation, since a participating member state gives up the right to monetize its debt. Moody's, on the other hand, would rate a country's euro-denominated debt at the same level as its local or domestic currency debt rating, on the basis that the euro will still be the domestic currency of each country and that participating member states still have extensive national tax raising powers in the euro.

As a consequence of the Triple-A ceiling for the EMU area, some companies, banks or local authorities could end up with higher credit ratings than their 'parent' government if the latter indeed has a lower credit rating. Both Moody's and Standard & Poor's have confirmed this possibility—however, if it happens at all, it is likely to be confined to regional, municipal or government-controlled institutions, rather than to private sector corporations.

Although it is unfortunate that the rating agencies do not agree on the approach towards sovereign credit ratings under EMU, the difference is largely semantic and more a point for academic debate, rather than a potential major influence on government bond spreads. For a start, many prospective member states have enjoyed a Triple-A rating on both their domestic and foreign debt, like Austria, France, Germany and the Netherlands, for example. For those countries where the foreign and domestic ratings of the various ratings agencies differed, there has been a convergence of the credit ratings. Following the decision of the May 1998 EU Summit on the participating member states for EMU, not only was the distinction between a domestic and foreign debt rating abolished for the eleven 'ins', other rating adjustments were also made. Both the pre- and post-May 1998 ratings are summarized in Figure 18.5. In addition, rating agencies have acknowledged that there is a general trend of euro-11 ratings to converge longer-term towards Triple-A.

If, in fact, the importance of credit in the assessment of relative bond yields will increase, then where will credit spreads of the EU sovereign states trade in the euro market? At the time of writing, with less than six months to go before the start of the monetary union, forward swap spreads to the 4 January 1999 indicate that at the long end of the curve, in the 10-year sector, spreads relative to Germany already trade virtually flat. This sharp convergence has taken place between the prospective EMU countries as they have economically converged, which has been reflected in the convergence of their credit rating and as people have anticipated that EMU will 'lock-in' tight credit spread levels, presumably for an indefinite period of time.

Different analysts have made different conclusions about the prospect of sovereign credit spreads under EMU. A number of analysts argue that credit spreads will become rather more volatile than they have been in the run-up to EMU. These analysts tend to have little confidence in the

Credit ratings: not much agency agreement...

| | Pre-EU Summit May 1998 | | | | New ratings | |
| | Moody's | | Standard & Poor's | | Moody's | S&P |
	Foreign	*Domestic*	*Foreign*	*Domestic*	*Domestic*	*Foreign*
Austria	Aaa	Aaa	AAA	AAA	Aaa	AAA
Belgium	Aa1	Aa1	AAA	AA+	Aa1	AA+
Finland	Aaa	Aa1	AAA	AA	Aaa	AA
France	Aaa	Aaa	AAA	AAA	Aaa	AAA
Germany	Aaa	-	AAA	AAA	Aaa	AAA
Ireland	Aaa	Aa1	AAA	AA	Aaa	AA+
Italy	Aa3	Aa3	AAA	AA	Aa3	AA
Luxembourg	-	-	AAA	AAA	-	AAA
Netherlands	Aaa	-	AAA	AAA	Aaa	AAA
Portugal	Aa2	Aa3	AAA	AA	Aa2	AA-
Spain	Aa2	Aa2	AAA	AA	Aa2	AA

Figure 18.5   Pre- and post-May 1998 sovereign credit ratings
Source: Moody's, S&P

enforceability of the Stability and Growth Pact. Some go even as far as to suggest that EMU will soon encounter tensions in the fiscal area, pointing to rising unemployment levels in many countries and the ballooning pension fund liabilities. Paribas, on the other hand, believes that the delivery of the single currency and the discipline imposed by the Maastricht Treaty and the stability pact will cause a further compression of credit spreads within Europe. Our regular EMU survey amongst international investors have shown that, although declining, scepticism on the sustainability of EMU has persisted with the weighted probability attached to EMU breaking up either during the transition period or post-2002 by investors still being 13 per cent in July 1998 (versus 87 per cent of investors believing that EMU will not break up). This belief is priced into spread levels. In addition, there has been a movement to improve the liquidity of government bond markets in many countries which will also lead to a spread tightening. Figure 18.6 summarizes our projected euro bond spreads for various sections of the curve relative to Germany. As

Government bonds will trade in a tight range...

	Basis point spread to Germany			
	2-yr	5-yr	10-yr	30-yr
Austria	0 to 5	0 to 5	0 to 5	0 to 5
Belgium	0 to 5	5 to 10	10 to 15	5 to 10
Finland	0 to 5	5 to 10	10 to 15	-
France	-5 to 0	-5 to 0	0 to 5	0 to 5
Ireland	0 to 5	5 to 10	10 to 15	-
Italy	5 to 10	10 to 15	10 to 20	10 to 20
Luxembourg	0 to 5	5 to 10	5 to 10	-
Netherlands	0 to 5	0 to 5	0 to 5	0 to 5
Portugal	5 to 10	10 to 15	15 to 20	-
Spain	0 to 5	10 to 15	10 to 15	5 to 15

Figure 18.6   Projected sovereign spreads post-EMU
Source: Paribas

illustrated, we forecast a narrow 20 basis point spread range across the 10-year sector in Europe beyond January 1999. We see potential for these spreads to narrow even further if the market adopts the view that EMU is sustainable and that policies being pursued will lead to an eventual unified credit rating across EMU countries.

The much larger emphasis on credit under EMU, together with the fact that the bond markets have already converged and absolute yield levels in G7 markets are at historical lows, have led to a surge of interest in credit products amongst investors this year. Accustomed to being able to pick up significant yield through country and currency diversification in the past, investors had to turn elsewhere to ensure the performance of their bond portfolios. However, a crisis in the emerging markets of Asia and most recently Russia have left investors with little other choice than to try and pick up yield through credit risk diversification. Particularly in Europe, where investors have traditionally held a defensive attitude towards credit, this has marked a significant change. As they have been forced to move down the credit curve, there is indeed evidence that investors are or have been able to amend their investment criteria. Non-sovereign bonds in European currencies, including domestic and corporate bonds, have therefore benefited from a larger interest. As an extension of this, the high yield bond sector in Europe, which in practice comprises corporate bond issues with a credit rating below BB+, has strongly emerged as well as other credit-driven products like mortgage- and asset-backed securities, subordinated debt and others (see Figure 18.7). It is generally expected that this trend will continue as the borrowing requirement of EMU sovereigns decline and as EMU will continue to transform the bond markets into credit driven markets. Besides, European corporates, who in the past have heavily relied on bank and syndicated loans for their financing, will find funding through bond issues increasingly attractive in an EMU environment. First, the process of rationalization and consolidation in the European banking sector will result in banks offering less favourable terms on loans. Secondly, bond markets will become more efficient as a result of the single currency, thus offering more attractive terms. The future of European bond markets will be characterized by a much greater sectoral, rather than country, approach—where credit analysis of issues will be vital in the identification of relative value.

The high-yield market is growing rapidly

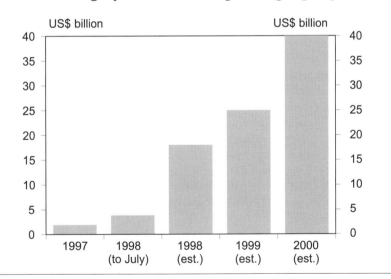

Figure 18.7   European high-yield issuance
Source: Paribas

In summary, one of the main implications of the advent of the euro will be the larger role that credit will play in the valuation of securities. With regard to sovereign ratings, EMU represents a unique situation for the credit rating agencies and it is unfortunate that the major agencies do not seem to agree on their approach towards sovereign ratings. That being said, all have confirmed a Triple-A rating as a sovereign ceiling for EMU and the credit ratings of the EMU sovereigns have tended to converge. Paribas projects a tight spread range of up to 20 basis points between the government bonds of the euro-11 countries. Driven by the prospect of the euro, developments in the credit domain of the non-sovereign sector are also already under way. Amongst the most important of these is a deeper and more liquid corporate bond market, which includes the development of a high-yield market in Europe. In this more credit-dominated environment, the 'winners' will be those with a fundamental understanding of credit risk.

3. Benchmark

The analysis in the previous section on sovereign credit risk highlights that there will be effectively eleven different sovereign yield curves under EMU, albeit all in euro. The reason is that, even among member states with a similar credit rating, differences in credit risk will exist as there will be differences in the level of financial flexibility of each state. It may appear as if securities of the various participating governments in the euro all lie on the same curve—assuming that the states have very similar economic and fiscal profiles, and no serious political tensions are present. But, however small these differences may be, if the credit risk of a country suddenly deteriorates, a rapid rise in the yield of its debt relative to the others will be observable. Therefore, debt of different sovereign borrowers should still be thought of as making up individual yield curves. At the very short end of the curve, money market rates will be much more—if not entirely— similar, as a result of the ECB setting one level of short-term interest rates for the whole EMU zone. Similarly, although there will be at least two euro interbank rates quoted (EURIBOR and euro LIBOR), one euro swap curve is likely to emerge.

Thus, with the euro market representing this unique situation of eleven different sovereign yield curves and one swap curve, the question arises as to which of these curves will become the benchmark. This has been a question of debate amongst financial analysts. The answer to this question largely depends also on the way in which a benchmark is defined. If a benchmark is the curve which is most often being used as the reference curve, then there is a lot to say for the euro swap curve to become the benchmark. As the euro bond market will become a more credit curve-driven market, more bonds will be priced on and quoted against the swap rate. The big advantage of the euro swap curve is also that, in contrast to the bond market, it is a single curve—which will therefore draw much liquidity.

Other analysts, however, argue that a benchmark comes closest to the risk-free rate of return—a concept born out of financial theory. The problem, though, is that under EMU (and as already identified by the credit rating agencies) governments lose their ability to monetize their debt and, as a result, government bond yield curves will contain more default risk, albeit at small absolute levels. The effect is that government bond yield curves become poorer approximations for the risk-free rate of return. However, swap rates represent counterparty risk—in that it contains default risk at the level of the counterparty in the swap—and are therefore not a good benchmark.

The right answer probably lies somewhere in the middle. Since, by comparison to the current situation, there is a shift in the whole concept of benchmark status in the case of the euro, we anticipate that both the swap curve and up to two sovereign yield curves will be used at different times as benchmark.

Which of the government bond curves, then, will be a benchmark under euro? The German government bond yield curve has been the benchmark in Europe for some time. The two principal factors behind this status are the size of the German economy (the largest in Europe in terms of GDP), and the proven ability of the Bundesbank in securing low inflation and a stable currency. However, with the creation of the euro, these factors will be shared with the rest of Euroland: Germany's economy will be absorbed in the single market and monetary policy will be set by the ECB. In the euro environment, it will be factors like liquidity, depth, sophistication, and transparency of a market and its procedures, that will be key in determining the benchmark. Comparing Germany and France, the only realistic contenders for euro benchmark status, reveals that it will be close call between French OATs and BTANs and German Bunds and BOBLs.

The French government has put in a tireless effort over the last decade to make its market more efficient. Amongst the numerous innovations have been larger size and more liquid issues, a regular auction calendar which is known in advance and new innovative products like Strips, TEC10 and, recently, inflation-linked bonds. Also, France has had a strong commitment to the single currency, shown through their domestic issuance programme in Ecu for many years and their determination to redenominate their existing government bonds into euros.

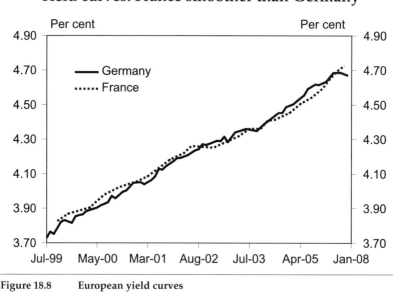

Yield curves: France smoother than Germany

Figure 18.8   **European yield curves**
Source: Paribas

This policy has borne fruit and the result has been that the average size of benchmarks is larger in France—contributing to a smoother yield curve—while issuing procedures contribute more to the efficiency and liquidity of the market in France than in Germany. The most important differences between the French and German markets lie in the fact that the repo market has always been more efficient in the former and also that, in France, Strips are actively traded. However, in many of these areas, Germany has been catching up with France during the last two years. For example, the issuance of long-term Bunds with a size of DM30bn has become the norm, the issuing calendar has become more transparent, Strips have been introduced (in July 1997) and minimum reserve requirements for repo operations have been abolished. The main advantage that Germany still has over France is that a much larger proportion of their debt is held with foreign investors—nearly 40 per cent, compared to only 11 per cent in France.

Paribas' conclusion to the benchmark issue is that it will be a combination of German and French securities. First of all, we anticipate that the German and the French curves will be trading very close to each other and that there will be many parts of the curve where the two government bonds will be interchangeable. Secondly, the curve is likely to be traded in sectors, rendering it possible for a different benchmark bond to be chosen for each sector. As the liquidity of the French market is better at the short end of the curve (out to four years), and again at the very long end (beyond 10 years), French government bonds would readily lend themselves as benchmarks in these sectors, with German government bonds in the remainder.

To summarize, the benchmark status for the euro market has been hotly contested—with both Germany and France playing hard to win the honours. In addition, it has to be recognized that the euro swap curve will become much more important and will also more frequently be used as a reference. The question as to which sovereign curve will become the benchmark lies with both the abilities of both Germany and France to modernize their capital markets. Although France took the lead in this area more than a decade ago, Germany has been able to catch up. Germany does have the additional advantage of being currently seen as the benchmark in Europe, and traditionally a more substantial part of their debt has been held outside their own domestic market. Paribas believes that in the sovereign sector the benchmark will consist of a combination of German and French securities.

4. Futures contracts

The rapid progress towards a euro benchmark curve has caused liquidity to consolidate around a restricted number of futures contracts. Trading volumes in the 10-year Austrian, Dutch, Belgium, Finnish, Ecu and, to a lesser extent, French bond futures have recently decreased. This is consistent with the rise in volumes for German 10-year Bund futures and with the strong convergence which has taken place in core Europe (Figure 18.9).

Consolidation is explained by financial and macroeconomic convergence, as well as credit issues. As futures are extensively used for hedging purposes, the fact that the correlation between the 10-year Deutschemark and other core European yields is virtually 1 now implies that hedging of these various bonds can easily be done by one and the same contract. Consolidation is also justified on credit grounds, as sovereign credit ratings have become very similar for the euro-11 countries.

The development in the futures market in southern European countries still offers, at this stage, a different picture. Indeed, volumes on Italian, Spanish and Portuguese 10-year bond futures show little sign of consolidating into the Bund futures contract. The correlation between 10-year lire, peseta and escudo yields and the Deutschemark is still too low to allow for an efficient hedge using Bund futures, while yield spreads

Bond futures trading moving to Germany

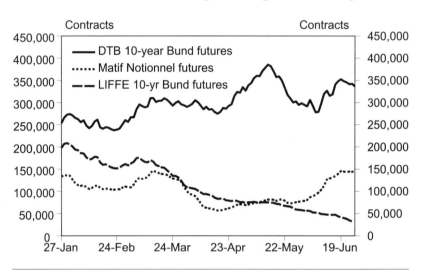

Contracts   Contracts

450,000 ── DTB 10-year Bund futures
400,000 ····· Matif Notionnel futures
350,000 ── LIFFE 10-yr Bund futures

450,000
400,000
350,000
300,000
250,000
200,000
150,000
100,000
50,000
0

27-Jan   24-Feb   24-Mar   23-Apr   22-May   19-Jun

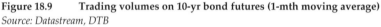

Figure 18.9   **Trading volumes on 10-yr bond futures (1-mth moving average)**
Source: Datastream, DTB

between southern and core Europe also need to decrease further. However, as the yield correlations to Germany increase, and market perceptions become more positive on former high-yielders, we should see lire, peseta and escudo futures consolidating into euro futures as well.

10-year Bund futures are currently traded by both LIFFE and DTB. In terms of volumes and open interest, DTB is experiencing substantial growth. Since February 1998, the open interest on DTB has risen above LIFFE and currently represents around 70 per cent of the market. The market perceives that one of the main elements behind the success of DTB is the use of electronic trading, which is considered as less expensive and more flexible than pit trading.

LIFFE and DTB also compete on 5-year BOBL futures, where DTB is again the leader. Furthermore, the Frankfurt-based exchange also quotes a 2-year futures contract, the open interest of which has risen from 52,000 in March 1997 to a current level of 170,000.

In the money market segment, the position of LIFFE is substantially stronger. In euro short-term interest rates, LIFFE dominates with a share of around 94 per cent, while DTB, which quotes a 3-month and a 1-month Euro-Deutschemark contract, has proved unable to attract substantial volumes so far.

However, this situation is likely to change as the leading position of LIFFE is challenged by the growing attractiveness of electronic trading. A number of US houses have suggested that they may favour a DTB 3-month Euro-Deutschemark contract, as this is electronically traded. Another critical factor for the success of short-term interest rate futures will be the choice of the reference rate. Both DTB and LIFFE currently use LIBOR rates. However, DTB has indicated that it considers introducing a contract based on EURIBOR, shortly before the start of EMU. EURIBOR is the alternative euro rate launched by the European Banking Federation and is based on quotations from a panel of sixty-four banks. The difference in the credit rating of the banks in the EURIBOR panel might lead euro LIBOR to trade at a negative spread to EURIBOR. Of course, this and other elements including the liquidity and the reliability of the reference rate, will be critical factors for the success of short-term interest rate contracts.

Rising volumes on Bund futures suggest that it has currently been selected as the benchmark contract in core Europe. However, this contract has a fundamental weakness, in that it only allows for bonds from one issuer to be delivered. Going forward the question arises whether: (i) a multiple deliverable basket will be introduced; or (ii) whether an alternative euro futures contract will be launched.

Various European exchanges have often mentioned the intention to introduce a multiple deliverable basket on the euro. In particular, MATIF recently announced the launch of a euro 'All Sovereigns' futures contract; its deliverable basket includes government bonds issued by Germany, France, Holland, Italy and Spain. In this case, lower-rated paper is virtually certain of being the cheapest-to-deliver (CTD). As far as other futures exchanges are concerned, the risks embedded in this decision have, so far, restrained LIFFE or DTB from action.

A suitable alternative to bond futures is a futures contract linked to euro swap rates. This prospect is currently being analysed by LIFFE. Indeed, a euro swap futures contract has a number of attractive features. For example, the fact that the contract is cash settled eliminates the inefficiencies linked to the physical delivery, including the likelihood of squeezes on the CTD. A further critical factor is the fact that the contract is based on swap rates. This may prove attractive for traders of corporate bonds and investors, as well as primary desks, who could be more inclined to use exchanged futures, rather than OTC swaps, to hedge their positions. A major boost to the contract should come from corporate bond trading. The European corporate bond market is still rather small, but is expected to develop strongly with the introduction of the euro. In addition, some market participants argue that the euro LIBOR curve might gradually supersede the euro bond yield curve and become the reference for government bond trading. The main rationale behind this would be the uniqueness and smoothness of the euro LIBOR curve compared to a euro bond curve, which some expect to be fragmented by different credit spreads.

In summary, trading volumes on European futures exchanges have recently staged a strong consolidation around Bund futures. This development, which will continue as we approach January 1999, is likely to result in the dominance of a few, selected futures exchanges.

Consolidation around Bund futures substantially augments the likelihood of squeezes on the CTD. In particular, these depend on who is holding the bond, conditions in the repo market and the supply in these bonds. Research indicates that squeezes on the Bund market are likely to accelerate in the coming months, especially if the Bund futures contract continues to be perceived as the benchmark for EMU.

5. Implications for investors

For investors, as the landscape of financial markets is changing, they very much need to change their investment strategy as well. Perhaps the most noticeable impact will be on the composition of their benchmark index. Most fund managers measure their performance against a benchmark index. They allocate a certain weight to each market and, on a frequent basis, fund managers decide how much the exposure of their investments should deviate from that of their index (where exposure is a combination of total allocation to a market and the duration of the allocation). A relatively higher exposure in an upward-trending market generally results in a better return relative to the index, and vice versa.

As illustrated in Figure 18.10, the largest component in the most widely-used benchmark indices is currently the US$-bloc, with an allocation of between 38 per cent and 44 per cent, followed by Japan with an allocation of between 14 per cent and 19 per cent. The largest European market, Germany, has an allocation of only around 9 per cent. Based on a simple summation of the percentage allocation to the individual markets of the monetary union, the arrival of the euro is expected to create one single component of between 32 per cent and 33 per cent (see Figure 18.11)

The effect of this larger euro component on portfolio allocations is likely to differ with the domestic base of investors. No large portfolio reallocation between the three major currency blocs of the US dollar, the euro and the Japanese yen should be expected from European investors, since most of them naturally hold a diversified European portfolio already. However, for European domestic institutions, the euro does imply that they can

Each EU country is represented by a separate index...

	Salomon Brothers WGBI	JP Morgan (traded)
US-bloc*	38.7	43.3
Japan	18.8	14.3
Germany	9.4	8.9
France	7.5	8.1
Holland	3.4	3.6
Austria	0.9	n/a
Belgium	2.6	2.9
Ireland	0.4	n/a
Finland	0.5	n/a
Italy	6.3	4.9
Spain	2.8	3.1
United Kingdom	6.5	7.1
Denmark	1.5	1.6
Sweden	1.4	1.6
Switzerland	0.5	n/a

Figure 18.10   Post-EMU benchmark bond indices
US, Canada, Australia
Source: Salomon Brothers DW, JP Morgan

...but the total euro weight is around one-third

	Salomon Brothers WGBI	JP Morgan (traded)
US-bloc*	38.7	43.3
Japan	18.8	14.3
Euro	**33.8**	**31.5**
United Kingdom	6.5	7.1
Denmark	1.5	1.6
Sweden	1.4	1.6
Switzerland	0.5	n/a

Figure 18.11   Post-EMU benchmark bond indices
US, Canada, Australia
Source: Salomon Brothers DW, JP Morgan

invest in the other EMU markets freely without imposing additional currency risk. Indeed, the decision in May 1998 of the EU heads of state to pre-announce the fixings of the conversion rates has greatly accelerated this process. As European domestic investors perceive that forex risk with other prospective euro-currencies has virtually dissipated, they have already started to explore other markets of the monetary union. Those investors who are still constrained by a currency-matching rule will be able to invest on a truly pan-European basis only from 1 January 1999. There is however also evidence that the traditional liking for currency diversification amongst the European has encouraged some to start considering more non-EMU countries and to even include these in their index going forward. The most likely candidates for inclusion are the Scandinavian countries, and countries like Poland, Hungary and the Czech Republic which have recently sought admission to the EU.

Non-European investors, on the other hand, may have had a tendency to de-emphasize Europe in their benchmark, as a heavy involvement in European markets would require knowledge of the economic and political situation of each individual country. Also, a number of European markets have hitherto been too small to accommodate large-scale trading, with the result that they have usually been the first to be removed from the benchmark. The euro, which will constitute a large part of their index, will thus provide these investors with one large domestic market, representing the same currency risk, and in which they can seek the instruments which represents the best risk/reward relationship. It is from these non-European investors that we can expect portfolio shifts into the euro, particularly if the euro establishes itself as a credible currency.

Investors world-wide have thus started to redefine their investment strategy and performance index in the light of EMU in terms of regions, sectors and products. In order to provide further insights into these decisions, which will determine the future shape of the euro capital markets, Paribas conducted an extensive survey among European and American bond portfolio managers in the first quarter of 1998. Some 98 portfolio managers in the US, and 55 portfolio managers in Europe, were extensively surveyed on the impact of EMU on their asset allocation process. The results of the survey can be classified into three different areas: credit risk changes, reallocations as a result of the euro and benchmark updates.

Indeed the most significant results of the survey were in the area of credit risk, as they clearly point to a substantial increase in the holdings of credit products, both in the US and in Europe. In fact, more than half of the US investors (57 per cent) who currently hold European non-sovereign paper, anticipates a rise in these holdings. The increase will mainly favour

European corporate and bank bonds, which are on average expected to rise a substantial 40 per cent. The impact of EMU on high-yield holdings is more subdued with 45 per cent of those who hold non-sovereign paper planning to increase their investment in this area. Likewise, in Europe, bond portfolio managers cited a greater willingness to diversify their credit risk. In particular, 85 per cent of the European respondents anticipates changes in the EMU non-sovereign holdings. Of these, 70 per cent expect the share of corporate and bank bonds in European portfolios to increase by an average of 21 per cent in the near future. Overall, therefore, the anticipated involvement of European investors in the euro credit market is greater than in the US. On the other hand, the stance towards European high-yield paper is more cautious with only 30 per cent of the Europeans expecting exposure to this sector to increase (Figure 18.12).

Investor survey highlights appetite for credit risk

Percentages anticipating changes in EMU non-sovereign holdings:

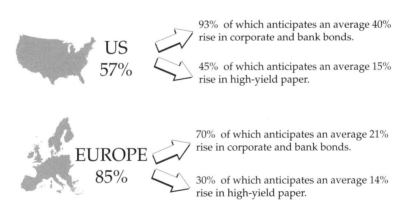

93% of which anticipates an average 40% rise in corporate and bank bonds.

45% of which anticipates an average 15% rise in high-yield paper.

70% of which anticipates an average 21% rise in corporate and bank bonds.

30% of which anticipates an average 14% rise in high-yield paper.

Figure 18.12   Changes in non-sovereign holdings
Source: Paribas EMU Investor Survey, Q1 1998

In the area of structural reallocations of the portfolio, the main changes in the US seem to be a rise in the Ecu/euro proportion from 12 per cent to 19 per cent of the overall European portfolio by January 1999. At this stage, no evidence can be found of an intended substantial portfolio shift away from the US dollar to the euro. In Europe, the only change of significance within the European portfolio is an expected increase in the holdings in Eastern Europe from zero per cent to three per cent by January 1999.

In the area of benchmark changes, it was evident that a majority of bond portfolio managers in both the US and Europe will start to treat Europe as one block in their index. The most interesting result here, though, was that the changes to the benchmark index are likely to take place sooner than many would expect. In the US, for example, over one-half (56 per cent) of those who anticipate to make changes to their benchmark indices would do so either during 1998, or shortly after 1 January 1999. Similarly, in Europe, a considerable 30 per cent of the portfolio managers indicated that the changes will be implemented during 1998.

To summarize, in the brave new world, there will be a reduced capacity to perform from country allocation within Europe for fund managers. This implication will particularly be felt with European investors, who traditionally have had a liking for diversification. In this environment, investors have sought to explore both other markets and credit products. This has been done within the context of a general reassessment of the asset allocation and investment strategy. A very important aspect of this is how the benchmark indices of investors will change, as this will anchor the process going forward and will reflect the decisions that various investors have made. The outcome of this process are likely to be felt in the form of portfolio reallocations, both within the European markets as well as globally, but more so in the area of credit as portfolio managers will seek to increase their holdings of European credit paper. Given the extent of the convergence of capital markets in Europe, this process is already largely underway.

6. Implications for borrowers

Without doubt, the euro also has important implications for issuers, not least the fact that they would be well advised to move in tandem with investors if they are to maintain competitive bids for funds. With the focus on credit increasing, in particular for European investors—which lag their US counterparts in this respect—the key to a successful placement programme will be an issuer's perceived credit status.

Borrowers have already started to act in anticipation of the single currency. January 1997 marked the birth of a new 'euro-style' bond market. Since then, this market segment has grown very rapidly to the extent that by the end of June 1998, a total of US$26.3bn euro-style bonds were placed in the market. The spectacular growth of this new market segment is illustrated in Figure 18.13, which shows that, despite the fact that the

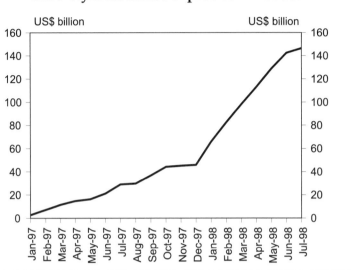

Figure 18.13   Cumulative growth of euro-style debt

Source: Capital Data Bondware

market had been growing steadily in the course of 1997, euro-style bonds gained their real momentum in 1998.

The rationale for tapping into the euro market, in one form or another, is obvious. As the official start date of EMU draws closer, investors want to build an exposure to euro-denominated bonds. Through launching euro-style issues, a borrower can create large, liquid issues denominated in the new single currency. This is indeed the crux of a euro-style issue as it includes specific clauses in the prospectus which either allow for a consolidation of a number of issues into one large size euro-denominated bond, or allow the bond to be denominated in euro prior to it officially coming into existence.

A euro-style issue allows borrowers to position their credit ahead of EMU. In particular, issuers who have infrequently tapped the individual European markets can pre-market their credit strength and enable their name to become familiar amongst a diverse range of domestic European investors. Issuers acting on behalf of those sovereigns or supranationals which have a positive attitude towards participation in EMU have been able to send a strong signal to the market, underlining their commitment to the euro, through the issuance of euro-style bonds. They were thus often the ones who led the way in the euro-style bond market. However, as the market has grown, with several euro-style bonds being greeted by an enthusiastic response from investors, bond issues from large European corporations and non-European sovereigns and others have followed suit.

A euro-style issue has proved to be an excellent vehicle to tap into a wide and growing investor base. Demand for these bonds has been good, and has emanated not only from across the whole of Europe, but also from the Middle East, Asia and the United States.

Euro-style issues have been launched in a variety of shapes and forms. Broadly speaking, three main structures can be distinguished: an exchangeable issue, a parallel bond and a euro issue. Below, we discuss each in turn:

Exchangeable bond

Through an exchangeable bond, a borrower issues a eurobond, denominated in one of the currencies which will participate in EMU, carrying the same coupon and maturity as a specific domestic issue. After EMU has started, both bonds will be re-denominated in euros allowing for an exchangeability between the two. A schematic representation of an exchangeable issue is given in Figure 18.14.

In the launch of its very first euro-style bond, the Republic of Austria introduced the first exchangeable bond. In this particular case, the exchange is unilateral from the eurobond into the domestic issue and is at the bondholder's discretion. The Kingdom of Spain went one step further in July 1997, by issuing a eurobond compulsorily exchangeable into a domestic issue.

Parallel bond

Through a parallel bond, a borrower launches two bonds with identical terms and conditions in two different currencies which will both participate in EMU. After EMU has started, both bonds will re-denominate into euro, allowing for the consolidation of both issues into one bond. Consolidation occurs without the explicit consent of the bond holder. A schematic representation of a parallel issue is shown in Figure 18.15.

There are different variations of the same parallel type structure. A parallel bond is also referred to as a 'twin bond' if there are only two tranches, or as a 'catamaran bond' if the coupon is floating. A 'tributary bond' is when the tranches (two or more) are issued at different dates. The last structure has the added advantage for borrowers in that it enables them to optimize the timing of the launch.

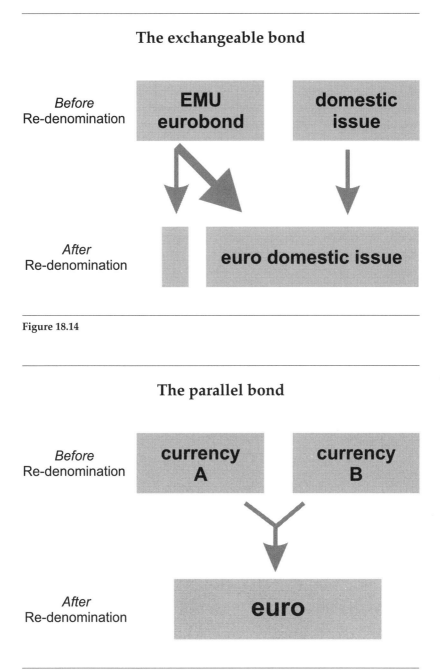

The exchangeable bond

Before
Re-denomination

EMU eurobond

domestic issue

After
Re-denomination

euro domestic issue

Figure 18.14

The parallel bond

Before
Re-denomination

currency A

currency B

After
Re-denomination

euro

Figure 18.15

Euro-issue

A euro-issue is a bond in which the payments are in euros. However, until EMU takes place, the borrower guarantees to pay in Ecu at an exchange rate of one Ecu for one euro. A schematic representation of a euro-issue is shown given in Figure 18.16. The first euro-issue was launched in January 1997 by the European Investment Bank. Although in 1997 all euro-issues were issued in eurobond format, the issuance of euro-issues in domestic format has emerged in 1998 (e.g. Kingdom of Sweden 5 per cent Jan 2009).

In turn, different variations on these three major structures exist. Moreover, 1998 saw the first euro-denominated FRNs, convertible bonds and the first German Pfandbriefe in euros. As new asset classes in euros were opened up, two other strong themes in the euro-style bond market can be distinguished. First, there has been a tendency to issue bigger size bonds. As investors were restructuring their portfolios in favour of the euro, demand for euro bonds far outstripped the redemption of Ecu/euro issues. For example, in the past, an issue of Ecu 1bn in the Ecu eurobond sector was already considered large but, in the first quarter of 1998, EUR1.5-2bn soon became the norm for a sovereign issuer. In February 1998, the Republic of Italy was even able to place a EUR4bn issue in the

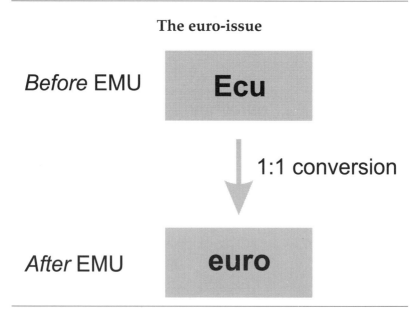

The euro-issue

Before EMU   Ecu

1:1 conversion

After EMU   **euro**

Figure 18.16   Euro issue

More and more issuance...

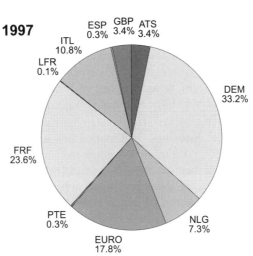

1997

ESP 0.3%
GBP 3.4%
ATS 3.4%
ITL 10.8%
LFR 0.1%
DEM 33.2%
FRF 23.6%
PTE 0.3%
NLG 7.3%
EURO 17.8%

Figure 18.17 Currency composition of euro-style debt issuance (1997)
Source: Capital Data Bondware

...in euro

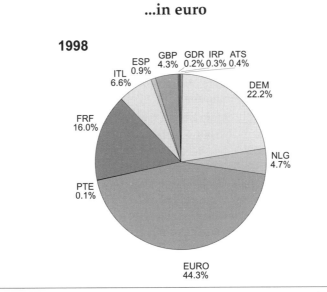

1998

ESP 0.9%
GBP 4.3%
GDR 0.2%
IRP 0.3%
ATS 0.4%
ITL 6.6%
DEM 22.2%
FRF 16.0%
NLG 4.7%
PTE 0.1%
EURO 44.3%

Figure 18.18 Currency composition of euro-style debt issuance (1998)
Source: Capital Data Bondware

market. This was the largest fixed rate eurobond in any currency, including the US dollar, ever.

The second theme has been for borrowers to continue to move away from national currencies to the euro. In 1997, parallel and tributary bonds became rather popular and as these tend to be issued in national currencies, euro-denominated issues accounted for less than 20 per cent of the overall euro-style issuance. In 1998, however, the share of euro-issues has shot up to 45 per cent, reflecting the fact that many borrowers have found it more attractive to issue in euros straight away (Figures 18.17 & 18.18).

To summarize, the euro-style debt market has achieved rapid success since the start of 1997. With many investors restructuring their portfolio and willing to increase their exposure to the euro, this should not come as a great surprise. In fact, for those borrowers who wish to position their credit, and their name, ahead of the creation of what will undoubtedly become a very large market, this sector represents a unique opportunity to do so. Now that the eleven member states for the monetary union have been chosen and the foreign exchange rate risk between the EMU currencies has been virtually eliminated, we expect this new market segment to continue to grow rapidly.

6. Conclusion

The introduction of the euro will have significant implications for European bond markets. In this chapter, we have analysed the impact of this new market in terms of size, notable features, credit aspects, benchmark choice and futures contracts. We have also analysed the implications for both investors and borrowers. In this final section, we shall briefly cover our main findings:

The euro will instantly create a bond market of a size of around US$6.3 trillion, second only to the US bond market. In terms of global government bond indices, the weight of Euroland will be greater than 30 per cent, while the US-bloc will constitute around 40 per cent.

The development of a deep and transparent bond market will be supported by the strong commitment made by the member states to redenominate all or part of their tradable debt from the domestic currency into euros. The conversion will take place during the first weekend in January. A further important step is the agreement on a common conventions for the bond, forex and money markets. These common conventions will be adopted for newly-issued debt after January 1999. In addition, EMU governments have decided to alter old conventions in order to bring them into line with the new ones.

The euro market will be a credit dominated market. With the elimination of currency risk, the valuation of securities will largely be done on the basis of credit aspects. Rating agencies, to whom EMU represents a unique case, agree that a Triple-A sovereign ceiling should apply, but they disagree in their approach towards sovereign ratings. Yet, with the recent convergence in sovereign credit rating, this is currently largely a matter of academic debate. Credit-driven products like high-yield bonds, subordinated debt and asset-backed securities have strongly emerged as a result of EMU as well, and it is widely expected that these trends will accelerate near term.

It will be conceptually right to think of different yield curves within the euro bond market, since sovereigns still have considerable tax raising and spending powers. At the very short end, one money market curve should emerge, as the ECB will operate one key interest rate for the entire euro zone. The latter is also likely to ensure that there will be one euro swap curve.

Of these difference yield curves, none will represent the true risk-free rate of return. Certainly, the swap curve will become a very important curve as the market becomes more credit driven. Benchmark status in the sovereign sector is expected to fall upon both Germany or France, where factors such as liquidity, depth and sophistication of their markets will determine exactly which of the two will be used for each sector of the sovereign segment.

Trading volumes on European futures exchanges have consolidated around Bund contracts, strengthening the position of Bunds in Euroland. This, however, substantially increases the chance of squeezes on the CTD and will affect the price action of the bonds in the deliverable basket. Therefore, it seems likely that a multiple deliverable basket will be introduced in the coming months.

The main implication for investors is the change in the composition of their benchmark index. This is likely to induce portfolio shifts into the euro from non-European investors. An extensive investor survey conducted by Paribas revealed that investors are prepared to take a greater credit risk in Euroland.

Borrowers have also already started to anticipate the single currency, as is evident from the issuance of euro-style debt since the start of 1997. Special structures like the euro-issue and parallel bonds have emerged, thereby allowing issuers to market their credit strength ahead of the establishment of the large euro market. The strong trends of 1998 are for larger issues and more issuance in euros compared to other currencies.

This chapter is by no means exhaustive and, and prior to the start of monetary union, further analysis of the impact of the euro on the bond market will no doubt be carried out. In addition, further in-depth analysis of each section in itself can, and almost certainly will, take place. Nevertheless, it is our hope that this chapter has enabled readers to gain a foundation into the principal effects of the euro on the European bond markets.

Of course, while EMU will require rapid and far-reaching changes to the market—some of which will be literally felt overnight in 1999—the wider implication of the single currency will only be realized over a longer period. It will take time to build a liquid and homogenous capital market of this size.

Chapter
18 APPENDIX
the *euro*

The redenomination of government debt

The following pages provide a tabular summary of the situation regarding the redenomination of government debt using information available as at 24 August 1998.

Member state	Affected issue	Date	Rounding basis	Rounding rule	Cash compensation	New minimum denomination	New minimum trading lot	ISIN charge	Interest conventions
Austria	Austrian government bonds traded on the Vienna Stock Exchange	1 Jan 99	Minimum denomination (top down)	Commercial rounding	No	EUR 0.01	EUR 0.01	No change	For newly-issued bonds from 4 Jan 99, interest calculation will be based on actual/actual. Decision is pending for existing issues
Belgium	Linear bonds (OLOs), Treasury certificates and Strips	2 Jan 99	Client position (bottom up)	Commercial rounding	No	EUR 0.01	Until 30.6.99: EUR 0.01. After 30.6.99: EUR 1, although investors are recommended to round up to EUR 1,000	No change	On 4 Jan 99, the interest calculation method for ALL issues, redenominated or not, will be as follows: OLOs: actual/actual; T-bills: actual/360. The new calculation rule will apply to the whole period since the last coupon payment.
Finland	Book entries of FIM serial bonds and obligations, Treasury bills	1 Jan 99	Client position (bottom up)	Commercial rounding	No	EUR 0.01	EUR 1,000. Odd lots can be traded, provided the amount exceeds the minimum trading lot. Possibility of issuers purchasing 'odd lots'	No change	The interest calculation method will change for new issues as follows: Bonds: actual/actual; T-bills: actual/360

Member state	Affected issue	Date	Rounding basis	Rounding rule	Cash compensation	New minimum denomination	New minimum trading lot	ISIN change	Interest conventions
France	All French government bonds, including CADES	1-3 Jan 99	Client position (bottom up)	Rounding down	Yes, at market prices + accrued interest. Legislation pending to cover tax implication	EUR 1 Stripped OAT coupons: EUR 0.25	EUR 1 Stripped OAT coupons: EUR 0.25	New ISIN	As existing interest rate calculation
Germany	All exchange-traded government bonds maturing after 20 Jan 1999	1 Jan 99	Client position (bottom up)	Commercial rounding	No	EUR 0.01	EUR 0.01	No change	For newly-issued bonds from 4 Jan 99, interest calculation will be based on actual/actual. For existing bonds, actual/actual will apply from first coupon date in 1999
Ireland	All government issues	1 Jan 99	Client position (bottom up)	Commercial rounding	No	EUR 0.01	EUR 0.01	No change	The interest calculation method will chnage for new issues as follows: Bonds: actual/actual T-bills: actual/360

Member state	Affected issue	Date	Rounding basis	Rounding rule	Cash compensation	New minimum denomination	New minimum trading lot	ISIN charge	Interest conventions
Italy	All tradable government debt	1 Jan 99	Minimum denomination (top down)	Rounding down	No	EUR 0.01	Intitially EUR 0.01, then subsequent repackaging of odd lots to EUR 1,000	No change	For new issues, the calculation will be: Bonds: actual/actual Money market instruments: actual/360 Reconventioning of existing debt is recommended but awaiting confirmation
Luxembourg	All OLUX issues. Other government issues will not be redenominated	1-3 Jan 99	Client position (bottom up)	Commercial rounding	No	To be confirmed	To be confirmed	No change	Interest calculation for all new government bonds issued wil be actual/actual
Netherlands	All government issues, with three exceptions	1 Jan 99	Client position (bottom up)	Issuer will round down and pay cash compensation but depository will round up at client level	Yes at depository level, not at client level	EUR 1	EUR 1	New ISIN	For new issues, the calculation will be Bonds: actual/actual Bills: actual/360 Reconventioning of existing debt is recommended but awaiting confirmation

Member state	Affected issue	Date	Rounding basis	Rounding rule	Cash compensation	New minimum denomination	New minimum trading lot	ISIN charge	Interest conventions
Portugal	All dematerialized government issues maturing after 31 Dec 1999	1 Jan 99	Client position (bottom up)	Commercial rounding	No	EUR 0.01	Not yet known	No change	For new issues, the calculation will be: Bonds: actual/actual Money market instruments: actual/360 Reconventioning of existing debt is recommended but awaiting confirmation
Spain	All government issues & public debt issues registered at Bank of Spain	1-3 Jan 99	Client position (bottom up)	Commercial rounding	No	EUR 0.01	Bonds and government notes: EUR 100. T-bills: EUR 10,000. Banks and brokers may purchase 'odd lots'	No change	For new issues, the calculation will be: Bonds: actual/actual Bills: actual/360 Will apply to existing debt

Figure 18.19 Redenomination table

Note: The above is accurate according to information available as at 15 May 1998
Source: Paribas Securities Services, Euroclear, Deutsche Borse Clearing, Bank of England

Chapter

19

Mike Young
& Peter Sullivan
Goldman Sachs

The euro and equity markets

EMU is here, or anyway nearly here. The only major unknowns for the transition to the single currency are the rate at which member currencies will translate into euros and the level at which short-term interest rates will converge. It is important at this juncture to remind ourselves that, while the recent focus has been on the European Central Bank and exchange rates, EMU is about more than its members sharing a currency. It is a further step in the process of creating the single market and it is about a shift in the philosophy of government being embraced by some, Italy and Spain, and being accepted grudgingly and with much opposition by others, most notably France. That philosophy reflects a more restrained role for national governments in managing economies and is forcefully reflected in the Maastricht Treaty limitations on government budgets and in the independence of the European Central Bank.

In prospect, EMU already has had substantial effects on the behaviour of investors, corporations and governments. We believe that these changes can be extrapolated into the future and will, in general, improve the European equity environment. Among the most important effects for equity investors, we expect that EMU will: (1) improve the risk reward opportunities for equity investors; (2) improve liquidity in equity markets; (3) accelerate the pace of restructuring, rationalization and consolidation in European industry; and (4) raise sustainable valuations through the present asset price cycle relative to history. These conclusions flow from our views regarding the impact of the changes in investor, corporate and government behaviour.

Parenthetically, we must add that these views are contingent on our assumption that for politicians in Euroland there is enormous pressure to make EMU 'work', in the sense of making the euro area a low-inflation, moderate-growth environment. While we would certainly not understate the potential economic problems and political conflicts likely to emerge, we would also not underestimate the political will to make EMU a success. For the political class of the continent having come this far, the risks of abandoning EMU clearly loom larger than the risks of pushing on.

While expectations of much of what we discuss below may be reflected in market prices, we would remind readers that as recently as 12 months ago there were still significant doubts that EMU would ever become reality and certainly serious questions that it would happen on schedule. Many of the major changes in corporate and investor behaviour are only now being implemented, or perhaps even considered.

To put all of this in perspective, we believe it is useful to focus on how monetary union is changing the behaviour of corporations and investors. Many of these changes are related, or are different aspects of the same things. We examine the likely impact on valuations and argue that the changes in government, corporate and investor behaviour are likely to combine to raise the average valuations in equity markets in Euroland markets relative to history. This may be the most important implication of EMU and perhaps the least appreciated. Finally, while many of the specific investment ideas attached to these issues are still very speculative, we offer some tentative conclusions and equities which may benefit from the changes we have identified.

Corporations: life gets more competitive

From a corporate perspective, the arrival of the single currency is one more step towards the creation of a single European market. That single market brings with it greater opportunities to exploit an increasingly seamless economic area which initially will include 290 million consumers and savers, reducing transaction costs, boosting scale and scope and increasing capital market opportunities. At the same time, it means that firms will face heightened competition from both other euro-zone firms as barriers to competition continue to fall and, perhaps, heightened competition from firms outside the euro zone attracted by the opportunity to view Euroland as one market with one currency and one interest rate. This evolutionary process has already had a profound effect on corporate strategy and tactics both within Europe and globally.

We propose to focus on only five issues that seem likely to affect equity valuations and investment opportunities in the near term. These include: (1) a further acceleration in the restructuring of the European financial services industry; (2) a push towards more pricing transparency; (3) prospects for a continuing high level of mergers and acquisition activity; (4) the likely geography of consolidation of production across Europe; and (5) pensions reform.

Restructuring

This continues to be one of the major themes in our European investment strategy. While it would have happened even without EMU, the single currency has clearly forced the pace within the financial services sector in Europe. Currency differentials have been one of the major barriers to cross-border competition within the sector. As reflected in Figure 19.1, while the return on equity of the continental banking sector has begun to rise, it remains well below the level achieved by US banks. The threat of more intense cross-border competition, the opportunity to pursue European-scale operations and the expected sharp increase in the asset management business are all accelerating the consolidation and restructuring process.

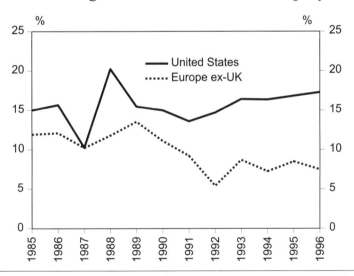

US banks generate a better return on equity...

Figure 19.1   Return on equity for the banking sector in US and FT/S&P-A Europe ex-UK

Source: Goldman Sachs

While the restructuring effect of EMU is most visible in the financial services sector at the moment, it is an important factor in accelerating the process across industry as a whole. In Figure 19.2 we compare the recent history of return on equity for the US and continental Europe. As shown, the European and US returns on equity were nearly equal in the mid-1980s. This is likely to have reflected the low ebb of US industry, reflecting the pressures of dollar strength while European industry was riding the wave of the same phenomenon. We believe that returns on equity capital on the two sides of the Atlantic are likely to converge going forward. The spread between the US and Europe in 1996/97 may be as large as it is likely to get. Restructuring efforts in Europe are likely to close the structural gap, while accelerating growth on the continent and slower growth in the US as we move into 1999 seem likely to close the cyclical gap.

If we are correct, then European restructuring can be expected to have an impact on earnings as large or proportionately larger than US restructuring has had on earnings there. Our best estimate is that US restructuring has added nearly 2 per cent a year to average EPS increases in the US over the period from the early 1980s to the late 1990s. Assuming a similar benefit in Europe in 10 years, the pool of earnings would be more than 20 per cent higher than historic trends would produce. If restructuring adds 2.5 per cent growth per year, then the pool of earnings could be nearly 30 per cent higher.

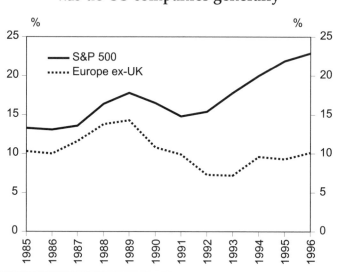

..as do US companies generally

Figure 19.2   **Return on equity for the S&P500 and FT/S&P-A Europe ex-UK**
Source: Goldman Sachs

Pricing transparency

The move to a single currency should make pricing comparisons more transparent for both consumers and corporations. There has been some concern that this will adversely affect earnings. To give some indication of the scale of the prospective changes, the European Commission recently fined VW Ecu102m for prohibiting Italian dealers from selling to customers in Austria and Germany where prices of similar models were 30 per cent more than in Italy. Elsewhere, surveys have identified pricing differentials on the same auto models of as much as 40 per cent across Europe. A survey by KPMG Management Consulting in the autumn of 1997 found that almost 50 per cent of corporate finance directors expected the euro to lead to lower prices for their products.

With sellers displaying prices in a common currency and continued pressure to eliminate the more overt forms of price support, many believe there will be irresistible pressure for common prices and that they are more likely to sink to the lower end of present spreads. This will certainly be true for some specific products, but we believe the impact in aggregate will be more modest. Some products are likely to see prices migrate toward an average. For others, price differentials may not change greatly as EMU is merely accelerating a trend that has already been in place as a result of the steady increase in competition we have already seen, reflecting the evolving single market and globalization. For example, Expert International, an association of electrical retailers, says that manufacturers' prices for consumer electronics diverged by as much as 35 per cent in the early 1990s but are broadly comparable throughout continental Europe today. Our best guess is that average prices across Europe are unlikely to differ greatly for most industries from what they would have been in the absence of EMU and that any impact from a narrowing of pricing differentials will be masked by improving economic prospects in the next few years.

Mergers and acquisitions

The enlarged domestic market for euro-11 firms is likely to increase the optimum size for firms and plants as economies of scale emerge. In some sectors excess capacity is likely to accelerate the consolidation process which has been visible for some years in areas like steel, auto components, chemicals, oil refining and other industries. Taken together these are expected to increase the pressures for combination or takeover of weaker firms.

The advent of the single currency has been widely heralded as a clarion call for M&A within the financial services sector and the single currency eliminates one of the most significant barriers to cross-border competition. There has already been a sharp rise in corporate activity in this sector within national markets. Mergers or acquisitions in Germany, Italy, Spain and France of varying sizes, both within banking and insurance and between companies in these two sectors have been widely publicized and have contributed to significant price appreciation in the stocks of many of the companies involved. But the anticipated cross-border corporate deals have not yet materialized. The *Financial Times* recently characterized the European cross-border mergers and acquisition activity as being much like Beckett's *Waiting for Godot*: a lot of entertaining conversation, but not much action. The market is still waiting for the first major cross-border acquisition/merger in the bank industry. The Merita/Nordbanken merger and the ING purchase of BBL are more realistically viewed as regional combinations to defend local positions from the expected invasion of non-domestic European firms. We continue to believe that cross-border mergers in this sector will come, but the single currency is only a further step in creating a single European banking market. Strong local effects continue to deter startups and, in the near term, we expect that attention will continue to focus on the gains from consolidation within national banking markets.

Outside the financial sector, cross-border combinations have been more common. We would point to the acquisition of Rover by BMW, the failed efforts of Volvo and Renault to forge an alliance, the consolidation of the power generation sector with the merger of divisions of GEC and Alsthom after a long history in a joint venture, and the ongoing rationalization

European M&A

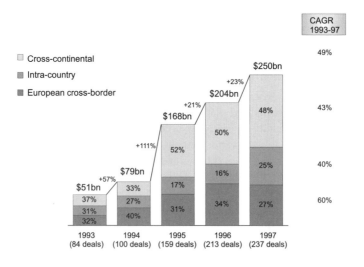

Figure 19.3   Total European M&A market - breakdown by deal type (deals over $200m)

Source: SDC

across Europe of chemicals, pharmaceuticals, defence, steel and other areas which have historically suffered from excess capacity. Again the advent of the single currency is accelerating a process that has been evident for some time. Figure 19.3 tracks the value of M&A activity in Europe by type of deal. Two key points from this data are the rapid increase in the value of transactions and the near equal split between cross-border and domestic activity, which have each been near 50 per cent of the total for the past three years.

Geographical effects

Despite the steps towards the single market we have seen in the past decade, significant barriers across Europe have contributed to corporations continuing to view Euroland as a group of largely discrete markets for many products and services. While this will not end with the single currency, it marks the elimination of one of the major barriers to viewing the countries as part of a single market. To this end, it is likely to facilitate concentration of production capabilities where economies of scale are available. While this will be evolutionary, we believe that it will favour low-cost areas. Because labour is not as mobile as in the US, capital mobility may be a key factor in adjusting wage and cost differentials.

Figure 19.4 compares 1996 data on compensation for countries in Euroland. In 1996, hourly compensation costs in Euroland manufacturing varied from near $32 per hour in the former West Germany, to less than $6 per hour in Portugal. Spain and Ireland were under $14 per hour and Italy at nearly $17.50 was still almost 20 per cent below the EU average and 45 per cent below German rates. While productivity, transportation costs, proximity to suppliers and customers, taxes and many other issues go into decisions on plant location, we believe that EMU is likely to facilitate the willingness of European producers to relocate new plant to lower-cost areas within Euroland. This is likely to be a stabilizing influence and act to speed the reduction of wage differentials that immobile labour has delayed. It is also likely to lead to growth differentials across Europe, with Germany continuing to be the slow growth economy in Europe for the foreseeable future as marginal investment disproportionately flows toward lower-cost areas. We believe that this suggests that investors should look to benefit from more rapid growth in domestic demand and production in these lower-cost areas including Portugal, Spain, Italy and Ireland. As reflected in Figure 19.5, for all except Italy, this merely extends the experience of the recent past.

Euroland: diverse labour costs...

	1996	Relative to EU Average
Austria	24.95	113
Belgium	25.89	117
Denmark	24.24	110
Finland	23.56	107
France	21.19	96
Germany	31.87	144
Greece	9.63	44
Ireland	13.85	63
Italy	17.48	79
Luxembourg	22.55	102
Netherlands	23.14	105
Norway	25.03	113
Portugal	5.58	25
Spain	13.40	61
Sweden	24.56	111
Switzerland	28.34	128
United Kingdom	14.13	64
European Union	22.06	100

Figure 19.4   **Hourly compensation costs in US dollars - production workers in manufacturing**
Source: US Department of Labour, Bureau of Labour Statistics, January 1998

..and GDP growth

	1990-95	1996	1997	1998E
Euroland	2.0	1.5	2.4	3.0
Ireland	5.5	7.7	7.5	7.3
Italy	1.3	0.7	1.5	2.3
Portugal	1.9	3.0	3.7	4.0
Spain	1.7	2.3	3.4	3.8

Figure 19.5   **Euroland GDP growth, constant prices, per cent CAR**
Source: Goldman Sachs, OECD

Pensions

The Maastricht budget criteria have created pressures for EMU governments to move pension liabilities from their own balance sheets and onto the private sector. This is likely both to create large new pools of investable funds and demands for capital market funding from corporations, particularly those which have historically carried pensions as an undifferentiated liability on the balance sheet. It is also likely to contribute to a rapid growth in the asset management business. In part reflecting the move to increased funded pensions, asset management is expected to be one of the growth industries in Europe over the next decade. Optimists expect organic growth of 10 per cent or more a year and the value of funds under management may rise by an average of 20 per cent or more. It also appears likely that equities will be an increasingly large segment of those funds.

Our colleague, Mark Griffin, has examined recent trends in this area in a recent piece, *The Global Pension Time Bomb and Its Capital Market Impact*. He identifies three issues regarding the pension sector in Europe: (1) a growing preference for defined contribution plans; (2) a shift towards higher risk/higher return investment profiles to cope with excess liabilities; and (3) outsourcing of management of pension assets. With the further integration of the European economies and efforts to promote labour mobility, we expect that the trend will clearly be towards private pension schemes on a portable, defined contribution basis. At the same time, we believe that a successful EMU will provide a favourable financial market environment supporting long-term investment planning and an increasing role for equity.

Investors: life gets more complicated

Many of the implications for investor behaviour, including a shift in the importance of sector versus country considerations in assessing portfolio risks and opportunities, have already been identified and are clearly visible. Media coverage of new Euroland-specific indices, which are likely to become widespread benchmarks for investors both inside and outside of the euro-11 area, have probably exaggerated the significance of benchmark shifts. What is perhaps less appreciated by the popular press and many professionals is the likely impact on the risk-reward opportunities for investors. The single currency and the elimination of regulatory restraints, that restricted pension funds and insurance company investment outside their domestic market, should result in a shift in the efficient frontier for many of these investors in a manner that may mean that they can raise expected return for any level of risk, or target an expected return at a lower level of risk.

Sectors versus countries

We have discussed various aspects of this in previous work and refer interested readers to *Sectors Versus Country, When Is an Asset Class an Asset Class*, 20 March 1998, and *European Asset Allocation, Asset Allocation After EMU*, February 1998. In these two documents, we have (1) argued that sectors have been as good a basis for strategic and tactical portfolio decisions as countries in Europe over the past five years; (2) indicated that available evidence suggests that sectors may be improving relative to countries as asset classes; and (3) proposed a systematic approach for translating evolving views of the economic environment into sector strategy decisions. Regardless of whether sectors have been an entirely appropriate asset class historically, it is clear that the signalling capability at the country level is likely to be vastly diminished when they share a common currency and interest rate regime, face similar fiscal policy restraints, and are migrating towards a more homogeneous legal and regulatory regime.

More efficient diversification

What has been lost in much of the speculation regarding a move to euro-zone benchmarks is the likely impact of opportunities for more efficient diversification on the equity risk premium and market valuations. Insurance companies and pension funds have been restrained in their asset liability mix in continental Europe. While the restraints on pension funds have varied greatly, the typical restraint on an insurer has been to hold about 80 per cent of assets in the currency of the liability.

A simple example will illustrate the opportunities: Chemicals and airlines represent less than 5 per cent of the Dutch market and there are no automobile producers, but Royal Dutch represents more than 20 per cent of the market capitalization of the CBS All Share index. Conversely, there are no oil stocks in the German market, where chemical, car and airline stocks comprise 30 per cent of the DAX index. What this has meant is that Dutch and German equity investors restrained to the domestic market were likely to be inefficiently diversified against volatility in the oil price. With the elimination of restrictions on investing in equities inside the euro zone, investors in both of these markets are likely to see the efficient frontier move outwards. Expected returns can be expected to rise for any given level of risk in an efficient portfolio, see Figure 19.6.

Moreover, even for investors who did not face restraints on investing outside the domestic market, the elimination of currency risk in investing

EMU shifts the risk/return trade-off

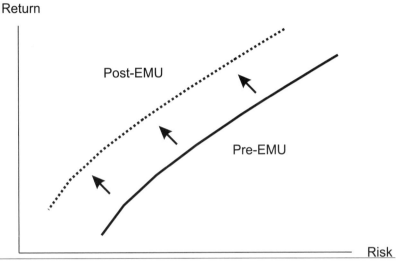

Figure 19.6   **EMU moves efficient frontier**
Source: Goldman Sachs

in non-domestic markets inside the euro zone is likely to mean that their efficient frontier has also moved in the direction indicated in the figure. Alternatively, for investors who might otherwise have chosen to hedge their foreign exchange exposure, the elimination of this risk/cost should increase expected returns for any level of portfolio volatility. We believe that, for a significant group of investors, the risk reward trade-off is likely to have improved. This should mean that the average equity risk premium demanded for these markets will fall. While the importance of this should not be overstated, our estimates suggest that a fall in the average risk premium of 25 basis points from an average of 3.1 per cent over the past decade could raise the average PE ratio by nearly 10 per cent.

Foreign investors are likely to share in this improved risk-reward environment. While they will continue to face an exchange rate risk, it is now one exchange rate with one monetary policy and one central bank to be monitored. We believe that this shift will ultimately attract an increasing number of domestic US investors to participate in the market. The cost of monitoring risk positions across the euro zone is likely to fall dramatically when there is only one currency and one central bank to monitor, and when the risks of fiscal profligacy have clearly fallen as a corollary to the Stability Pact. We believe that the increased number of investors may improve liquidity and in the first instance may benefit large cap stocks at the expense of small capitalization stocks.

Liquidity

The combination of new international investors, funded pensions and a continuing increase in the market capitalization of listed firms through both the consolidation of European industry and privatization of state businesses, is expected to improve liquidity of the equity market. As

Euroland companies small relative to the US

Euroland	Mkt Cap (US$bn)	United States	Mkt Cap (US$bn)
Royal Dutch	124	General Electric Co	279
Allianz Ag Hldg.	75	Microsoft Corp	218
Intl. Nederlanden Group	65	Coca-Cola	188
France Telecom	55	Exxon Corp	186
ENI	54	Pfizer	146
Daimler Benz	51	Merck & Co	139
Unilever (N/V)	51	Intel	134
Telefonica De Espana	43	Wal-Mart Stores	114
Deutsche Bank	41	International Bus Machns.	114
Aegon	40	Procter & Gamble	112
Telecom Italia Spa	40	Bristol Myers Squibb Co	106
AXA-UAP	39	AT&T	98
Munich Re	39	Lucent Technologies Inc.	98
Telecom Ital Mobile	38	Johnson & Johnson	94
ABN Amro Hldgs.	37	Amer Intl Group	93
Elf Aquitaine	36	Philip Morris	91
Banco Bilbao Vizcaya	35	Disney (Walt) Prods	85
Siemens	33	Du Pont E I De Nemours	85
Veba	33	Berkshire Hathaway Inc.	83
Phillips Electronics	33	SBC Communications	77
L'Oreal	33	Bell Atlantic	76
Generali (Assicurazioni)	31	Cisco Systems	75
Alcatel Alsthom	31	Nationsbank Corp	75
Nokia A	30	Hewlett-Packard	75
Total	29	Lilly (Eli)	74
Average	**45**	*Average*	**117**

Figure 19.7   Market capitalization of top 25 companies in Euroland and the United States

Source: FT/S&P-A Indices, Worldscope

indicated in Figure 19.7, the average market capitalization of the 25 largest companies within the FT/S&P-A indices for the US is more than twice the average value of the largest companies in Euroland. While some of this may reflect excess valuations of the US dollar, much of it is a reflection of the historic limits of the much smaller domestic European markets. Globalization is likely to have eliminated much of this differential in any case, but the increasingly homogeneous nature of the single market is accelerating this process.

Large versus small capitalization stocks

There has been much speculation regarding potential impacts of the process of diversifying from domestic markets to a euro level. Our own view is that, aside from the change in the risk-reward opportunities, there are likely to be few discernible value impacts resulting from the flow of funds. Cataclysmic views that suggest that Dutch pension fund managers will sell equity holdings in their own market to buy Italian stocks are unlikely. Adjustments will be made at the margin. New inflows will be used to adjust to desired allocations. At the mutual fund level, new products will focus on new euro-zone benchmarks. Since these marginal

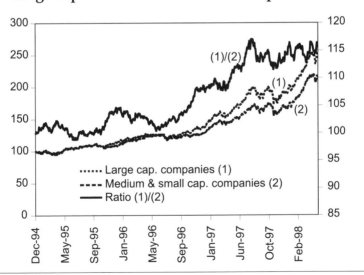

Large capitalization stocks have outperformed

Figure 19.8   **Large caps versus small caps, FT/S&P-A Europe ex-UK**
Source: FT/S&P-A Indices

moves will reflect flows from every part of Euroland into every other part of Euroland, we may see much noise and little trend.

It is also important to recognize that portfolio rebalancing is likely to focus on sectors rather than markets. Dutch investors do not have to buy French oils, retailers and banks because they get exposure to many of the same risk and reward opportunities through their own oils, retailers and banks.

The one area in which predictions do seem to have more weight is in the view that large capitalization issues may benefit at the expense of small. The key points in support of this view are: (1) the new euro indices have a bias towards large capitalization stocks; if they become benchmarks, marginal flows are likely to flow disproportionately towards them; and (2) that for investors looking to move into new sectors or new markets, larger, more liquid issues may be regarded as less risky. As reflected in Figure 19.8, any tendency in this direction will simply extend the broad trend for larger issues to outperform over the past three years.

Valuations: the air gets thinner

We believe higher sustained valuations may be the single most important and immediate impact of EMU. The combination of restructuring benefits, fiscal restraint leading to lower real bond yields, and a lower equity risk premium as a result of more efficient diversification of portfolios, is likely to lead to higher average equity valuations over the next cycle than we have seen historically. We believe these effects appear to justify much, if not most, of the expansion in traditional valuation measures (see Figure 19.9).

Lower real bond yields

The Stability Pact agreed by the EMU countries commits governments to average deficits of 1 per cent. On estimates that our colleague Martin Brookes in the Goldman Sachs European Economic Research Group has made of the impact of the Stability Pact on deficits and debt ratios, if governments were to live with this restraint it would reduce the European debt/GDP ratio over the next decade from over 70 per cent to near 50 per cent, Figure 19.10. This could lower the debt/GDP ratio for the global economy by 10 per cent. The IMF has estimated that, for every 1 per cent fall in the global debt/GDP ratio, the real bond yield can be expected to fall by about 10 basis points. This could imply a fall in the average real bond

Higher P/E ratios are partly justified...

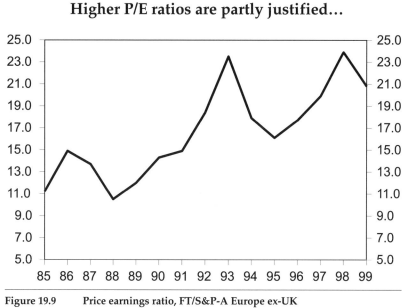

Figure 19.9   **Price earnings ratio, FT/S&P-A Europe ex-UK**
Source: Goldman Sachs

...by an expected fall in real yields

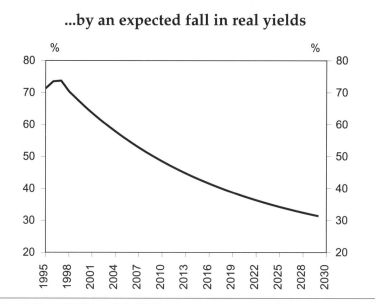

Figure 19.10   **EMU area debt/GDP at 1 per cent average deficit**
Source: Goldman Sachs

Higher equity prices justified by lower real yields?

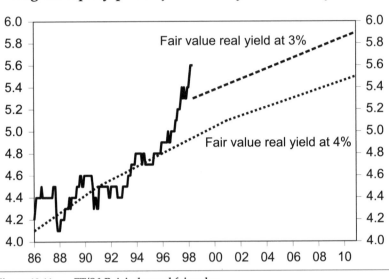

Figure 19.11   FT/S&P-A index and fair value
Source: Goldman Sachs

yield of as much as 100 basis points. This decline would have a direct impact on sustainable market valuations.

In Figure 19.11 we compare the expected evolution of the fair value of continental European equity markets, assuming that real bond yields, inflation, real earnings growth, risk premiums and payout ratios remain constant with fair value with a real bond yield that is lower by 100 basis points. Fair value increases by nearly 40 per cent on our estimates. If the market were fully discounting this change now, it could nearly justify the present differential between historic average PEs and present levels.

Earnings impact of restructuring

We believe European corporate restructuring would have happened under the pressures of globalization and the effects of the Single Market Act even without EMU, but EMU is accelerating and intensifying the pressures. Our estimates suggest that, over the decade from the mid 1980s to the mid-1990s, US restructuring increased average EPS growth by about two per cent. We see no reason to believe that it will have any less impact on Europe and there are several compelling arguments that it might well have a greater impact. On unchanged market multiples, and with a return to trend growth after 10 years, restructuring would add more than 20 per cent to market values at a two per cent a year gain and nearly 30 per cent at a 2.5 per cent a year improvement in average EPS growth. Even assuming that the market does not value those increased earnings until they occur, and discounting the value back at six per cent, improvements on this order of magnitude add 10 per cent to 15 per cent to present fair values of the market.

What is all of this likely to mean? If we assume that real bond yields fall by 50 basis points, that the equity risk premium falls by 25 basis points and that restructuring is worth two per cent a year additional earnings growth over the next 10 years, the appropriate market multiple on earnings should be between 20 and 22. If real bond yields fall by 100 basis points, the risk premium by 35 basis points and restructuring gains are nearly 2.5 per cent per year for a decade, the appropriate market multiple on earnings is likely to be nearer to 28.

Is all of this already in the market? While expectations of much of this may be reflected in market prices, we would remind readers that, as recently as 12 months ago, there were still significant doubts that EMU would ever become reality and certainly serious doubts that it would happen on schedule. Many of the major changes in corporate and investor behaviour are only now being implemented, or perhaps even considered.

Investment implications

As might be gathered from the above comments, we remain optimistic about equity market prospects in the medium term. To benefit from the dynamic described above, we would: (1) focus on restructuring themes particularly in the financial services area; (2) look for exposure to firms with a strong market position in asset management; and (3) look to benefit from continuing stronger growth in areas like Portugal, Spain and Ireland. We note that the competitive pressures will force European firms to focus much more intensely on cost control. We believe that increasing efforts to close the technology gap with the US, gain a leg-up on local competitors, conversion to the euro and the millennium problem will keep spending levels on information technology high into the next decade. This suggests that investors might: (4) look for exposure to the continuing spend on IT and outsourcing.

Finally we note that much of the impact of EMU is likely to be evolutionary and medium term. We will not know whether our conclusions on valuations, growth prospects, asset management earnings trends and consolidation are working out as expected for at least five, and perhaps, ten years.

Chapter
20

Peter Oppenheimer
HSBC Securities

Pension funds and EMU

Demographic trends

In 1993, some 15 per cent of the population of Europe was aged over 65. A further 11 per cent of the population was aged in the range 55-64. This combined total of some 96 million people is heavily dependent upon pay-as-you-go (PAYG) pensions systems, which are not sustainable if substantial tax increases are to be avoided and/or sociably-unacceptable cuts made in the level of welfare to pensioners.

The number of over 65s is set to grow rapidly, both in absolute terms and as a proportion of under 65s working and paying taxes (see Figure 20.1).

Demographic projections show that the number over 60 will rise until around 2050, before gradually falling, but still remaining at far higher levels than today. In OECD countries, the number of people over 60 will account for 27 per cent of the population in 2010, peaking at 31 per cent in 2050.

Between 1960, at the end of the post-war baby boom, and 1990, the fertility rate has dropped from 2.7 children to 1.8, against a replacement level (to keep the population stable) of 2.1. At the same time, life expectancy for men has risen from 64 in 1951 to 75, while that for women has risen from 70 to 77.

The result of these shifts is a pronounced increase in the dependency burden.

Pensions

Pensions account for around 25 per cent of government expenditure across Europe.

Without change, pensions expenditure is set to increase by between 50 per cent and 100 per cent, raising government expenditure significantly and implying either an unsustainable increase in taxation or borrowing.

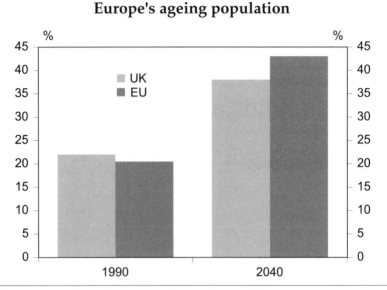

Europe's ageing population

Figure 20.1   Ratio of over 65s to those aged 15-64 (%)

Any move away from unfunded pension arrangements is likely to be organized on a collective—rather than individual—basis, using the defined contribution model. This will massively increase demand for equities.

Ultimately, compulsory pensions saving is likely to become the norm and fiscal relief will be modest.

Irrespective of the relative degrees of compulsion and incentivization, significant changes will occur on both the demand and supply side of the savings market. These changes will lead to the development of new and alternative distribution channels and intense competition, leading to further consolidation of the savings and financial services industry.

On modest assumptions, a partial switch to funded arrangements will result in a real ten-fold increase in pension fund assets in the next 20 to 25 years.

Growth to this extent can only be absorbed by European fund managers adopting a global approach to asset allocation, and by huge growth in the European securities market. The implied growth of funds managed in Europe over the next 20 years is, in real terms, $27 trillion, compared to the current global stock of assets of fund managers of $22 trillion.

The size of the pension fund industry

Pension funds now account for some 40 per cent of assets managed globally, and mutual funds and insurance funds account for the balance in roughly equal amounts.

Pension funds have 40% of global assets

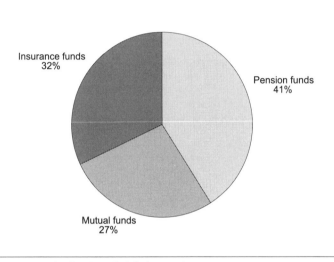

Figure 20.2   **Distribution of global assets by type**

The bulk of assets are managed in the USA (see Figure 20.3)—at just under half the world total—although Europe now manages around one-third of global assets. The USA also dominates the pension fund market as shown in Figure 20.4. Pension funds' non-domestic portfolios are increasing, even in Europe. In proportionate terms, the UK has the greatest global exposure.

In a global context, therefore, Europe has a significant fund management industry. Replacing Europe's unfunded pension liabilities with funded arrangements is set to raise the size of the industry dramatically, possibly by a factor of 10 by the year 2020.

Bulk of global assets managed in the US

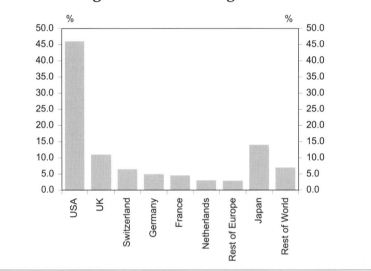

Figure 20.3   Distribution of global assets managed by ownership

US also dominates pension fund assets

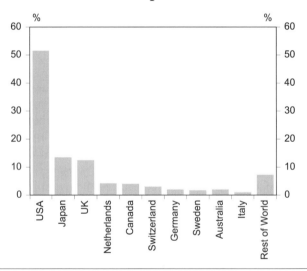

Figure 20.4   Distribution of pension fund assets
Source: InterSec Research Corp, Stamford, Conn.

Deposit taking

While Europe still accounts for a small proportion of the worlds pension assets, there remains a very large pool of savings in Europe which will be tapped for investment purposes as the emphasis of pension provision shifts to the private sector. The distribution of deposits on a global basis is shown in Figure 20.5.

$16 trillion of bank deposits

	$ billion	Share
Japan	4,418.8	27.8%
USA	2,289.3	14.4%
Canada	347.0	2.2%
Euro-11	4,252.4	26.7%
Other EU	1,585.0	10.0%
Switzerland	347.5	2.2%
Other Europe	334.6	2.1%
China	725.2	4.6%
Other Asia	753.2	4.7%
Australia & Oceania	503.5	3.2%
S&Central America	208.3	1.3%
Africa	157.7	1.0%
Total	*15,922.5*	

Figure 20.5 **Distribution of global bank domestic bank deposits**
Source: derived form IMF International Financial Statistics

Europe accounts for 41 per cent of global bank deposits. In total, excluding saving in housing stock, world savings amounted to around US $60 trillion as at the end of 1996, of which approximately one-third is attributable to Europe.

Pension liberalization

The ageing of Europe's population is taking place at a time when the political imperative has moved to reducing taxation and reducing government borrowing, the former because of global competitive issues, the latter because of high debt levels and the constraints on fiscal policy under EMU. However, even if these schemes were closed today, and only those benefits paid that have been earned to date, the impact on public finances would still be dramatic. At present, the expenditure on current pensioners is only the tip of the iceberg. The accrued rights that have been built up in respect of the current workforce are getting on for twice that of the existing pensioners, and all these liabilities are unfunded.

Even if the various state PAYG pension schemes stopped today and were replaced by some alternative, the existing liabilities would add significantly to government debt, unless governments were to default on those liabilities.

Discontinuance of existing schemes implies that no further contributions would be paid and, in effect, the accrued liabilities would become government debt if taxation was not to be raised. The effect of this is shown in Figure 20.7.

The build-up in these accrued rights means that an inexorable rise in taxation is required if reforms are not made to state pension arrangements.

Italy has the major problem, the funding cost being expected to rise to around 22 per cent of GDP, before falling back to 16 per cent. The cost of the French scheme is expected to rise steadily to around 14 per cent of GDP, the cost of the German scheme is expected to rise to 18.5 per cent of GDP before settling back, while the UK scheme should mature at around 11 per cent of GDP. Since the OECD study was published, the Italian government has introduced reforms designed to reduce the level of liabilities.

Without any change to the schemes, or contributions through payroll taxes, the shortfalls to be met by government through general taxation indicate the potential impact on public finances.

Liberalization of pension funds in Europe has just begun. In the case of Italy for example, pension legislation aimed at freeing-up this sector was passed in 1993, but it has taken three further reforms for the market to begin in earnest. The country's first non-bank private sector pension, Fonchim, which was set up for the workers of the chemical and pharmaceutical union, received authorization on 10 December 1997. It already covers about 67,000 employees. Another 101 pension funds have already applied for authorization from the independent commission that monitors pension funds. According to this body, there will be 3.9 million people, or 23 per cent of the workforce, registered in pension schemes by 2001—with the market projected to reach 500 trillion lire by 2020. These growth rates are similar to those that are likely elsewhere in Europe.

Public pensions: a hefty bill...

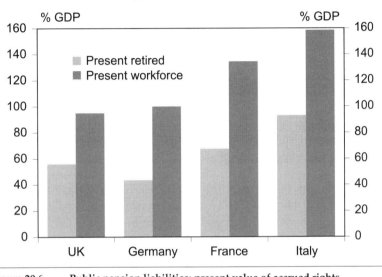

Figure 20.6   Public pension liabilities: present value of accrued rights
Source: OECD

..which dwarfs current debt levels

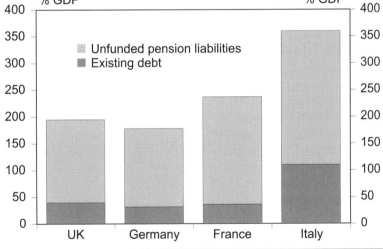

Figure 20.7   Cumulative unfunded pension liabilities and debt (1990)
Source: OECD

The impact of EMU

EMU will have a dramatic impact on the capital market. Under a single currency, institutions will be able to match liabilities with assets across the single currency areas, rather than only in the home market. The main changes that will result from this will depend on the UK joining the single currency. At that time, investors across Europe will tend to invest to replicate a pan-European equity market.

While the UK will be the biggest component of the new pan-European market—roughly 38 per cent—there will be significant capital flows out of the UK as UK institutions raise the amount of money that they hold in other European stocks. While there will also be a flow in the other direction, it will not be as big, since other European pension assets are tiny compared to those in the UK—see Figure 20.8. The UK has over 80 per cent of European equity funds in equities. Consequently, they have more to redistribute to the rest of Europe than other Europeans have for investing in the UK. The same is true if one looks at life assurance funds.

	Total	Foreign	Local	% of Local in Europe total
UK	628,560	185,976	442,584	84.1
France	8,983	1,409	7,574	1.4
Germany	9,754	2,280	7,474	1.4
Italy	2,212	0	2,212	0.4
Netherlands	89,508	51,639	37,869	7.2
Spain	878	176	702	0.1
Portugal	750	0	750	0.1
Sweden	19,495	6,338	13,157	2.5
Denmark	8,214	1,912	6,301	1.2
Austria	263	214	49	0.0
Belgium	4,045	2,314	1,731	0.3
Ireland	15,283	9,161	6,122	1.2
Total	787,943	261,420	526,524	100.0

Figure 20.8   **Pension fund assets allocated to equities, 1995 (US$ million)**

	Automobiles	Bank	Building	Chemicals	Consumer goods	Electronics	Insurance	Media	Capital Goods	Oils	Paper & packaging	Pharmaceuticals	Retail	Services & transport	Telecomms	Textiles	Utilities	Total
UK	0.29	8.38	1.16	0.67	2.88	0.64	1.55	1.74	2.59	5.00	0.27	3.52	3.16	3.63	1.82	0.00	0.59	37.90
France	0.62	1.44	1.20	0.70	1.90	1.22	0.81	0.55	0.19	1.77	0.11	0.55	1.39	0.35	0.00	0.02	0.93	13.76
Germany	2.24	2.73	0.30	2.16	0.10	1.44	2.54	0.11	1.48	0.00	0.07	0.69	0.15	0.21	0.00	0.00	1.96	16.20
Italy	0.46	0.83	0.07	0.00	0.19	0.09	1.06	0.19	0.02	1.33	0.02	0.00	0.05	0.00	1.93	0.03	0.16	6.43
Neths	0.00	0.84	0.04	0.42	1.47	0.93	1.94	0.99	0.14	3.28	0.10	0.03	0.41	0.43	0.51	0.00	0.00	11.52
Spain	0.00	1.75	0.08	0.00	0.10	0.01	0.08	0.00	0.13	0.35	0.02	0.00	0.00	0.00	0.77	0.00	1.48	4.77
Portugal	0.00	0.00	0.00	0.00	0.00	0.00	0.00	0.00	0.00	0.00	0.01	0.00	0.00	0.00	0.11	0.00	0.00	0.12
Sweden	0.50	0.77	0.00	0.14	0.00	1.74	0.18	0.07	0.68	0.00	0.52	0.80	0.00	0.03	0.06	0.00	0.19	5.69
Denmark	0.00	0.23	0.00	0.00	0.18	0.00	0.05	0.00	0.00	0.00	0.00	0.18	0.00	0.02	0.11	0.00	0.00	0.77
Austria	0.00	0.16	0.06	0.00	0.03	0.01	0.02	0.00	0.19	0.11	0.03	0.00	0.01	0.03	0.00	0.01	0.10	0.76
Belgium	0.00	0.49	0.00	0.28	0.00	0.00	0.35	0.07	0.04	0.25	0.00	0.00	0.12	0.00	0.00	0.00	0.40	1.99
Ireland	0.00	0.00	0.00	0.00	0.00	0.00	0.00	0.00	0.00	0.00	0.10	0.00	0.00	0.00	0.00	0.00	0.00	0.10
Europe	4.12	17.62	2.91	4.37	6.85	6.08	8.58	3.73	5.48	12.10	1.24	5.76	5.29	4.70	5.29	0.06	5.82	100.0

Figure 20.9   Before EMU: 12 separate portfolios*

*Figures in per cent

	Automobiles	Bank	Building	Chemicals	Consumer Goods	Electronics	Insurance	Media	Capital Goods	Oils	Paper & packaging	Pharmaceuticals	Retail	Services & transport	Telecomms	Textiles	Utilities	Total
UK	-1.9	-53.7	-7.5	-4.3	-18.5	-4.1	-10.0	-11.2	-16.6	-32.1	-1.7	-22.6	-20.3	-23.3	-11.7	0.0	-3.8	-243.0
France	2.9	6.8	5.7	3.3	9.0	5.7	3.8	2.6	0.9	8.4	0.5	2.6	6.5	1.6	0.0	0.1	4.4	64.9
Germany	10.8	13.1	1.4	10.4	0.5	6.9	12.2	0.5	7.1	0.0	0.4	3.3	0.7	1.0	0.0	0.0	9.4	77.8
Italy	2.3	4.1	0.3	0.0	1.0	0.4	5.2	1.0	0.1	6.5	0.1	0.0	0.3	0.0	9.5	0.2	0.8	31.6
Neths	0.0	1.7	0.1	0.8	2.9	1.8	3.8	2.0	0.3	6.5	0.2	0.1	0.8	0.8	1.0	0.0	0.0	22.8
Spain	0.0	9.0	0.4	0.0	0.5	0.1	0.4	0.0	0.7	1.8	0.1	0.0	0.0	0.0	3.9	0.0	7.6	24.4
Portugal	0.0	0.0	0.0	0.0	0.0	0.0	0.0	0.0	0.0	0.0	0.0	0.0	0.0	0.0	-0.1	0.0	0.0	-0.1
Sweden	1.5	2.3	0.0	0.4	0.0	5.1	0.5	0.2	2.0	0.0	1.5	2.4	0.0	0.1	0.2	0.0	0.6	16.8
Denmark	0.0	-0.7	0.0	0.0	-0.5	0.0	-0.1	0.0	0.0	0.0	0.0	-0.5	0.0	-0.1	-0.3	0.0	0.0	-2.2
Austria	0.0	0.8	0.3	0.0	0.2	0.0	0.1	0.0	1.0	0.6	0.1	0.0	0.0	0.2	0.0	0.0	0.5	3.9
Belgium	0.0	2.2	0.0	1.2	0.0	0.0	1.5	0.3	0.2	1.1	0.0	0.0	0.5	0.0	0.0	0.0	1.8	8.8
Ireland	0.0	0.0	0.0	0.0	0.0	0.0	0.0	0.0	0.0	0.0	-5.6	0.0	0.0	0.0	0.0	0.0	0.0	-5.6
Europe	16	-15	1	12	-5	16	18	-5	-4	-7	-4	-15	-11	-20	3	21	0	0

Figure 20.10   After EMU: net inflows/outflows*
*Figures in US$ billion

It is impossible to calculate with accuracy the scale of the net flows in and out of each sector and country that might result from a move away from domestic investment towards a European-wide investment. Nonetheless, we can make an estimate. If we assume that every pension fund in Europe replicates their domestic index weightings (with a structure as set out in Figure 20.9) and will diversify to replicate the pan-European index, we can use the distribution of assets shown in Figure 20.9 to calculate the implied net flow.

Figure 20.10 summarizes these flows (in $ billion). The UK is clearly a major loser—over $200bn in theory (roughly 15 per cent of the current market capitalization)—and the rest of Europe would enjoy a major net capital inflow.

Section

VIII

The *euro*

The impact on companies & consumers

Chapter
21

John Hegarty
Secretary General, Fédération des Experts Comptables Européens (FEE)

The euro and accounting practices

Introduction

For those who feel that the few months remaining until 1 January 1999 provide inadequate time to prepare for the introduction of the euro, the news from the accounting front is likely to be unwelcome: in participating countries, the advent of the single currency should be accounted for in the financial statements for the year ending 31 December 1998, a reporting period which has already begun. This is irrespective of whether accounts are drawn up in euro or national currency denominations. Bearing in mind the possible taxation consequences, it is obvious that planning for the impact of the euro must begin now, and the purpose of this chapter is to give an overview of some of the considerations which should be taken into account. As befits a complex subject, however, there are many details and nuances which cannot be covered in a limited number of pages. Information is therefore provided on where more extensive material may be obtained.

Financial reporting - the key issue

In accounting terms, the main impact of the introduction of the euro is to realize previously unrealized exchange gains and losses between participating currencies. For example, the French franc and Deutschemark will cease to be foreign currencies with respect to each other on 1 January 1999, when they simply become different expressions of the same currency, the single currency. Traditional rules for foreign currency translation cease to apply, and new treatments for the new euro take effect.

Two questions must be answered, to come up with the appropriate treatment:

- When should exchange gains and losses be considered realized ?

- How should realized exchange differences be accounted for ?

The preponderant view amongst accountancy professionals and regulators is that realization takes place in the period ending 31 December 1998. Because of the one-to-one relationship between the Ecu and the euro, closing exchange rates between the participating currencies on 31 December 1998 will be the same as the irrevocable conversion rates on 1 January 1999, so that convergence is an event in 1998, not 1999. In reality, therefore, the impact on companies already using the closing rate method should be nil. However, for companies not using the closing rate method (for example in Germany, where prudence requires the use of the lower of historical rate or closing rate), the choice of 1998 or 1999 is not a neutral one. This is at the origin of the controversy described below.

As regards how the realized differences should be accounted for, the majority opinion is clear-cut: they should be taken direct to the profit and loss account for the period ending 31 December 1998. Again, this should not have any impact on companies already using the closing rate. This will not be the case, though, if prudent German-style treatments have been applied to date. The latter will have ensured that all unrealized losses are taken into account as they arise, but not unrealized gains. There is therefore the potential for a one-off upwards earnings blip for those companies, for example, having outstanding debts in a participating currency which has weakened against the participating currency in which they report (e.g. a German company which borrowed French francs). Since those countries with conservative accounting practices tend also to be those with a very strong link between tax and financial reporting, the introduction of the euro could lead to an additional tax bill.

Given the wish of all concerned that the advent of the single currency should be tax neutral, there are two ways to deal with this problem. The preferable one would be to make the necessary amendments to the taxation legislation in the countries in question, to ensure that there is no tax on good accounting. Unfortunately, it now seems likely that some countries will leave the tax laws unchanged and instead achieve fiscal neutrality by manipulating the accounting treatment. This is explained in greater detail below.

European Commission: 'Accounting for the introduction of the euro'

In June 1997, as part of a series of actions to provide enterprises with some form of certainty as to the regulatory consequences of the advent of the single currency, the European Commission published a non-binding paper on accounting for the introduction of the euro. The document was the result of consultations, undertaken since Summer 1996, between the Commission, the Accounting Directives Contact Committee of member state officials responsible for the national implementation of EU financial reporting legislation, and the Fédération des Experts Comptables Européens (FEE), which represents the accountancy profession at European level. The paper makes clear that, although a majority favoured realization in 1998 and the taking of differences direct to the profit and loss account, a minority did not. Rather than opt for one approach or the other, the document accommodates both, so that:

- Countries may permit the impact of the euro to be accounted for in 1999, instead of 1998.

- Countries may require or allow the deferral of positive exchange differences, instead of taking them immediately to the profit and loss account.

Since the ultimate decision will be made at the level of each individual member state, companies should pay very close attention to the different national dispositions will be adopted, and should assume that divergences in treatment will exist. Given that one of the objectives of the single currency is to strengthen the single market, it is to be regretted that a single accounting approach seems unlikely. Equally, companies that wish to comply simultaneously with national requirements and other standards— such as International Accounting Standards (IASs), or United States generally accepted accounting principles (US GAAP)—will have to cope with the fact that not all options included in the Commission paper are considered compatible with IASs or US GAAP.

Other accounting issues

Exchange differences on consolidation

Only those exchange gains and losses relating to monetary assets and liabilities become realized on the introduction of the euro. No adjustments are required, for example, to fixed assets purchased in another participating currency. Equally, exchange differences on consolidation, which arise because of the impact of fluctuating exchange rates on foreign currency denominated investments in subsidiaries, will not be realized because of the euro, but only when the investment is disposed of.

Comparative information

Because of stock exchange or other requirements, companies may wish to restate in euro financial information relating to dates or periods predating the introduction of the single currency. This is problematical, because no national currency/euro rates exist until 1 January 1999. Two second-best alternatives present themselves: either the national currency/Ecu rate for the date in question, or the irrevocable national currency/euro rate. For purely pragmatic reasons, since neither is theoretically perfect, the balance of opinion has come down in favour of the latter. This has the advantage that year-on-year trends previously expressed in national currency remain intact (e.g. percentage growth in sales or earnings-per-share) and it avoids the counter-intuitive phenomenon of exchange gains and losses arising in companies which had no foreign currency transactions or exposure. However, unlike the use of the national currency/Ecu rate, it ignores all previous fluctuations between participating currencies, and therefore distorts any comparisons of prior-period information between companies with accounts previously denominated in different participating currencies.

Conversion costs

The decision whether to capitalize or expense costs associated with the introduction of the euro will be governed by the same tests and rules as apply to other expenditure. In this sense, there is nothing different about the euro, such that costs should be written-off as incurred unless there is some identifiable future benefit. Equally, existing rules will determine whether a company can establish a provision for costs associated with the introduction of the euro, but not yet incurred. Unfortunately, these rules are not the same in all member states, so the introduction of the single currency for the single market will be accompanied by different accounting treatments in participating countries.

Disclosure

In light of the many issues to which the single currency gives rise, and the likelihood of different treatments in different countries, companies should ensure that sufficient footnote disclosure is made in their accounts to allow users to have a clear understanding of the underlying events and transactions, and of the policies adopted to account for them.

Accounting records and publication of accounts

The realization of exchange gains and losses on monetary assets and liabilities denominated in other participating currencies, as described above, is triggered by the introduction of the euro, irrespective of whether a company prepares its accounts in euro or national currency denominations. In this regard, a company has no choice.

In line with the Madrid scenario, however, and the rule of 'No compulsion, no prohibition' during the 3-year period of Phase B, a company should be free to choose when, during that period, it wishes to begin keeping its accounting records in euro and publishing its accounts in euro.

The timing of this switch will, in principle, be driven by a number of factors, including:

- The rate at which the company's transactions will switch to being denominated in euro, which in many cases will depend on decisions made by business partners rather than the company itself.

- The readiness of the company's accounting systems (for both internal and external reporting) to cope with the switch.

These considerations are largely academic, however, unless regulatory requirements permit the company to make a free choice. For example, many countries have stipulations (often enshrined in primary legislation) which oblige companies to maintain their accounting records and publish financial statements in national currency, so that changes are required to make operative the supposed freedom of action underlying the Madrid scenario.

Initially, the outlook was not positive. Public administrations in many countries took the view that 'no compulsion, no prohibition' applied equally, if not more so, to them, and that they were not inclined to switch until the latest date possible i.e. 1 January 2002. With the exception of those member states where companies were already free to use any currency of their choice (e.g. Ireland or the Netherlands), companies were confronted with not being able to switch, even if they wanted to, unless they were willing to incur the costs required to keep records and publish financial statements in both euro and national currency.

However, the situation has improved. Led by Belgium, all participating member states have now published comprehensive national changeover plans which commit their public administrations to being able to deal in the euro, at least with companies if not always every citizen, from 1 January 1999. This will allow companies to choose the best course of action for themselves. Germany, unfortunately, is an exception. There, the administration of the taxation system is devolved to the Länder, which have indicated that they will need until 2002 to prepare themselves. The federal government has introduced relaxations as far as record-keeping and accounts publication are concerned, but if tax authorities still require the use of Deutschemark denominations, the option to switch will remain unattractive.

Taxation - administrative issues

The likelihood of differences of approach in both the accounting and the taxation fields between participating countries reflects the reluctance of the European Commission to propose harmonizing legislation at EU level to facilitate the introduction of the euro and to ensure a consistent approach by all member states. With the exception of the two regulations establishing the legal framework for the use of the euro, no further proposals are likely to be forthcoming. To a certain extent, this is due to the lack of time to steer legislation through the normal decision-making process, but it also reflects a preference for allowing the operation of subsidiarity. In part, though, it is a consequence of an unwillingness of member states to agree to fresh legislation, especially in the taxation field where, despite the Treaty of Amsterdam, unanimity is still required.

To the problems of filing tax returns and making payments/refunds in euro should be added the issue of penalties for errors and omissions. Based on the experience of introducing the transitional VAT regime, it is inevitable that the changeover to the euro will lead to inadvertent mistakes in the making of declarations and returns. It seems unjust that these should be penalized, yet many countries' legislation leaves no room for discretion in the levying of penalties in such cases. In particular for SMEs, for whom the relative burden will be higher, member states should introduce the amendments required to ensure a more pragmatic and equitable approach.

Taxation - technical issues

There is universal agreement in principle that the introduction of the euro should be tax neutral, but the earlier comments on accounting indicate how this may not be the case unless changes are made to the law in some member states. The question of the tax treatment of exchange gains triggered by the single currency has already been explained. Also of concern is the tax treatment of conversion costs. Unless clarification is provided, there is the risk in some countries that, irrespective of the accounting treatment adopted, companies may not be able to deduct such spending for tax purposes as incurred, but may have relief spread over a number of years. This seems inequitable, as does the possibility that tax losses carried forward may be lost if the euro leads to the discontinuation of certain activities, e.g. treasury operations involving participating currencies. Companies should not delay in examining their exposure to risks such as these.

In relation to indirect taxes, particularly value added tax, the potential problems are less acute in scale for business as a whole, although individual companies may find themselves at a particular disadvantage. Financial institutions, for example, can recover little or any of their input VAT, because output VAT is not levied on most financial services. As a consequence, VAT on supplies associated with preparing for the euro (e.g. computer hardware and software, consultancy fees) is irrecoverable, adding materially to the cost of conversion.

Helping business prepare for the euro

As the leading advisers to Europe's business community, from the smallest SME to the largest multinational, the accountancy profession has recognized its particular responsibility to help ensure as smooth a transition as possible to the single currency. This has been acknowledged by the European Commission which, as part of its overall communications programme on the euro, has provided very generous financial assistance for work by the Fédération des Experts Comptables Européens (FEE). FEE is the representative organization for the accountancy profession in Europe, grouping together 38 professional bodies in 26 countries with a combined membership of approximately 400,000 individuals. Of these, roughly 45 per cent are in public practice, with the other 55 per cent working in industry, commerce, government or education.

A key element of FEE's euro project is an internet-accessible database of detailed information and guidance on the practical aspects of the introduction of the euro. In addition to coverage of tax and accounting issues, it also deals with legal, IT, general and financial management, personnel and public sector topics, and is regularly updated to take account of new developments and information. Those wishing to explore in greater depth some of the subject s raised in this chapter should therefore visit the FEE euro website at:

www.euro.fee.be.

or turn for advice to their accountants and auditors.

Copies of a regular euro newsletter are also available from FEE at:

rue de la Loi 83
B - 1040 BRUXELLES
Belgium
Tel: + 32 (2) 285 40 85
Fax: + 32 (2) 231 11 12

Graham Bishop
*Salomon Smith Barney**

Chapter 22	The euro

The impact on financial services

The creation of an economic and monetary union (EMU) that eventually spans an enlarged European Union will be an historic business opportunity for the financial services industry. It will occur at a time of continued technological change and in the context of an ageing population.

The conclusion of this chapter is that these driving forces for change may well lead to a dramatic increase in the 'securitization' of credit in Europe. Securitization—the process whereby assets are packaged together and sold as securities—has been a familiar feature of the US financial market for some years. The new environment is conducive to its development in Europe. That may undermine the position of the traditional banks. But the technology that enables securitization to occur will also keep its costs down. This is likely to lead to an environment of intense competition in financial services, with perhaps the customer being the main long-term beneficiary.

Three main forces

Three main forces will change the financial landscape of Europe over the coming years.

- **European integration**—incorporating the introduction of the euro as well as the expansion of the EU and of the single market—is an obvious 'driver' and has several possible outcomes which are discussed below.

- **Demographic trends** mean that there will be a steadily ageing European population in coming years. That ageing population will

---

*The views expressed are the author's own and are not shared by Salomon Smith Barney, nor any of its affiliates.

have a substantial pool of savings and is likely to become ever more financially sophisticated. An ageing electorate may also have different political priorities: namely preserving the purchasing power of their assets.

- **Technology** is a global driving force that will have a profound impact. The increasing power of computing and communications technology will continue to change the face of the financial services sector.

We discuss each of these forces below.

European integration

There are three broad scenarios which can be envisaged for European integration over the next decade or so:

- 1) That the broad EMU which starts with 11 participating states on 1 January 1999 endures and, indeed, enlarges as the EU itself enlarges. On this view the euro could be the currency used by as many as 500 million people within the next twenty years and the euro would emerge as a major rival to the US dollar as a reserve currency.

- 2) One of the initial eleven EMU members 'drops out', but the rest carry on. A manager with businesses in that 'drop-out' state will face exceptional difficulties.

- 3) EMU disintegrates after a time, and the EU follows suit. This outcome could be catastrophic for a business structured for a pan-European market.

The analysis of this chapter is based on the first scenario. It also assumes that the drive to a wider EMU is based on the liberal and competitive economic model of the single market. The other two main changes— demographics and the impact of technology—will also have a great impact in financial services. But before considering these, it is useful to step back and consider the most basic function of a financial market.

Principles of a financial market

The most basic function of a financial market is to facilitate intermediation between savers and the eventual users of their funds. There are two main ways in which this intermediation is carried out in modern financial markets: through banks or the securities market.

Deposit-taking bank

When intermediation is carried out through a bank, a saver makes a deposit, for a particular term, and is certain that the capital is secure. The bank will manage a diversified portfolio of assets—using that deposit. Public regulators in all countries require that the bank's shareholders put up ample capital to buffer losses so that the saver's capital is safe. But the bank's shareholders demand a proper return on their capital. Therefore, the saver's maximum net return is the return on the bank's asset portfolio *less* the bank's management and regulatory expenses *less* the bank shareholders' return.

The securities market

The securities market offers a different type of intermediation. The saver pays a fee to engage directly with the user of the funds, bearing the full risk of market movements and credit problems. To achieve an adequate degree of credit diversification, the saver could pay the management expenses of a mutual fund (or other institution).

If the management expenses of the bank equalled those of a mutual fund, then the saver could increase return simply by capturing the bank shareholders' portion of the return provided by the underlying assets. However, this analysis can only be performed if the type of assets available to the bank are also available for purchase in the securities market. But, in Europe today, they are not. If EMU has the side-effect of bringing those assets to the market, then the playing field will tilt a little. If technology shifts the 'management expenses' goal posts as well, then the entire structure of the financial market could change.

The impact of the euro on financial market structure

In order to assess the chance of the euro's introduction bringing about a shift from intermediation by banks to intermediation by securities markets, it is useful to review the development of the dollar markets.

Development of the US financial market over the last 20 years

Figure 22.1 shows the change in the relative role of banks and securities markets since 1975. The shift in favour of securities as the principal method

US securitization

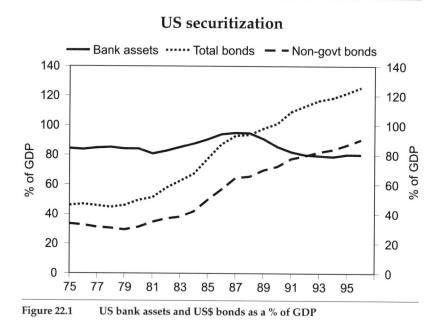

Figure 22.1   US bank assets and US$ bonds as a % of GDP

US dollar security matrix

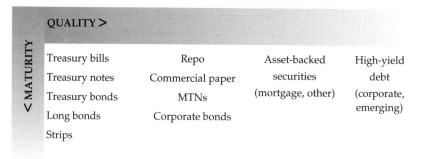

QUALITY >			
Treasury bills	Repo	Asset-backed	High-yield
Treasury notes	Commercial paper	securities	debt
Treasury bonds	MTNs	(mortgage, other)	(corporate,
Long bonds	Corporate bonds		emerging)
Strips			

Figure 22.2   Maturity and quality matrix for the US dollar bond market

30-year government bonds and all the way through the spectrum of creditworthiness from 'risk-free' to highly-risky bonds where the expected default rate is explicitly factored into the required yield.

However, two decades ago, the US market was much more straightforward—with three comparable segments: government and government agency, municipal, and corporate bonds. At that time, however, the Eurodollar market was already developing and other sectors became significant in the 1980s:

- In 1984 non-agency mortgage-backed bonds.

- In 1986 high-yield corporate bonds and bonds issued by foreign institutions (termed 'Yankee bonds').

- In 1989 other types of asset-backed bonds (that is backed by assets other than mortgages).

Figure 22.3 shows how the growth of these bonds issued by institutions other than the government has been a key factor behind the overall growth of the bond market. Figure 22.4 shows the relative importance of bond issuers other than the government in the current structure of the US dollar

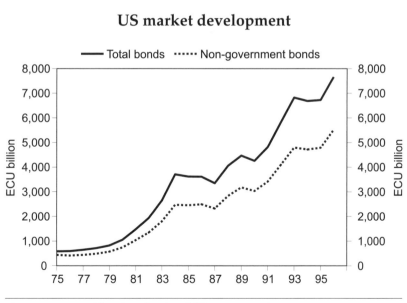

Figure 22.3   US bond market (Ecu billion, 1975-1996)

US bond market structure

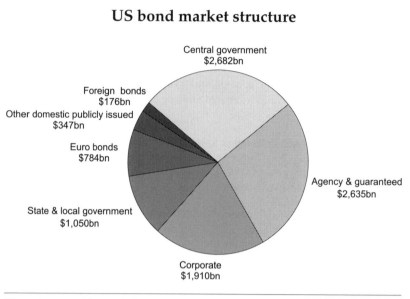

Figure 22.4   The US dollar bond market (US$, end-96)

Source: Salomon Brothers, 'How Big is the World Bond market?', September 1997

Figure 22.3 shows how the growth of these bonds issued by institutions other than the government has been a key factor behind the overall growth of the bond market. Figure 22.4 shows the relative importance of bond issuers other than the government in the current structure of the US dollar bond market. In the US, it was the build up of these extra components of the bond market, as well as the agency market, that was the raw material for the mortgage bond market. Many of the securities that were issued might otherwise have been bank assets. But, for example, high-yield bond issuers were often trying to escape from the onerous debt amortization provisions or the restrictive covenants that banks would have required. In fact, during 1989-1991, US banks themselves became active securitizers. This enabled them to comply with the new risk-based capital requirements yet maintain their customer relationships. That opened the door to new competitors such as speciality credit card companies where economies of scale became a key competitive advantage, or non-banks such as the automobile finance companies, and even mutual funds that invest in bank loans. Even loans to small- and medium-sized companies—a traditional area of strength of the banks—have now been securitized.

In effect, investors can now extend credit directly to virtually all the sectors of the US economy that were formerly the preserve of the banks. New technology has been of key importance in this process: first, in

Euro market development

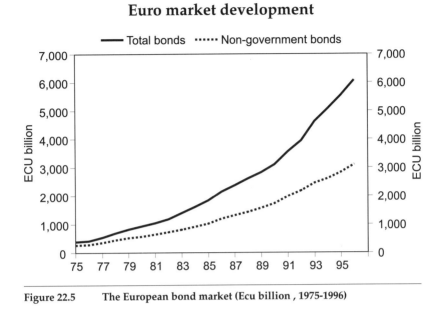

Figure 22.5   **The European bond market (Ecu billion , 1975-1996)**

Euro bond market structure

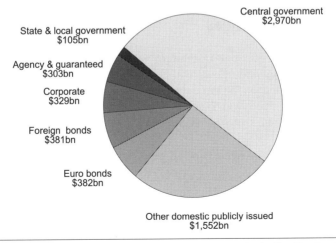

Figure 22.6   **The European bond market (US$, end-96, including Ecu bonds)**

Source: Salomon Brothers, 'How Big is the World Bond market?', September 1997

Development of European financial markets in the last 20 years

The development of European financial markets has been rather different. There has been a substantial increase in the size of the bond market—from 28 per cent to 86 per cent of GDP over the last twenty years—but well over half the increase was accounted for by government issuance. The result is that bond markets are now dominated by government issuance (see Figure 22.6). Indeed, the amount of marketable government debt in the euro area is larger than in the US market.

It is true that some Treasury debt managers have sought to minimize funding costs by issuing securities directly to end-investors, reducing reliance on the commercial banks. But this market is nowhere near as well developed as in the US.

The key problem for launching a new sector is to get the initial critical mass. Investors are reluctant to buy securities that are both unfamiliar in their credit nature and destined to be illiquid. This is where EMU may have a key influence. EMU will remove the importance of currency-matching rules, whereby investors in each country typically have to hold a high proportion of their assets in their own 'domestic currency'. Once the euro is launched, the domestic currency is the euro and 'currency-matching' will entail matching domestic euro liabilities, for example, with euro assets. There should therefore be a substantial increase in the range of institutions that can purchase the new types of securities.

Demographic changes

The population of Europe—in common with the rest of the industrialized world—is ageing. The effects will begin to become quite pronounced within the next decade. By 2009, almost 20 per cent of the population of the euro area will be aged over 65 and that proportion will continue rising (see Figure 22.7). The process has several consequences for financial markets.

Ageing populations need funded pensions

Public pay-as-you-go systems will not be able to cope, so a move to—at least partial—funding by individuals of their own retirement is generally accepted. That eventual imperative has been brought into sharp focus by governments' collective agreement to avoid 'excessive deficits' in the future—an immediate benefit of EMU. The ultimate result of this trend was illustrated by the previous UK government's proposal for every citizen to build up a personal pension fund. For EMU, this has the practical

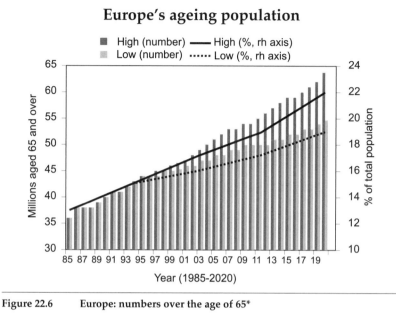

Europe's ageing population

Figure 22.6   Europe: numbers over the age of 65*

*actual data to 1996, projected numbers thereafter
Source: Eurostat and the United Nations

result of enlarging the size—and therefore, power—of the financial markets.

The majority of electors will fear for the safety of their pensions.

If we (arbitrarily) assume that once people are over 45 years old they become concerned about their retirement income, then we already have a group of people representing well over half the electorate. Once this group grasps that their self-interest lies in price stability and the safety of their capital, they are likely to vote for conservative financial policies.

Extra return will be sought

The bulk of these retirement savings will be intermediated by financial institutions that sell their services on the basis of performance. For the fixed-income component of the savings portfolio, taking on the market risk of the underlying assets is an easy boost to performance versus a bank deposit. But the process of seeking higher return is unlikely to stop there.

The preferred asset mix changes at the moment of retirement

During the earning years, a saver may go for higher returns in the equity market but—on retirement—many people will buy an annuity. Indeed,

The preferred asset mix changes at the moment of retirement

During the earning years, a saver may go for higher returns in the equity market but—on retirement—many people will buy an annuity. Indeed, pension schemes often require that. At that moment, the insurance company that offers the highest annuity rate gets the business. In what assets will they invest the money? Bank deposits, government bonds and AAA corporates, or credit card receivables plus a leavening of really high yielders? Early retirement of the 'baby boomers' of 1946 onwards should have a rising impact after 2002. In effect, the rise in the number of retirements that will parallel the early years of EMU should prompt an institutional search in Europe for incremental yield.

If continuing price stability succeeds in keeping government bond yields at the lowest levels for a generation or two, the scramble to maintain yields as high as possible should provide the critical mass to start up new security sectors denominated in the euro. Perhaps the opening of the Deutschemark-denominated high yield sector is just a foretaste?

Technological change

The key questions for financial institutions are: How will these products be delivered? Will 'add-on' services be provided by the deposit-taking bank, or will the securities firms dominate? Or will money managers be the winners?

Technology will resolve this debate. The advances in recent years are quite startling (see Figure 22.7). In the past quarter century, processing power has risen 30,000 fold; the cost of storage has been divided by 100,000 and communication speeds multiplied by over 40,000—a revolution that has brought us to the dawn of cybersociety.

The heart of any financial activity is making the final payment, and, at that moment, security is of paramount importance. Until technology offers security that is at least as good as existing systems, that final link will be an impediment to any attempts to achieve the ultimate disintermediation: Direct contact between saver and borrower.

Once customers are convinced that the security problems have been overcome, the unbundling of financial services can proceed. At one level, electronic 'money on a chip', such as the Mondex system originally developed by NatWest, will eventually enable payments in euros to be made anywhere in the EU (or elsewhere) instantly and securely for the price of a telephone call. The payments system of a bank—traditionally a key to its grip on the financial flows of its customers—may be about to move over to the telecom company. Similarly, home banking will

The IT revolution

PROCESSING POWER

1972

1997

Intel 4004 microprocessor:
  2300 transistors
  108 KHz clock speed
  4-bit bus width

Intel Pentium Pro:
  5.5 million transistors
  200 MHz clock speed
  64-bit bus speed

Transistors: x2400
Speed: x1900
Performance
  (speed x bus width): x30,000

STORAGE CAPACITY

1972   *1997*

1Kbit Dram about $60
IBM 3340 disk drive:
  60Mb about $100,000

16Mbit Dram about $10
IBM Ultrastar disk drive:
  9 Gigabytes about $1000

Dram storage: x16,000
Hard disk storage: x150
Dram unit cost: 100,000
Hard disk unit cost: 15,000

COMMUNICATION SPEED

1972

1997

Analogue modem 2.4 Kbit / sec.   Fast ethernet: 100Mbit / sec.

Communication speed: x42,000

Figure 22.7   Advances in IT performance and cost over the last 25 years

However, once the customer has taken that step, the purchase (and sale) of securities may be just one of the products on offer. The customer now has access to just the same training systems as an investment professional. Information service providers are ready to supply—cheaply—the same services to the end-customer as those available to the trader. Systems such as Financial Information Exchange (FIX) enable a customer to deal directly in equities around the globe from their PC. These order-driven systems have pushed the cost of a $20,000 share trade down from perhaps $200 a few years ago to barely $10 for an 'e-trade' today.

At present, bond dealers seem safe from these systems because the dealer acts as a principal rather than an agent. However, the forthcoming wave of securitizing Europe's credit markets should increase activity in the bond markets to such an extent that even bond dealers should wonder what is round the next technological corner.

Conclusions

Two basic conclusions can be drawn. First, that the simple model of a traditional bank—taking a deposit, making payments and giving loans—will come under increasing pressure from the combination of the introduction of the euro, the single market and new technology. Second, that euro-denominated securities markets seem set for explosive growth as the cost of dealing continues to fall and markets go ever more 'straight through'.

The financial institutions that intermediate these flows are already into a process of dramatic transition. The euro will simply accelerate and intensify that because the combined driving forces of EMU, demographics and technology may have a lot of surprises still in store for us all.

Chapter
23
The euro

Paul Temperton
*The Independent Economic Research
Company (TIER)*

Retail sector and consumer impact

Euro notes and coin will not be available in 1999...

When the euro is introduced in 1999, euro cash—notes and coin—will not be available immediately. These will be introduced on 1 January 2002. A period of dual circulation of national currency and euro cash will then follow but, by 1 July 2002 at the latest, national currencies will no longer be legal tender and will be withdrawn from circulation. In some countries, a shorter period of dual circulation will take place—for example, in Germany, where this period will last only from 1 January 2002 until 28 February 2002.

If the euro is to become generally established outside the financial sector before 2002, it would clearly be desirable for it to be used for retail and consumer transactions as soon as possible after its introduction. The absence of euro notes and coin is not necessarily an impediment to this: after all, many consumer transactions already take place by non-cash means—cheque, credit card, debit card, etc. But notes and coin are psychologically important and without them it may well be difficult to encourage a widespread switch to use of the euro for consumer transactions. This chapter considers that particular point, together with other issues to be faced in the retail and consumer sectors.

...but conversion rates will be fixed from 1 January

Conversion rates between euro area member currencies will be fixed from 1 January 1999. The conversion rates will be more than just 'fixed exchange rates'—'fixed' exchange rates can, after all, be changed. These will be irrevocably-locked conversion rates between national currencies and the euro. Thus national currency amounts will simply be another manifestation of the euro amount.

Certainly, the conversion rates that link national currency amounts to the euro will not be round amounts such as 2:1 or 10:1, but rather will be fractions. It has already been agreed that conversion factors between national currencies and the euro will be expressed to six significant figures.

...so 'dual pricing' could occur from that time

Suppose, for example, that Ireland is a member of the euro area and that its conversion rate is set at:

1 euro = I£0.732393

This conversion rate would then be used for converting all Irish £ prices into euro and vice versa. An article priced at I£4.99 would then have an equivalent price of 6.81 euros.

Dual pricing: euro prices rounded

Figure 23.1

The question arises as to how the retailer and consumer will react once such conversion rates have been set. Some consumer associations have called for the use of 'dual prices'—i.e. national currency and euro amounts—to be made compulsory in the period from 1 January 1999 until euro notes and coin are introduced. But, despite such pressure, this will not be the case: dual pricing will be voluntary. Dual pricing involves costs—double labelling, modifications of computer systems, staff training and so on—which firms themselves will have to bear.

It is possible that consumers and retailers will continue to operate predominantly in domestic currency right up until the time that euro cash is introduced. The equivalent euro price of the national currency amount could be little more than a detail of interest to some.

On the other hand, suppose the retailer wanted to shift to pricing his goods predominantly in euro. Suppose also that he wanted to preserve a price described in 'units plus 99 cents'. Then to use the earlier example once more, he might round the price up from 6.81 euros to 6.99 euros or down to 5.99 euros. Moreover, *when* this change takes place is of importance. One technique might be to 'phase in' euro pricing throughout the 1999-2002 transition period, but this would involve regular re-labelling of goods (see Figure 23.2).

Dual pricing: how price tags might look

Figure 23.2

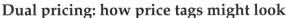

But relative prices might be affected...

There are major implications for the price of the product in question. If, as suggested in Figure 23.2, the price is rounded up, the price of the product increases by 2.6 per cent; alternatively, if the price is rounded down, to 5.99

euros, the price of the product falls by 12 per cent. Of course, such simple pricing strategies (i.e. using 99 as the subsidiary unit) may already have fallen out of fashion to some extent. And it would be possible (for some goods) to correct for any price change by making compensating changes to quantities (the *Mars* bar becomes bigger, loaf of bread smaller, etc.).

Even so, there could potentially be quite large changes in the relative prices of different goods, acting to distort the pattern of production and consumption.

...and there is a risk of consumer confusion

There is also a risk of consumer confusion. The situation has been likened to that following decimalization in the UK. There was widespread concern at the time that changing from 'pounds, shillings and pence' to 'pounds and new pence' would push prices up (see Figures 23.3 & 23.4).

It is true that UK inflation rose sharply soon after decimalization, but it was not the cause: expansionary government fiscal policies, a rapid expansion of money and credit and the quadrupling of oil prices provide an altogether better explanation.

There are already examples of multiple pricing

There are already, well before the start of 1999, examples of retailers using price tags with prices expressed in various European currencies. For example, some UK retailers have used price tags similar to that shown in Figure 23.5. Such multiple pricing, however, uses relationships between prices in different currencies which are not based just on current exchange rates. Clearly, production costs, tax regimes and pricing strategies are different in different countries at the moment.

So this type of multiple pricing is quite different to that envisaged with dual pricing between national currency and euro amounts which would legally have to use the fixed conversion rates for converting national currencies into euro. The implication is that the current types of multiple pricing may be illegal after 1 January 1999.

Costs of dual pricing

Of more practical concern to retailers and consumers, however, are the actual costs involved in switching from prices in national currencies to those—initially—in two currencies (national currency and euros) and then to prices in euros only. Retailers have made various estimates of the costs

UK inflation rose sharply...

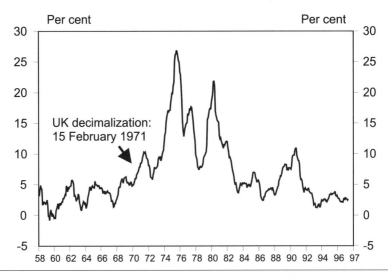

Figure 23.3   UK retail prices, per cent change on a year earlier

...after decimalization in 1971

Figure 23.4

A current example of multiple pricing

Figure 23.5

Retailers: some cost estimates

DM terms	**Euro-11**	**Per head**
Bottom-up		
(M&S estimate)	DM30bn	DM80
Top-down		
(Eurocommerce)		
1.8%	DM75bn	DM200
2.5%	DM105bn	DM280

Figure 23.6

involved. Marks & Spencer, for example, puts the cost of installing all the new systems and technology at £100 million, which implies a much larger figure for the retail sector as a whole. Very crudely, the Marks & Spencer figure, grossed up for the euro-11 retail sector would imply a cost of DM30bn. That 'bottom-up' estimate is, however, much smaller than other estimates. *Eurocommerce*, representing retailers throughout the EU, initially estimated the costs at 1.8 per cent of turnover, but revised these upward to 2.5 per cent in November 1997. A comparison of 'top-down' and 'bottom-up' estimates of the costs involved is given in Figure 23.6. This would suggest that, for all euro-11 countries, the overall cost of switching to the euro could amount to as much as DM105 billion. For comparison, that amounts to a one-off cost of DM280 per head.

Given the difficulties associated with dual pricing, the fact that it may be difficult to get consumers to switch over to 'thinking in euros' rather than national currencies, that relative prices might change and that the entire process will be quite costly, is it worth it?

The costs need to be set alongside the benefits that will come from the use of a single currency across a wide area. There will be benefits to consumers and retailers alike.

For consumers, there will be much greater transparency in the pricing of goods between countries. No longer will the consumer have to think in terms of which exchange rate to apply and the transaction costs involved in switching between currencies. The price of a good will be set in euros in all of the countries in the euro area. This transparency will be coupled with greater freedom of movement of goods and services within the single market and the overall effect should be to encourage competition and drive prices lower. That there are wide price differentials in the euro area is demonstrated by a comparison on prices for two basic goods (see Figure 23.7).

That will be a disadvantage to retailers, who will find it increasingly difficult to differentiate prices between markets. But, offsetting this, retailers will benefit from generally much lower costs in conducting cross border business in the euro area. No longer need they be concerned about currency exchange rates and hedging currency exposure. Furthermore, whereas the costs of switching to the euro are generally 'one-off'—changing cash registers, training of staff, dual pricing for the interim period—the benefits are continuing.

This was recently demonstrated in a submission by the European tourist industry to the European parliament: the costs of moving to euro pricing were a one-off 1.5 per cent of turnover (i.e. a cost similar to those estimated by retailers) whereas the benefits of operating in euros were a continuing three per cent per year (see Figure 23.8).

The impact of the euro on price transparency

		Current price in local currency		Price in euros[1]	
COCA-COLA 1.5 LITRE					
Belgium	*francs*	48	*euros*	1.22	
France	*francs*	6.5	*euros*	1.02	
Germany	*Deutschemarks*	3.02	*euros*	1.57	
Ireland	*punts*	0.93	*euros*	1.19	
Italy	*lire*	2,460	*euros*	1.29	
Luxembourg	*francs*	42	*euros*	1.06	
Portugal	*escudos*	199	*euros*	1.02	
Spain	*pesetas*	125	*euros*	0.77	
UK	*pounds*	1.09	*euros*	1.36	
MACDONALD'S *BIG MAC*					
Austria	*schillings*	36	*euros*	2.67	
Belgium	*francs*	109	*euros*	2.76	
Finland	*markka*	19.9	*euros*	3.47	
France	*francs*	17.5	*euros*	2.69	
Germany	*Deutschemarks*	4.9	*euros*	2.55	
Ireland	*punts*	1.62	*euros*	2.06	
Italy	*lire*	4,500	*euros*	2.36	
Netherlands	*guilders*	5.45	*euros*	2.53	
Portugal	*escudos*	440	*euros*	2.26	
Spain	*pesetas*	365	*euros*	2.26	
UK	*pounds*	1.79	*euros*	2.23	

Figure 23.7

[1]*euro prices are derived from the likely conversion rates of national currencies per euro (apart from sterling which is based on the current market rate versus the Ecu). These conversion rates will be formally announced on 31 December 1998.*

Source: Bureau Européen des Unions des Consommateurs

European tourism

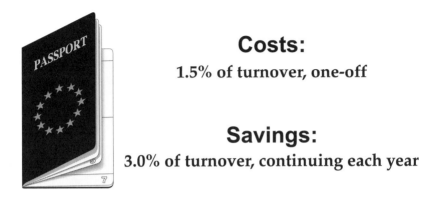

Figure 23.8   Tourism: costs and savings from the euro
Source: Estimates presented to the European Parliament by the European tourist industry

Conclusion

The transition from national currency to euro prices for the consumer is unlikely to be straightforward. From 1999 to 2002, the absence of euro notes and coin may impede the use of the euro for consumer transactions. And there are problems associated with dual pricing. But these costs to the consumer and the firm—which are essentially one-off costs—are likely to be easily offset by the longer terms benefits of greater price transparency, lower transactions costs and greater competition.

Section

VIII

The *euro*

Regulations &
Provisions

Article 235 Regulation

COUNCIL REGULATION (EC) No 1103/97

of 17 June 1997

on certain provisions relating to the introduction of the euro

THE COUNCIL OF THE EUROPEAN UNION,

Having regard to the Treaty establishing the European Community, and in particular Article 235 thereof,

Having regard to the proposal of the Commission (1), [*]

Having regard to the opinion of the European Parliament (2), [**]

Having regard to the opinion of the European Monetary Institute (3), [***]

(1) Whereas, at its meeting held in Madrid on 15 and 16 December 1995, the European Council confirmed that the third stage of Economic and Monetary Union will start on 1 January 1999 as laid down in Article 109j (4) of the Treaty; whereas the Member States which will adopt the euro as the single currency in accordance with the Treaty will be defined for the purposes of this Regulation as the 'participating Member States';

(2) Whereas, at the meeting of the European Council in Madrid, the decision was taken that the term 'ECU' used by the Treaty to refer to

[*] OJ No C 369, 7. 12. 1996, p. 8
[**] OJ No C 380, 16. 12. 1996, p. 49
[***] Opinion delivered on 29 November 1996

the European currency unit is a generic term; whereas the Governments of the fifteen Member States have achieved the common agreement that this decision is the agreed and definitive interpretation of the relevant Treaty provisions; whereas the name given to the European currency shall be the 'euro'; whereas the euro as the currency of the participating Member States will be divided into one hundred sub-units with the name 'cent'; whereas the European Council furthermore considered that the name of the single currency must be the same in all the official languages of the European Union, taking into account the existence of different alphabets;

(3)   Whereas a Regulation on the introduction of the euro will be adopted by the Council on the basis of the third sentence of Article 109l (4) of the Treaty as soon as the participating Member States are known in order to define the legal framework of the euro; whereas the Council, when acting at the starting date of the third stage in accordance with the first sentence of Article 109l (4) of the Treaty, shall adopt the irrevocably-fixed conversion rates;

(4)   Whereas it is necessary, in the course of the operation of the common market and for the changeover to the single currency, to provide legal certainty for citizens and firms in all Member States on certain provisions relating to the introduction of the euro well before the entry into the third stage; whereas this legal certainty at an early stage will allow preparations by citizens and firms to proceed under good conditions.

(5)   Whereas the third sentence of Article 109l (4) of the Treaty, which allows the Council, acting with the unanimity of participating Member States, to take other measures necessary for the rapid introduction of the single currency is available as a legal basis only when it has been confirmed, in accordance with Article 109j (4) of the Treaty, which Member States fulfil the necessary conditions for the adoption of a single currency; whereas it is therefore necessary to have recourse to Article 235 of the Treaty as a legal basis for those provisions where there is an urgent need for legal certainty; whereas therefore this Regulation and the aforesaid Regulation on the introduction of the euro will together provide the legal framework for the euro, the principles of which legal framework were agreed by the European Council in Madrid; whereas the introduction of the euro concerns day-to-day operations of the whole population in participating Member States; whereas measures other than those in this Regulation and in the Regulation which will be adopted under

the third sentence of Article 109l (4) of the Treaty should be examined to ensure a balanced changeover, in particular for consumers;

(6)   Whereas the ECU as referred to in Article 109g of the Treaty and as defined in Council Regulation (EC) No 3320/94 of 22 December 1994 on the consolidation of the existing Community legislation on the definition of the ECU following the entry into force of the Treaty on European Union* will cease to be defined as a basket of component currencies on 1 January 1999 and the euro will become a currency in its own right; whereas the decision of the Council regarding the adoption of the conversion rates shall not in itself modify the external value of the ECU; whereas this means that one ECU in its composition as a basket of component currencies will become one euro; whereas Regulation (EC) No 3320/94 therefore becomes obsolete and should be repealed; whereas for references in legal instruments to the ECU, parties shall be presumed to have agreed to refer to the ECU as referred to in Article 109g of the Treaty and as defined in the aforesaid Regulation; whereas such a presumption should be rebuttable taking into account the intentions of the parties;

(7)   Whereas it is a generally accepted principle of law that the continuity of contracts and other legal instruments is not affected by the introduction of a new currency; whereas the principle of freedom of contract has to be respected; whereas the principle of continuity should be compatible with anything which parties might have agreed with reference to the introduction of the euro; whereas, in order to reinforce legal certainty and clarity, it is appropriate explicitly to confirm that the principle of continuity of contracts and other legal instruments shall apply between the former national currencies and the euro and between the ECU as referred to in Article 109g of the Treaty and as defined in Regulation (EC) No 3320/94 and the euro; whereas this implies, in particular, that in the case of fixed interest rate instruments the introduction of the euro does not alter the nominal interest rate payable by the debtor; whereas the provisions on continuity can fulfil their objective to provide legal certainty and transparency to economic agents, in particular for consumers, only if they enter into force as soon as possible;

---

* *OJ No L 350. 31. 12. 1994, p. 27.*

(8)   Whereas the introduction of the euro constitutes a change in the monetary law of each participating Member State; whereas the recognition of the monetary law of a State is a universally accepted principle; whereas the explicit confirmation of the principle of continuity should lead to the recognition of continuity of contracts and other legal instruments in the jurisdictions of third countries;

(9)   Whereas the term 'contract' used for the definition of legal instruments is meant to include all types of contracts, irrespective of the way in which they are concluded;

(10)   Whereas the Council, when acting in accordance with the first sentence of Article 109l (4) of the Treaty, shall define the conversion rates of the euro in terms of each of the national currencies of the participating Member States; whereas these conversion rates should be used for any conversion between the euro and the national currency units or between the national currency units; whereas for any conversion between national currency units, a fixed algorithm should define the result; whereas the use of inverse rates for conversion would imply rounding of rates and could result in significant inaccuracies, notably if large amounts are involved;

(11)   Whereas the introduction of the euro requires the rounding of monetary amounts; whereas an early indication of rules for rounding is necessary in the course of the operation of the common market and to allow a timely preparation and a smooth transition to Economic and Monetary Union; whereas these rules do not affect any rounding practice, convention or national provisions providing a higher degree of accuracy for intermediate computations;

(12)   Whereas, in order to achieve a high degree of accuracy in conversion operations, the conversion rates should be defined with six significant figures; whereas a rate with six significant figures means a rate which, counted from the left and starting by the first non-zero figure, has six figures,

HAS ADOPTED THIS REGULATION:

Article 1

For the purpose of this Regulation:

—   'legal instruments' shall mean legislative and statutory provisions, acts of administration, judicial decisions, contracts, unilateral legal acts, payment instruments other than banknotes and coins, and other instruments with legal effect,

–   'participating Member States' shall mean those Member States which adopt the single currency in accordance with the Treaty,

–   'conversion rates' shall mean the irrevocably-fixed conversion rates which the Council adopts in accordance with the first sentence of Article 109l (4) of the Treaty,

–   'national currency units' shall mean the units of the currencies of participating Member States, as those units are defined on the day before the start of the third stage of Economic and Monetary Union,

–   'euro unit' shall mean the unit of the single currency as defined in the Regulation on the introduction of the euro which will enter into force at the starting date of the third stage of Economic and Monetary Union.

Article 2

1.   Every reference in a legal instrument to the ECU, as referred to in Article 109g of the Treaty and as defined in Regulation (EC) No 3320/94, shall be replaced by a reference to the euro at a rate of one euro to one ECU. References in a legal instrument to the ECU without such a definition shall be presumed, such presumption being rebuttable taking into account the intentions of the parties to be references to the ECU as referred to in Article 109g of the Treaty and as defined in Regulation (EC) No 3320/94.

2.   Regulation (EC) No 3320/94 is hereby repealed.

3.   This Article shall apply as from 1 January 1999 in accordance with the decision pursuant to Article 109j (4) of the Treaty.

Article 3

The introduction of the euro shall not have the effect of altering any term of a legal instrument or of discharging or excusing performance under any legal instrument, nor give a party the right unilaterally to alter or terminate such an instrument. This provision is subject to anything which parties may have agreed.

Article 4

1.   The conversion rates shall be adopted as one euro expressed in terms of each of the national currencies of the participating Member States. They shall be adopted with six significant figures.

2.   The conversion rates shall not be rounded or truncated when making conversions.

3.   The conversion rates shall be used for conversions either way between the euro unit and the national currency units. Inverse rates derived from the conversion rates shall not be used.

4.   Monetary amounts to be converted from one national currency unit into another shall first be converted into a monetary amount expressed in the euro unit, which amount may be rounded to not less than three decimals and shall then be converted into the other national currency unit. No alternative method of calculation may be used unless it produces the same results.

Article 5

Monetary amounts to be paid or accounted for when a rounding takes place after a conversion into the euro unit pursuant to Article 4 shall be rounded up or down to the nearest cent. Monetary amounts to be paid or accounted for which are converted into a national currency unit shall be rounded up or down to the nearest sub-unit or in the absence of a sub-unit to the nearest unit, or according to national law or practice to a multiple or fraction of the sub-unit or unit of the national currency unit. If the application of the conversion rate gives a result which is exactly half-way, the sum shall be rounded up.

Article 6

This regulation shall enter into force on the day following that of its publication in the Official Journal of the European Communities.

This regulation shall be binding in its entirety and directly applicable in all Member States.

Article 109l(4) Regulation

Proposal for a Council Regulation [ ]
on the introduction of the euro

THE COUNCIL OF THE EUROPEAN UNION,

Having regard to the Treaty establishing the European Community, and in particular Article 109 1 (4) third sentence thereof,

Having regard to the proposal from the Commission,

Having regard to the opinion of the European Central Bank,

Having regard to the opinion of the European Parliament,

(1)   Whereas this regulation defines monetary law provisions of the Members States which have adopted the euro; whereas provisions on continuity of contracts, the replacement of references to the ECU in legal instruments by references to the euro and rounding have already been laid down in Council Regulation [...]; whereas the introduction of the euro concerns day-to-day operations of the whole population in participating Member States; whereas measures other than those in this regulation and in the regulation on some provisions relating to the introduction of the euro should be examined to ensure a balanced changeover, in particular for consumers;

(2)   Whereas, on the occasion of the meeting of the European Council, held at Madrid on 15/16 December 1995, it was decided that the term "ECU" used by the Treaty to refer to the European currency unit as a generic term; whereas "the Governments of the fifteen Member States have achieved the common agreement that this decision is the agreed and definitive interpretation of the relevant Treaty provisions"; whereas the name given to the European currency shall be the "euro"; whereas the euro as the currency of the participating

Member States shall be divided into one hundred sub-units with the name "cent"; whereas the definition of the name "cent" does not prevent the use of variants of this term in common usage in the Member States; whereas the European Council furthermore considered that the name of the single currency must be the same in all the official languages of the European Union, taking in account the existence of different alphabets;

(3)   Whereas the Council when acting according to Article 109 1 (4), third sentence of the Treaty shall take the measures necessary for the rapid introduction of the euro other than the adoption of the conversion rates;

(4)   Whereas whenever under Article 109 k (2) of the Treaty a Member State becomes a participating Member State, the Council shall according to Article 109 1 (5) of the Treaty take the other measures necessary for the rapid introduction of the euro as the single currency of this Member State;

(5)   Whereas according to Article 109 1 (4) of the Treaty the Council shall at the starting date of the third stage adopt the conversion rates at which the currencies of the participating Member States will be irrevocably fixed and at which irrevocably-fixed rate the euro will be substituted for these currencies;

(6)   Whereas given the absence of exchange rate risk either between the euro unit and the national currency units or between these nation currency units, legislative provisions should be interpreted accordingly;

(7)   Whereas the term "contract" used for the definition of legal instruments is meant to include all types of contracts, irrespective of the way in which they are concluded;

(8)   Whereas in order to prepare a smooth changeover to the euro a transitional period is needed between the substitution of the euro for the currencies of the participating Member States and the introduction of the euro banknotes and coins; whereas during this period the national currency units will be defined as sub-divisions of the euro; whereas thereby a legal equivalence is established between the euro unit and the national currency units;

(9)   Whereas in accordance with Article 109 g of the Treaty and with Council Regulation [...] on some provisions relating to the introduction of the euro, the euro will replace the ECU as from 1

January 1999 as the unit of account of the institutions of the European Communities; whereas the euro should also be the unit of account of the European Central Bank (ECB) and of the central banks of the participating Member States; whereas, in line with the Madrid conclusions, monetary policy operations will be carried out in the euro unit by the ESCB; where as this does not prevent national central banks from keeping accounts in their national currency unit during the transitional period, in particular for their staff and for public administrations;

(10) Whereas each participating Member State may allow the full use of the euro unit in its territory during the transitional period;

(11) Whereas during the transitional period contracts, nation laws and other legal instruments can be drawn up validly in the euro unit or in the national currency unit; whereas during this period, nothing in this regulation should affect the validity of any reference to a national currency unit in any legal instrument;

(12) Whereas, unless agreed otherwise, economic agents have to respect the denomination of a legal instrument in the performance of all acts to be carried out under that instrument;

(13) Whereas the euro unit and the national currency units are units of the same currency; whereas it should be ensured that payments inside a participating Member State by crediting an account can be made either in the euro unit or the respective national currency unit; whereas the provisions on payments by crediting an account should also apply to those cross-border payments, which are denominated in the euro unit or the national currency unit of the account of the creditor; whereas it is necessary to ensure the smooth functioning of payment systems by making provision dealing with the crediting of accounts by payment instruments credited through those systems; whereas the provisions on payments by crediting an account should not imply that financial intermediaries are obliged to make available either other payment facilities or products denominated in any particular unit of the euro; whereas the provisions on payments by crediting an account do not prohibit financial intermediaries from co-ordinating the introduction of payment facilities denominated in the euro unit which rely on a common technical infrastructure during the transitional period;

(14) Whereas in accordance with the conclusions reached by the European Council at its meeting held in Madrid, new tradable public

debt will be issued in the euro unit by the participating Member States as from 1 January 1999; whereas in order to allow issuers of debt to redenominate outstanding debt in the euro unit; whereas the provisions on redenomination should be such that they can also be applied in the jurisdictions of third countries; whereas issuers should be enabled to redenominate outstanding debt if the debt is denominated in a national currency unit of a Member State which has redenominated part or all of the outstanding debt of its general government; whereas these provisions do not address the introduction of additional measures to amend the terms of outstanding debt to alter, among other things, the nominal amount of outstanding debt, these being matters subject to relevant national law; whereas in order to allow Member States to take appropriate measures for changing the unit of account of the operating procedures of organised markets;

(15) Whereas further action at the Community level may also be necessary to clarify the effect of the introduction of the euro on the application of existing provisions of Community law, in particular concerning netting, set off and techniques of similar effect;

(16) Whereas any obligation to use the euro can only be imposed on the basis of Community legislation; whereas in transactions with the public sector participating Member States may allow the use of the euro unit; whereas in accordance with the reference scenario decided by the European Council at its meeting held in Madrid, the Community legislation laying down the time frame for the generalisation of the use of the euro unit might leave some freedom to individual Member States;

(17) Whereas according to Article 105a of the Treaty the Council may adopt measures to harmonize the denominations and technical specifications of all coins;

(18) Whereas banknotes and coins need adequate protection against counterfeiting;

(19) Whereas banknotes and coins denominated in the national currency units lose their status of legal tender at the latest six months after the end of the transitional period; whereas limitations on payments in notes and coins, established by Members States for public reasons, are not compatible with the status of legal tender of euro banknotes and coins, provided that other lawful means for the settlement of monetary debts are available;

(20) Whereas as from the end of the transitional period references in legal instruments existing at the end of the transitional period will have to be read as references to the euro according to the respective conversion rates; whereas a physical redenomination of existing legal instruments is therefore not necessary to achieve this result; whereas the rounding rules defined in Council Regulation [...] shall also apply to the conversions to be made at the end of the transitional period or after the transitional period; whereas for reasons of clarity it may be desirable that the physical redenomination will take place as soon as appropriate;

(21) Whereas point 2 of the protocol n°11 on certain provisions relating to the United Kingdom of Great Britain and Northern Ireland stipulates that, inter alia, point 5 of that protocol shall have effect if the United Kingdom notifies the Council that it does not intend to move to the third stage; whereas the United Kingdom gave notice to the Council on 16 October 1996 that it does not intend to move to the third stage; whereas point 5 stipulates that, inter alia, Article 109 1 (4) shall not apply to the United Kingdom;

(22) Whereas Denmark, referring to point 1 of the protocol no°12 on certain provisions relating to Denmark has notified, in the context of the Edinburgh decision of 12 December 1992, that it will not participate in the third stage; whereas. therefore, according to point 2 of this protocol, all Articles and provisions of the Treaty and the Statute of the ESCB referring to a derogation shall be applicable to Denmark;

(23) Whereas, according to Article 109 1 (4), the single currency will be introduced only in the Member States without a derogation;

(24) Whereas this regulation, therefore, shall be applicable pursuant to Article 189 of the Treaty, subject to Protocols n°11 and 12 and Article 109 k l.

HAS ADOPTED THIS REGULATION:

PART I

DEFINITIONS

Article 1

For the purpose of this regulation:

– "participating Member States" shall mean [Countries A, B......]
– "legal instruments" shall mean legislative and statutory provisions, acts of administration, judicial decisions, contracts, unilateral legal acts, payment instruments other than banknotes and coins, and other instruments with legal effect.

– "conversion rate" shall mean the irrevocably-fixed conversion rate adopted for the currency of each participating Member State by the Council according to Article 109l(4) first sentence of the Treaty.

– "euro unit" shall mean the currency unit as referred to in the second sentence of Article 2.

– "national currency units" shall mean the units of the currencies of participating Member States as those units are defined on the day before the start of the third stage of Economic and Monetary Union.

– "transitional period" shall mean the period beginning on 1.1.1999 and ending on 31.12.2001.

– "redenominate" shall mean changing the unit in which the amount of outstanding debt is stated from a national currency unit to the euro unit, as defined in Article 2, but which does not have through the act of redenomination the effect of altering any other term of the debt, this being a matter subject to relevant national law.

Part II

SUBSTITUTION OF THE EURO FOR THE CURRENCIES OF THE PARTICIPATING MEMBERS STATES

Article 2

As from 1.1.1999 the currency of the participating Member States shall be the euro. The currency unit shall be one euro. One euro shall be divided into one hundred cent.

Article 3

The euro shall be substituted for the currency of each participating Member State at the conversion rate.

Article 4

The euro shall be the unit of account of the European Central Bank (ECB) and of the central banks of the participating Member States.

Part III

TRANSITIONAL PROVISIONS

Article 5

Article 6-9 apply during the transitional period.

Article 6

(1) The euro shall also be divided into the national currency units according to the conversion rates. Any sub-division thereof shall be maintained. Subject to the provisions of this Regulation the monetary law of the participating Member States shall continue to apply.

(2)

Where in a legal instrument reference is made to a national currency unit, this reference shall be as valid as if reference were made to the euro unit according to the conversion rates.

Article 7

The substitution of the euro for the currency of each participating Member State shall not in itself have the effect of altering the denomination of legal instruments in existence on the date of substitution.

Article 8

(1) Acts to be performed under legal instruments stipulating the use of or denominated in a national currency unit shall be performed in that national currency unit. acts to be performed under legal instruments stipulating the use of or denominated in the euro unit shall be performed in this unit.

(2)   The provisions of paragraph 1 are subject to anything which parties may have agreed.

(3)   Notwithstanding the provisions of paragraph 1, any amount denominated either in the euro unit or in the national currency unit of a given participating Member State and payable within that Member State by crediting an account of the creditor, can be paid by the debtor either in the euro unit or in that national currency unit. The amount shall be credited to the account of the creditor in the denomination of his account, with any conversion being effected at the conversion rates.

(4)   Notwithstanding the provisions of paragraph 1, each participating Member State may take measures which may be necessary in order to:

–   redenominate in the euro unit outstanding debt issued by that Member State's general government, as defined in the European System of Integrated Accounts, denominated in its national currency unit and issued under its own law. If a Member State has taken such a measure, issuers may redenominate in the euro unit debt denominated in that Member State's national currency unit unless redenomination is expressly excluded by the terms of the contract, this provision shall apply to debt issued by the general government of a Member State as well as to bonds and other forms of securitised debt negotiable in the capital markets, and to money market instruments, issued by other debtors;

–   enable the change of the unit of account of their operating procedures from a national currency unit to the euro unit by:

a)   markets for the regular exchange, clearing and settlement of any instrument listed in section B of the annex of Directive 93/22/EEC on investment services in the securities field and of commodities; and

b)   systems for the regular exchange, clearing and settlement of payments.

(5)   Other provisions than those of paragraph 4 imposing the use of the euro unit may only be adopted by the participating Member States according to any time-frame laid down by the Community legislation.

(6)   National legal provisions of participating Member States which permit or impose netting, set-off or techniques with similar effects shall apply to monetary obligations, irrespective of their currency

denomination, if that denomination is in euro or in a national currency unit, with any conversion being effected at the conversion rates.

Article 9

Banknotes and coins denominated in a national currency unit shall retain their status as legal tender within their territorial limited as of the day before the entry into force of this regulation.

Part IV

EURO BANK NOTES AND COINS

Article 10

At a date to be decided, in accordance with the Madrid scenario, when the present regulation is adopted, the ECB and the central banks of the participating Member States shall put into circulation banknotes denominated in euro. Notwithstanding Article 15, these banknotes denominated in euro shall be the only banknotes which have the status of legal tender in all these Member States.

Article 11

At a date to be decided, in accordance with the Madrid scenario, when the present regulation is adopted, the participating Member States shall issue coins denominated in euro or in cent and complying with the denominations and technical specifications which the Council may lay down in accordance with Article 105 a (2) second sentence of the Treaty. Notwithstanding Article 15, these coins shall be the only coins which have the status of legal tender in all these Member States. Except of the issuing authority and for those persons specifically designated by the national legislation of the issuing Member State, no party shall be obliged to accept more than fifty coins in any single payment.

Article 12

Participating Member States shall ensure adequate sanctions against counterfeiting and falsification of euro banknotes and coins.

Part V

FINAL PROVISIONS

Article 13

Articles 14-16 apply as from the end of the transitional period.

Article 14

Where in legal instruments existing at the end of the transitional period reference is made to the national currency units, these references shall be read as references to the euro unit according to the respective conversion rates. The rounding rules laid down in Council Regulation [...] shall apply.

Article 15

(1)   Banknotes and coins denominated in a national currency unit as referred to in Article 6 (1) shall remain legal tender within their territorial limits until six months after the end of the transitional period at the latest; this period may be shortened by national law.

(2)   Each participating Member State may, for a period of up to 6 months after the end of the transitional period, lay down rules for the use of the banknotes and coins denominated in its national currency unit as referred to in Article 6(1) and take any measures necessary to facilitate their withdrawal.

Article 16

In accordance with the laws or practices of participating Member States, the respective issuers of banknotes and coins shall continue to accept, against euro at the conversion rate, the banknotes and coins previously issued by them.

Part VI

ENTRY INTO FORCE

Article 17

This Regulation shall enter into force on 1st January 1999.

This Regulation shall be binding in its entirety and directly applicable in all Member States, in accordance with the Treaty, subject to Protocols n° 11 and 12 and Article 109 k 1.

Continuity of contract:
State of New York legislation

STATE OF NEW YORK

5049—A

Section 1. Article 5 of the General Obligations Law is amended by adding a New Title 16 to read as follows:

Title 16

Continuity of Contract

Section   5-1601.   Definitions.
             5-1602.   Continuity of Contract.
             5-1603   Effect of Agreements.
             5-1604.   Application.

5-1601. Definitions. As used in this Title the following terms shall have the following meanings:

1. "Euro" shall mean the currency of participating member states of the European Union that adopt a single currency in accordance with the Treaty on European Union signed February Seventh, Nineteen Hundred Ninety Two.

2. "Introduction of the Euro" shall mean and include the implementation from time to time of economic and monetary union in member states of the European Union in accordance with the Treaty on European Union signed February Seventh, Nineteen Hundred Ninety-Two.

3.   "ECU" or "European Currency Unit" shall mean the currency basket that is from time to time used as the unit of account of the European Community as defined in European Council Regulation No. 3320/94. When the euro first becomes the monetary unit of participating member states of the European Union, references to the ECU in a contract, securities or instrument that also refers to such definition of the ECU shall be replaced by references to the euro at a rate of one euro to one ECU. References to the ECU in a contract, security or instrument without such a definition of the ECU shall be presumed, unless either demonstrated or proven to the contrary by the intention of the parties, to be references to the currency basket that is from time to time used as the unit of account of the European Community.

5-1602. Continuity of Contract

1.   (A) If a subject or medium of payment of a contact, security or instrument is a currency that has been substituted or replaced by the euro, the euro will be a commercially reasonable substitute and substantial equivalent that may be either: (I) used in determining the value of such currency; or (ii) tendered, in each case at the conversion rate specified in, and otherwise calculated in accordance with, the regulations adopted by the Council of the European Union.

(B) If a subject or medium of payment of a contract, security or instrument is the ECU, the euro will be a commercially reasonable substitute and substantial equivalent that may be either: (I) used in determining the value of the ECU; or (ii) tendered, in each case at the conversion rate specified in, and otherwise calculated in accordance with, the regulations adopted by the Council or the European Union.

(C) Performance of any of the obligations described in paragraph (A) or (B) of this subdivision may be made in the currency or currencies originally designated in such contract, security or instrument (so long as such currency or currencies remain legal tender) or in euro, but not in any other currency, whether or not such other currency (i) has been substituted or replaced by the euro or (ii) is a currency that is considered a denomination of the euro and has a fixed conversion rate with respect to the euro.

2.   None of: (A) the introduction of the Euro; (B) the tendering of euros in connection with any obligation in compliance with paragraph (A) or (B) of subdivision one of this section ; (C) the determining of the value of any obligation in compliance with paragraph (A) or (B) of

subdivision one of this section ; or (D) the calculating or determining of the subject or medium of payment of a contract, security or instrument with reference to interest rate or other basis has been substituted or replaced due to the introduction of the euro and that is a commercially reasonable substitute and substantial equivalent, shall either have the effect of discharging or excusing performance under any contract, security or instrument, or give a party the right to unilaterally alter or terminate any contract, security or instrument.

5-1603. Effect of Agreements.

The provisions of this Title shall not alter or impair and shall be subject to any agreements between parties with specific reference to or agreement regarding the introduction of the euro.

5-1604. Application.

1. Notwithstanding the uniform commercial code or any other law of this State, this title shall apply to all contracts, securities and instruments, including contracts with respect to commercial transactions, and shall not be deemed to be displaced by any other law of this State.

2. In circumstances of currency alteration, other than the introduction of the euro, the provisions of this Title shall not be interpreted as creating any negative inference or negative presumption regarding the validity or enforceability of contracts, securities or instruments denominated in whole or in part in a currency affected by such alteration.

Section 2. This act shall take effect immediately.

Continuity of contract:
ISDA Provision

International Swaps and Derivatives Association, Inc. (ISDA)

EMU Continuity Provision

[16]. EMU; Continuity of Contract.[*]

(a)   The parties confirm that, except as provided in subsection (b) below, the occurrence or non-occurrence of an event associated with economic and monetary union in the European Community will not have the effect of altering any term of, or discharging or excusing performance under, the Agreement or any Transaction, give a party the right unilaterally to alter or terminate the Agreement or any Transaction or, in and of itself, give rise to an Event of Default, Termination Event or otherwise be the basis for the effective designation of an Early Termination Date.

This clause on European monetary union may be (i) included in Part 5 of the Schedule to a 1992 Multicurrency-Cross Border ISDA Master Agreement or in Part 4 of the Schedule to a 1992 Local Currency-Single Jurisdiction ISDA Master Agreement, in each case as an additional section in the Master Agreement, or (ii) added as an amendment to an existing 1987 or 1992 Master Agreement. If the parties would also like to confirm in their Agreement the allocation of responsibility for assessing and understanding the risks associated with EMU, they may consider adding the Representation Regarding Relationship Between Parties released by ISDA on March 6, 1996, where that representation accurately reflects how the parties are acting, their capabilities and the nature of their relationship. Different language should be used, for example, if one of the parties has agreed to act as an adviser to the other party.

"An event associated with economic and monetary union in the European Community" includes without limitation, each (and any combination) of the following:

(i)   the introduction of, changeover to or operation of a single or unified European currency (whether known as the euro or otherwise);

(ii)   the fixing of conversion rates between a member state's currency and the new currency or between the currencies of Member States;

(iii)   the substitution of that new currency for the ECU as the unit of account of the European Community;

(iv)   the introduction of that new currency as lawful currency in a member state;

(v)   the withdrawal from legal tender of any currency that, before the introduction of the new currency, was lawful currency in one of the Member States; or

(vi)   the disappearance or replacement of a relevant rate option or other price source for the ECU or the national currency of any member state, or the failure of the agreed sponsor (or a successor sponsor) to publish or display a relevant rate, index, price, page or screen.

(b)   Any agreement between the parties that amends or overrides the provisions of this Section in respect of any Transaction will be effective if it is in writing and expressly refers to this Section or to European monetary union or to an event associated with economic and monetary union in the European Community and would otherwise be effective in accordance with Section 9(b).

Index